R. M. Ballantyne

The Fugitives

The Tyrant Queen of Madagascar

R. M. Ballantyne

The Fugitives
The Tyrant Queen of Madagascar

ISBN/EAN: 9783337320492

Printed in Europe, USA, Canada, Australia, Japan

Cover: Foto ©Thomas Meinert / pixelio.de

More available books at **www.hansebooks.com**

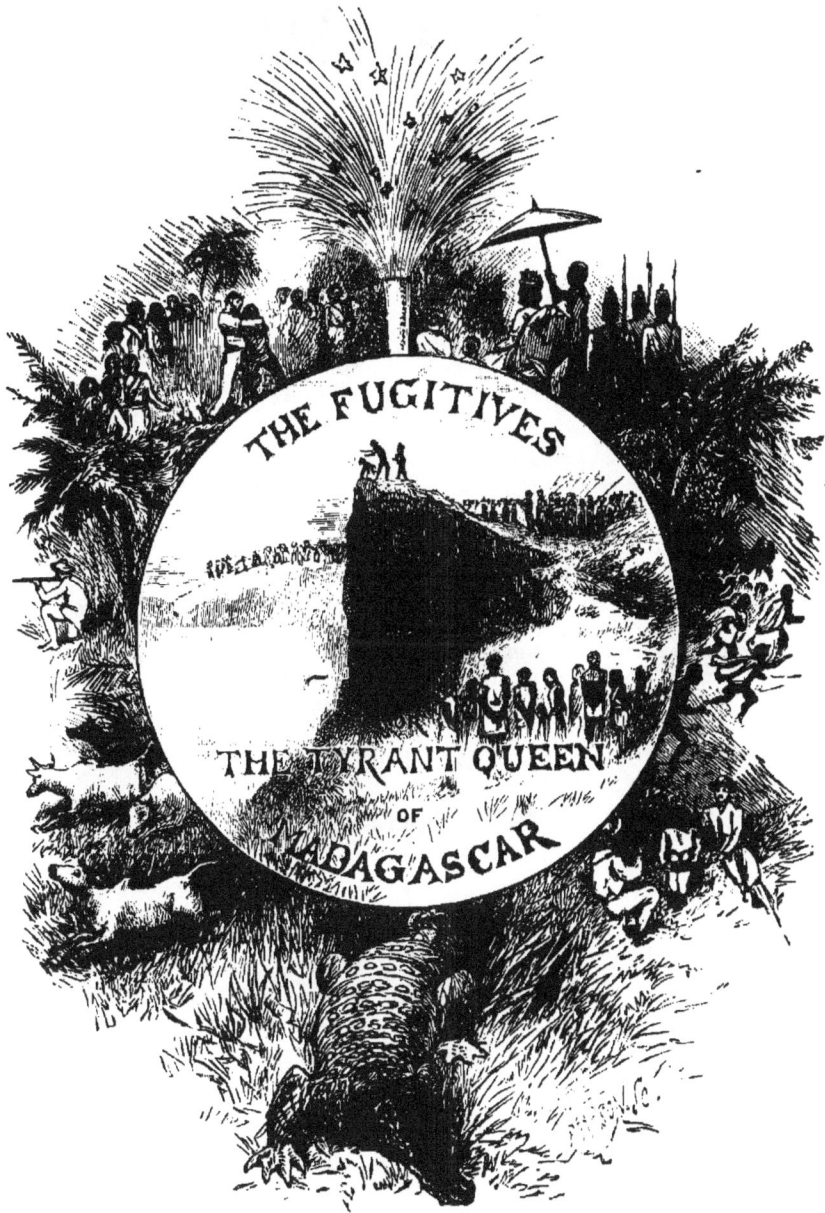

THE FUGITIVES

THE TYRANT QUEEN
OF
MADAGASCAR

THE FUGITIVES

OR

THE TYRANT QUEEN OF MADAGASCAR.

BY R. M. BALLANTYNE,

AUTHOR OF "RED ROONEY;" "THE ROVER OF THE ANDES;" "THE WILD MAN OF THE
WEST;" "THE RED ERIC;" "FREAKS ON THE FELLS;" "THE YOUNG TRAWLER;"
"DUSTY DIAMONDS;" "THE BATTERY AND THE BOILER;" "POST HASTE;"
"BLACK IVORY;" "THE IRON HORSE;" "FIGHTING THE FLAMES;"
"THE LIFEBOAT;" ETC. ETC.

With Illustrations.

SEVENTH THOUSAND.

LONDON:
JAMES NISBET & CO., 21 BERNERS STREET.

PREFACE.

IT is almost allowable, I think, to say that this is a true story, for fiction has only been introduced for the purpose of piecing together and making a symmetrical whole of a number of most interesting facts in regard to Madagascar and the terrible persecutions that took place there in the early part and middle of the present century.

I have ventured to modify time and place somewhat, as well as to mix my characters and their deeds a little, in order to suit the conditions of my tale; but in doing so I have striven to avoid exaggeration and to produce a true picture of the state of affairs, at the period treated of, in what may be styled one of the most interesting and progressive islands of the world.

I take this opportunity of thanking the Rev. George Cousins, of the London Missionary Society,

and formerly of Madagascar, for kindly supplying
me with much valuable information, and of acknow-
ledging myself indebted, among others, to the works
of Messrs. Sibree, Ellis, and Shaw.

R. M. BALLANTYNE.

HARROW-ON-THE-HILL, 1887.

CONTENTS.

PAGE

CHAP. I.—INTRODUCES THE CHIEF ACTORS AND A FEW MYSTERIES,   1

II.—HARKS BACK A LITTLE, ...   15

III.—DESCRIBES THE DEED OF AN AMATEUR MATADOR AND
THE WORK OF A ROUGH-AND-READY SHOEMAKER,   25

IV.—THE DOCTOR FINDS UNEXPECTED WORK IN THE
WILDERNESS, AND A MYSTERIOUS STRANGER IS
INTRODUCED, ...   40

V.—THE OUTLAW'S FRIENDS — THREATENED DANGER
CURIOUSLY AVERTED, ...   55

VI.—THE GUIDE BECOMES COMMUNICATIVE, AND TELLS OF
TERRIBLE DOINGS, ...   72

VII.—DESCRIBES A MEEK MOTHER AND CROCODILE-SON—
JOURNEY RESUMED AND STRANGE TREATMENT OF
THE KING OF THE WATERS, ...   85

VIII.—A FRIEND APPEARS UNEXPECTEDLY, AND OUR TRA-
VELLERS SPEND A DISTURBED NIGHT, . . .   101

IX.—A JOVIAL CHIEF, AND NEW EXPERIENCES OF VARIOUS
KINDS, ...   114

X.—TELLS OF A GRAND HUNT AND OTHER THINGS, .   126

XI.—AN UNINVITED GUEST APPEARS WITH NEWS THAT
DEMANDS INSTANT ACTION, ...   141

PAGE

CHAP. XII.—A NARROW ESCAPE AND THREATENING CLOUDS, . 157

XIII.—ARRIVAL AT THE CAPITAL—QUEEN RANAVALONA'S
TROUBLES AND PERPLEXITIES, ... 173

XIV.—THE PRIME MINISTER LAYS DEEP PLANS—SO DOES
HIS NEPHEW—THE GREAT MARKET-PLACE—A
FRIEND IN DEADLY PERIL, AND OUR THREE
HEROES COME TO GRIEF, ... 193

XV.—THE SPIES AND THE SECRET MEETING—THE PRIME
MINISTER FOILED BY THE PRINCE, . . . 208

XVI.—IN PRISON—EFFECTS OF A FIRST SIGHT OF TORTURE, 222

XVII.—MAMBA IS SUCCOURED BY ONE OF THE "ANCIENT
SOOT," AND FULFILS HIS MYSTERIOUS MISSION, 234

XVIII.—UNEXPECTED DELIVERANCE AND SEVERAL SUR-
PRISES, ... 252

XIX.—A MALAGASY GARDEN PARTY—THE CLOUD GROWS
BLACKER, ... 268

XX.—A GREAT KABÀRY IS HELD, FOLLOWED BY DREADFUL
MARTYRDOMS, ... 281

XXI.—MAMBA, SUBJECTED TO THE ORDEAL OF THE "TAN-
GENA," ESCAPES, BUT AFTERWARDS ACCUSES
HIMSELF AND IS CONDEMNED, ... 294

XXII.—THE COURT PHYSICIAN PRESCRIBES FOR THE QUEEN
—A BLOW-UP, AND MYSTERIOUS PREPARATIONS
FOR TREMENDOUS SURPRISES, ... 305

XXIII.—IN WHICH MARK CARRIES OUT HIS PLANS SUCCESS-
FULLY, AND POWERFULLY ASTONISHES HIMSELF
AS WELL AS EVERY ONE ELSE, ... 318

XXIV.—FLIGHT AND PURSUIT OF RAVONINO AND RAFARA-
VAVY, ... 336

XXV.—THE FOREST REFUGE—VOALAVO IS WARLIKE,
RAVONINO PEACEFUL, AND FALSE FRIENDS DAN-
GEROUS, ... 349

CONTENTS.

PAGE

CHAP. XXVI.—DR. BREEZY PRESCRIBES FOR THE QUEEN, AND
    ATTAINS TO TEMPORARY "PERFIK F'LICITY,"   361

XXVII.—IN WHICH A HAPPY CHANGE FOR THE BETTER IS
    DISASTROUSLY INTERRUPTED,   .   .   .   374

XXVIII.—IN WHICH TERRIBLE BUT TRUE MARTYRDOMS ARE
    DESCRIBED, ...   387

XXIX.—THREATENED DEATH AVERTED—BURIED ALIVE
    —END OF THE TYRANT QUEEN — REVOLT
    CRUSHED AND RADAMA II. CROWNED,   .   .   404

XXX.—THE LAST, ...   420

LIST OF ILLUSTRATIONS.

A SCRAMBLE FOR LIFE (p. 5),   .   .   . *Frontispiece*

ILLUSTRATED TITLE-PAGE.

AN AMATEUR MATADOR,   .   .   . *facing page* 35

NOCTURNAL VISITORS, ... 107

A FUGITIVE MEETING, ... 210

HIDING IN A SWAMP, .   ,   .   ,   .   . 345

A SCRAMBLE FOR LIFE.—Page 5. (*Frontispiece.*)

AN AMATEUR MATADOR. Page 35.

NOCTURNAL VISITORS.—Page 107.

A FUGITIVE MEETING.—Page 270.

HIDING IN A SWAMP.—Page 345.

THE FUGITIVES

OR

THE TYRANT QUEEN OF MADAGASCAR.

CHAPTER I.

INTRODUCES THE CHIEF ACTORS AND A FEW MYSTERIES.

INTENSE action is at all times an interesting object of contemplation to mankind. We therefore make no apology to the reader for dragging him unceremoniously into the middle of a grand primeval forest, and presenting to his view the curious and stirring spectacle of two white men and a negro running at their utmost possible speed, with flashing eyes and labouring chests—evidently running for their lives.

Though very different in aspect and condition, those men were pretty equally matched as runners, for there was no apparent difference in the vigour with which they maintained the pace.

The track or footpath along which they ran was so narrow as to compel them to advance in single file. He who led was a tall agile youth of nineteen

A

or thereabouts, in knickerbocker shooting-garb, with short curly black hair, pleasantly expressive features, and sinewy frame. The second was obviously a true-blue tar—a regular sea-dog—about thirty years of age, of Samsonian mould, and, albeit running for very life, with grand indignation gleaming in his eyes. He wore a blue shirt on his broad back, white ducks on his active legs, and a straw hat on his head, besides a mass of shaggy hair, which, apparently, not finding enough of room on his cranium, overflowed in two brown cataracts down his cheeks, and terminated in a voluminous beard.

The third fugitive was also a young man, and a negro, short, thickset, square, tough as india-rubber, and black as the Emperor of Zahara. Good-humour wrinkled the corners of his eyes, the milk of human kindness played on his thick lips and rippled his sable brow, and intense sincerity, like a sunbeam, suffused his entire visage.

James Ginger—for that was his name, though his friends preferred to call him Ebony—scorned a hat of any kind ; his simple costume consisting merely of two garments—canvas trousers and a guernsey shirt.

The sailor wore a cutlass in his belt. Ebony was unarmed. The youthful leader carried a short fowl-ing-piece.

A yell in the far distance, as if from a hundred fiends, told that the pursuers had discovered the trail of the fugitives, and were gaining on them.

"We'll have to fight for it, doctor," growled the sailor in a savage tone, "better stop while we've got some wind left."

"The wood seems more open ahead," replied the youth, "let's push on a bit further."

"Hi!" exclaimed the negro in surprise, not un-mingled with alarm, as they suddenly emerged on an open space and found themselves on the edge of a stupendous precipice.

The formation of the region was curious. There was a drop in the land, as it were, to a lower level. From their elevated position the three men could see a turbulent river rushing far below, at the base of the cliffs on the edge of which they stood. Beyond lay a magnificent and varied stretch of forest scenery, extending away to the horizon, where the prospect terminated in a blue range of hills. No path was at first visible by which the fugitives could reach the plain below. The precipice was almost perpendicular. They were about to leap recklessly over, and trust to descending by means of an occasional bush or shrub which grew on the rocky face, when the negro uttered one of his falsetto exclamations.

"Hi! here am a track."

He dashed aside the branches of an overhanging bush, and ran along a narrow path, or ledge, which sloped gently downwards. It was a fearfully giddy position, but this in the circumstances, and to men accustomed to mast-heads and yard-arms, was of small moment. On they ran, at a more cautious pace indeed, but still with anxious haste, until about a quarter of the distance down the face of the precipice, when, to their horror, they came to a turn in the path where it suddenly ended. A mass of rock, apparently detached from the cliff by recent rains, had fallen from above, and in its thundering descent had carried away fully ten yards of the path into the stream below, where they could see its shattered fragments in the rushing river. The gap in front of them was absolutely impassable. On the right, the cliff rose sheer upwards. On the left, it went sheer down.

A sort of groan escaped from the doctor.

"What's to be done now, Hockins?" he asked sharply, turning to the sailor.

"Die!" replied Hockins, in a tone of savage bitterness.

"Stuff an' nonsense! we no' die yit," said the negro, pointing to the snake-like branches of a climbing plant which, spreading over the naked face of the cliff, turned into a crevice and disappeared round a jutting point.

" Will it bear our weight, lad ? " asked the sailor doubtfully.

" It leads to nothing that I can see," said the young doctor, "and would only ensure our being dashed to pieces instead of speared."

" Nebber fear, massa Breezy. Dis not de fus' time I's goed troo de forests. If you stop here you die. James Gingah he go on an' lib."

" Go on then, Ebony; we will follow," returned Breezy, slinging his gun on his shoulder so as to leave his hands free.

A yell of disappointment on the cliffs above accelerated their movements. It was evident that the pursuers had come out on the open plateau, but had not observed the path by which they descended. As it was certain, however, that they would find it in a few minutes, Ebony sprang upon the creeping plant and clambered along its tortuous limbs like a monkey. Young Breezy followed, and Hockins came last.

The plant was tough. It stood the strain well. If it had given way, death on the jagged rocks below would have been the result. But death by savage spears was behind them, so they did not hesitate. A few seconds and all three had passed round the jutting rock and into the crevice, where they were completely hidden from the view of any one standing on the path they had just left.

In the crevice they found a ledge or platform sufficiently large to admit of their standing together. They had scarcely obtained a footing on it when another shout announced that the pursuer had traced their trail to the head of the track.

We know not, reader, whether you have ever experienced that heart-melting qualm which comes over one at the sudden and unexpected approach of what, at least, appears to be death. If you have, you will be able to understand the intense relief and thankfulness felt by the fugitives when, safe from immediate danger, they listened to their pursuers as they held excited conversation at the end of the broken track. Not knowing the language they could not, of course, understand what was said, and being just beyond the range of vision—owing to the jutting cliff that concealed them—they could not see what their pursuers were doing, but they heard a suggestive crash and a sharp exclamation.

Had they been able to see, they would have understood the situation well enough without the aid of language.

Two of the natives, who were dark-skinned and almost naked savages, had come to the place where the track had been broken away. They gazed at the profound depths on the left and the inaccessible cliffs on the right, and then glanced at each other in solemn surprise.

No doubt the creeping plant would in a few seconds have attracted special attention, had not an incident turned their minds in another direction. While the foremost savage was craning his neck so as to see as far round the projecting cliff as possible, the piece of rock on which his advanced foot rested was dislodged, and he had the narrowest possible escape from plunging headlong after the rock, which went bounding and crashing into the gulf below.

Instantly the faces of the two men gleamed with intelligence; they nodded with energy, grinned with satisfaction, and pointed to the abyss in front of them with the air of men who had no doubt that their enemies were lying down there in quivering fragments.

Something of this James Ginger did indeed manage to see. Curiosity was so powerfully developed in that sable spirit, that, at the imminent risk of his life, he reached out by means of a branch, and so elongated his black neck that he got one of his brilliant eyes to bear for a moment upon his foes. He appreciated the situation instantly, and drew back to indulge in a smothered laugh which shut up both his eyes and appeared to gash his face from ear to ear.

"What's wrong with you, Ebony?" whispered Mark Breezy, who was in anything but a laughing mood just then.

"Oh! nuffin, nuffin, massa; only dem brown niggers are sitch asses dat dey b'lieve a'most anyting. Black niggers aint so easy putt off de scent. Dey tinks we's tumble ober de precipis an' busted ourselbes."

"Lucky for us that they think so," said Hockins, in a soft tone of satisfaction. "But now, what are we to do? It was bad enough clamberin' up here in blazin' excitement to save our lives, but it will be ten times worse gettin' down again in cold blood when they're gone."

"Time enough to consider that when they *are* gone," muttered Breezy. "Hush! Listen!"

The sounds that reached their place of concealment told clearly enough that a number of the savages had descended the cliffs, presumably to look at the place over which the white men had fallen. Then there was much eager conversation in an unknown tongue, mingled with occasional bursts of laughter—on hearing which latter the huge mouth of our negro enlarged in silent sympathy. After a while the voices were heard to retire up the narrow track and become fainter until they died away altogether, leaving no sound save the murmur of the rushing river to fill the ears of the anxious listeners who stood like three statues in a niche on the face of that mighty precipice.

"Now, you know," said Breezy, with a sigh of

relief, "this is very satisfactory as far as it goes, and we have reason to be thankful that we are neither speared nor dashed to pieces; nevertheless, we are in an uncomfortable fix here, for night is approaching, and we must retrace our steps somehow or other, unless we make up our minds to sleep standing."

"That's so, doctor. There's not room to lie down here," assented the sailor, glancing slowly round; "an', to tell ee the plain truth, I feel as funky about trustin' myself again to that serpent-like creeper as I felt the first time I went up through the lubber-hole the year I went to sea."

"What you's 'fraid ob, Mr. 'Ockins?" asked Ebony.

"Afraid o' the nasty thing givin' way under my weight. If it was a good stout rope, now, I wouldn't mind, but every crack it gave when I was comin' aloft made my heart jump a'most out o' my mouth."

"What have ee found there, doctor?" asked the seaman, on observing that his companion was groping behind a mass of herbage at the back part of the niche in which they stood.

"There's a big hole here, Hockins. Perhaps we may find room to stay where we are, after all, till morning. Come here, Ebony, you've got something of the eel about you. Try if you can wriggle in."

The negro at once thrust his head and shoulders into the hole, but could not advance.

"Bery strange!" he said, drawing out his head, and snorting once or twice like a dog that has half-choked himself in a rabbit-hole. "Seems to me dere's a big block o' wood dere stoppin' de way."

"Strange indeed, Ebony. A block of wood could not have grown there. Are you sure it is not a big root?"

"Sartin' sure, massa. I hab studied roots since I was a babby. Hold on, I try again."

The negro tried again, and with such vigour that he not only displaced the block of wood, but burst in several planks which concealed the entrance to a cavern. They fell on the stone floor with a crash that aroused a multitude of echoes in the dark interior. At the same moment something like a faint shriek or wail was heard within, causing the hearts of the three listeners to beat faster.

"Did you hear that, Hockins?"

"Ay, I heard it sure enough. What is it, think ee, lad?" said the seaman to the negro.

Ebony, who was gazing into the dark cavern with glaring eyeballs and distended nostrils, replied—

"My 'vice to you is let's go back de way we come. Dis no place for 'spectable Christians."

"Do you fear ghosts?" asked Mark, smiling, yet at the same time bringing his gun into a convenient position, with his finger ready on the trigger.

"I fears nuffin," returned the negro with a proud look, while beads of perspiration stood on his brow.

"Then ye're a braver man than I am, Ebony, for I fear that climbin' plant worse than a ghost; so here goes to find out what it is."

Although the sailor spoke thus boldly, and tried to look cool, it is certain that he also was afflicted with sensations of an unusual description, which, of course, he would have scorned to admit were the result of fear! His power of will, however, was stronger than his fears. Drawing his cutlass, he was about to enter the cavern, when Mark laid a hand on his shoulder.

"Come, Hockins, you have accepted my lead hitherto. It is not fair to take it out of my hands at this critical point."

So saying he glided past his comrade, and was almost lost to sight immediately in the deep gloom.

"Softly, softly, doctor," whispered the seaman, as he followed, "there may be holes or pits within—"

"All right; I'm feeling my way carefully. Keep close."

As he spoke a slight, indescribable sound was heard—almost like a sigh.

"Hist! Did ee hear that?" said Hockins in the lowest possible whisper.

"Oh! massa, let's go back de way we come," urged Ebony, in the same low but earnest tone.

Mark Breezy did not reply, but the click of his gun as he cocked it showed that he was on the alert.

For nearly a minute the three men stood in absolute silence, listening for a repetition of the mysterious sound, and, though it did not recur, there was an indescribable feeling in the heart of each that they were not alone in that cavern.

"Have you not flint and steel?" asked Mark.

"Yes; but to strike a light would only show our whereabouts if there *is* any one here."

The seaman accidentally touched Ebony on the elbow as he spoke, and sent that worthy's heart, or something like it, into his throat with such violence as nearly to choke him.

"Git along, massa," he said in a gaspy whisper, when able to articulate, "we's got to go troo wid it *now*."

Acting on this advice the young man continued to advance cautiously, feeling his way step by step and fully expecting every moment to reach the inner wall of the cavern.

Presently the explorers were again brought to a stand by the sudden appearance of a light in the far distance. As, however, it did not move, they continued to advance, and soon were convinced that it was daylight shining through an opening in that direction. Every step convinced them more and more that they were right, and their spirits rose with the hope of escaping, though the light made no appreciable difference as yet in the darkness that surrounded them.

Suddenly a sharp, loud, short cry filled the cavern for an instant, and almost froze their blood! The loudness and abrupt stoppage of the cry left the impression that the creature which uttered it had been suddenly and effectively killed, for it ended in a sharp gasp or gurgle, and then all was still,—but only for a moment, for the shock to Mark's nerves was such that his finger inadvertently pressed the trigger of his gun, which exploded with a deafening crash, and awoke shrieks and cries that were not to be accounted for by mere echoes.

This was too much for ordinary human beings. Fabled knights of old in armour of proof might have stood it, but the two white men and the black, being ordinary heroes, regardless of pride and honour, went in for a regular stampede, and it is but simple justice to say that Ebony won, for he reached the outlet of the cavern first, and sprang through it into daylight like a black thunderbolt. It is also due to his comrades to add that they were not far behind him.

Their courage, however, was soon restored. Day·

light has a celebrated power of restoring courage. On clearing the bushes which concealed the entrance to the cave they simultaneously stopped, turned round, and resolutely faced their foe!

But no foe was to be seen! Once again all was still as death. After glaring for a few seconds at the spot whence the expected enemy should have issued, the three fugitives relaxed their frowning brows and turned inquiring eyes on each other.

"Dis beats cockfightin' a'most," said Ebony, with a sigh of intense relief.

" Ay, an' every other sort o' fightin' as I ever heard on," responded Hockins.

"Come, friends," said their young leader, "whatever it may have been, it behoves us to get as far away from this spot as possible, and that as fast as we can."

CHAPTER II.

HARKS BACK A LITTLE.

THE spot where our adventurers found themselves
on issuing from the mysterious cave was a peculiarly
rugged one.   It formed a sort of hollow or depression in the forest-land in which we introduced the
three men as fugitives.   From this hollow there
descended a narrow track or pathway to the extensive valley which had been seen from the summit
of the precipice that barred their flight, and had so
nearly proved fatal.

So confused was the nature of the ground here,
and so intricate were the tracks—originally formed
no doubt by wild animals, though made use of by
wandering men—that it became impossible for Mark
Breezy to know in what direction he was leading his
comrades as he wound in and out among large rocks
and fallen trees.   In fact it was more by chance
than guidance that they ultimately hit upon the
path which finally led them to the lower region or
plateau of forest-land; and it is certain that they

would have found it impossible to find their way
back to the cave, even had they desired to do so.

Their chief object, however, was to put as much
space as possible between themselves and their late
pursuers, and to this end they pushed forward at
their best speed, until they reached a small river
which appeared to be a tributary to, or a branch of,
that which they had seen from the heights earlier
in the day.

> " ' Come to a ribber—couldn't git across,
> Gib a couple o' dollars for an' old blind hoss,"

murmured Ebony, quoting an ancient ditty.

" We shall have to swim it, I fear," remarked
Breezy, " for there is no horse here, blind or otherwise. Perhaps that fallen tree may prove strong
enough to serve as a bridge."

He pointed to a slender tree which had evidently
been placed there, with several others, for the purpose
of forming a rough and ready bridge ; but its companions had been removed by floods, for they lay
tossed on the bank further down among other
wreckage.

" It 'll be somethin' like tight-rope dancin'," said
the sailor. " We 'll have to repair the bridge."

" Nuffin ob de sort ! Look here."

Ebony ran to the tree referred to, and skipped
over with admirable agility, though it bent under
him not unlike a tight-rope.

"But *I* can't do that," said Hockins, "not bein' a black monkey, d'ee see?"

With a sudden expression of intense pity the negro exclaimed—"Oh! I beg pardin'. Didn't I forgot; you's on'y a white man. But stop; I come ober agin an' took you on my back."

He pretended to be on the point of recrossing, but the sailor had already got upon the bridge, and, with much balancing and waving of his long arms, passed over in safety. Mark was about to follow, when Hockins called out, "Better pitch over the powder-flask in case you fall in."

"That's true, for I mayn't be as good as you or Ebony on the tight-rope. Look out!"

He pulled the powder-flask out of his pocket and threw it towards his comrades. Unfortunately the branch of an overhanging bush had touched his hand. The touch was slight, but it sufficed to divert the flask from its proper course, and sent it into the middle of the stream.

Ebony followed it head first like an otter, but soon reappeared, gasping and unsuccessful. Again and again he dived, but failed to find the flask, without which, of course, their gun was useless, and at last they were obliged to continue their flight without it.

This was a very serious loss, for they had not an ounce of provisions with them, and were in a land the character and resources of which were utterly unknown at least to two of them, while the youth who had become their leader knew very little more than the fact that it was the island of Madagascar, that it lay about 300 miles off the eastern shores of Africa, and that the tribes by whom they were surrounded were little if at all better than savages.

That day they wandered far into the depths of a dark and tangled forest, intentionally seeking its gloomiest recesses in order to avoid the natives, and at night went supperless to rest among the branches of an umbrageous tree, not knowing what danger from man or beast might assail them if they should venture to sleep on the ground.

Although possessed of flint and steel, as well as tinder, they did not use them for fear of attracting attention. As they had nothing to cook, the deprivation was not great. Fortunately the weather at the time was pleasantly warm, so that beyond the discomfort of not being able to stretch out at full length, the occasional poking of awkward knots and branches into their ribs, and the constant necessity of holding on lest they should fall off, their circumstances were not insufferable, and might have been worse.

While they are enjoying their repose, we will tell in a few sentences who they were and how they got there.

When Mark Breezy, in the closing years of his

medical-student career, got leave to go on a voyage to China in one of his father's ships, the *Eastern Star*, for the benefit of his health and the enlargement of his understanding, he had no more idea that that voyage would culminate in a bed up a tree in the forests of Madagascar than you, reader, have that you will ultimately become an inhabitant of the moon! The same remark may with equal truth be made of John Hockins when he joined the *Eastern Star* as an able seaman, and of James Ginger—*alias* Ebony—when he shipped as cook. If the captain of the *Eastern Star* had introduced those three,—who had never seen each other before —and told them that they would spend many months together among savages in the midst of terrestrial beauty, surrounded by mingled human depravity and goodness, self-denial and cruelty, fun and tragedy such as few men are fated to experience, they would have smiled at each other with good-natured scepticism and regarded their captain as a facetious lunatic.

Yet so it turned out, though the captain prophesied it not—and this was the way of it.

Becalmed off the coast of Madagascar, and having, through leakage in one of the tanks, run short of water, the captain ordered a boat with casks to be got ready to go ashore for water. The young doctor got leave to land and take his gun for the purpose of procuring specimens—for he was something of a naturalist—and having a ramble.

"Don't get out of hail, Doctor," said the captain, as the boat shoved off.

"All right, sir, I won't."

"An' take a couple o' the men into the bush with you in case of accidents."

"Ay ay, sir," responded Mark, waving his hand in acknowledgment.

And that was the last that Mark Breezy and the captain of the *Eastern Star* saw of each other for many a day.

"Who will go with me ?" asked Mark, when the boat touched the shore.

"Me, massa," eagerly answered the negro cook, who had gone ashore in the hope of being able to get some fresh vegetables from the natives if any were to be found living there. "Seems to me dere's no black mans here, so may's well try de woods for wild wegibles."

"No no, Ebony," said the first mate, who had charge of the boat, "you'll be sure to desert if we let you go—unless we send Hockins to look after you. He's the only man that can keep you in order."

"Well, I'll take Hockins also," said Mark, "you heard the captain say I was to have two men. Will you go, Hockins ?"

"Ay ay, sir," answered the seaman, sedately, but with a wrinkle or two on his visage which proved that the proposal was quite to his taste.

All the men of the boat's crew were armed either with cutlass or carbine—in some cases with both; for although the natives were understood to be friendly at that part of the coast it was deemed prudent to be prepared for the reverse. Thus John Hockins carried a cutlass in his belt, but no fire-arm, and the young doctor had his double-barrelled gun, with powder-flask and shot-belt, but Ebony— being a free-and-easy, jovial sort of nigger—went unarmed, saying he "didn't want to carry no harms, seein' he would need all de harms he had to carry back de fresh wegibles wid."

Thus those three went into the bush, promising to keep well within ear-shot, and to return instantly at the first summons.

That summons came—not as a shout, as had been expected, but as a shot—about an hour after the landing. Our explorers ran to the top of a neighbouring mound in some surprise, not unmixed with anxiety. Before they reached the summit a volley from the direction of the sea, followed by fierce yells, told that some sort of evil was going on. Another moment, and they reached the eminence just in time to behold their boat's crew pulling off shore while a band of at least a hundred

savages attacked them—some rushing into the
water chest-deep in order to seize the boat. Cutlass and carbine, however, proved more than a
match for stone and spear.

The fight had scarce lasted a minute, and our
trio were on the point of rushing down to the
rescue, when a white cloud burst from the side of
the *Eastern Star*, the woods and cliffs echoed with
the roar of a big gun, and a shot, plunging into the
crowd of natives, cut down many of them and went
crashing into the bushes.

It was enough. The natives turned and fled
while the boat pulled to the ship.

Uncertainty as to what should be done kept
Mark Breezy and his companions rooted for a few
seconds to the spot. Indecision was banished,
however, when they suddenly perceived a band of
thirty or forty natives moving stealthily towards
them by a circuitous route, evidently with the
intention of taking them in rear and preventing
them from finding shelter in the woods.

It was the first time that the young student's
manhood had been put severely to the test. There
was a rush of hot blood to his forehead, and his
heart beat powerfully as he saw and realised the
hopelessness of their case with such tremendous
odds against them.

" We can die but once," he said with forced calmness, as he cocked his gun and prepared to defend himself.

"I's not a-goin' to die at all," said the negro, hastily tightening his belt, "I's a-goin' to squatilate."

"And you?" said Mark, turning to the seaman.

"Run, says I, of coorse," replied Hockins, with something between a grin and a scowl; "ye know the old song—him wot fights an' runs away may live to fight another day!"

"Come along, then!" cried Mark, who felt that whether they fought or ran he was bound to retain the leadership of his little party.

As we have seen, they ran to some purpose. No doubt if they had started on equal terms, the lithe, hardy, and almost naked savages would have soon overtaken them, but fortunately a deep gully lay between them and the party of natives who had first observed them. Before this was crossed the fugitives were over the second ridge of rolling land that lay between the thick woods and the sea, and when the savages at last got upon their track and began steadily to overhaul them, the white men had got fairly into the forest.

Still there would have been no chance of ultimate escape if they had not come upon the footpath down the precipice which we have described as having been partly carried away by falling rocks, thus enabling Hockins and his companions to make a scramble for life which no one but a sailor, a monkey, or a hero, would have dared, and the impossibility of even attempting which never occurred to the pursuers, who concluded, as we have seen, that the white men had been dashed to pieces on the rocks far below.

Whether they afterwards found out their mistake or not we cannot tell.

The reason—long afterwards ascertained—of this unprovoked attack on the boat's crew, was the old story. A party of godless white men had previously visited that part of the coast and treated the poor natives with great barbarity, thus stirring up feelings of hatred and revenge against *all* white men —at least for the time being. In this way the innocent are too often made to suffer for the guilty.

We will now return to our friends in the tree.

CHAPTER III.

DESCRIBES THE DEED OF AN AMATEUR MATADOR AND THE WORK
OF A ROUGH-AND-READY SHOEMAKER.

WHEN the day began to break Hockins awoke, and his first impulse was to shout "hold on!" Ebony's first action was to let go, thereby bringing himself to the ground with an awful thud, which would have told severely on any one less akin to india-rubber.

For a few minutes Mark Breezy, holding tight to his particular branch, looked down at his companions, yawned heavily, and smiled a little. Then a sudden impulse of memory caused him to look grave.

"Come," he said, dropping lightly from his perch, "these natives may have been searching for us all night, and are perhaps nearer than we suppose. I vote that we push on at once."

"Agreed," said Hockins, stretching himself.

"No fear, Massa," remarked the negro. "If it wur moonlight dey might 'ave search, but whar de nights am dark dey knows better. De niggahs in dis yer island hab got skins an' eyes an' noses. If dey was to go troo such woods in de dark, dey hab no skins or eyes or noses in de mornin—leas'wise nuffin wuth mentionin'. Cause why? Dey'd all git knocked into a sorter mush. Plenty ob time for breakfast 'fore we start."

"That's true, boy," said Hockins, "but where's the breakfast to come from?"

"What! you no bringed nuffin in your pockits?" asked the negro with a look of visible anxiety on his expressive face.

Hockins turned his various pockets inside out by way of reply.

"I am equally destitute," said Mark.

The negro groaned as he slowly drew from his breeches pockets two sea-biscuits and a cold sausage.

"I meant dat," he said, "as a light lunch for *one* yisterday."

"It'll have to do dooty, then, as a heavy breakfast for three this morning, Ebony. Come, divide, and let's have fair play."

"Here, massa," said Ebony, handing the food to Mark, "you divide, I ain't got de moral courage to do it fair. Number one is too strong in me when I's hungry!"

With a laugh at this candid admission the youth did his best at a fair division. In a few minutes the scanty meal was finished, and the fugitives proceeded straight into the interior of the country at the utmost speed which was compatible with sustained exertion.

They could see the faint outlines of a mountain range in the far distance, and towards that they directed their steps, knowing that in the event of sustained pursuit they had a much better chance of escaping among the rugged fastnesses of a mountain region than in the forests or on the plains. But they saw plainly that there was many a weary mile to traverse before the sheltering mountains could be reached.

At first they walked rapidly and in silence, one behind the other—Mark leading—but as time passed, and the danger of being overtaken decreased, they fell more into line and began to talk of their plans and prospects.

Of course they thought about the *Eastern Star*, and the possibility of her hanging about the coast in the hope of picking them up; but as there was no certainty upon that point, and a return to the coast would be like rushing into the very jaws of the lion from which they were fleeing, they soon dismissed the idea as untenable.

"Now then, the question is, sir, Wot are we agoin' for to do?" said Hockins.

"Ay, dat's de question," added Ebony with much force, and more than Shakspearean brevity.

"Well now, lads," said Mark, "I 've been thinking over that, and it seems to me that there's not much to choose between. Unfortunately, I know uncommonly little about this island—not that my geographical education has been neglected, but the class-books I have used did not give much information about Madagascar. I know, however, that the Mozambique Channel, which divides us from Africa, is a little too wide to swim. I also know that there is a capital somewhere near the middle of the island, the name of which begins with an ' Ant,' and ends with a 'rivo.' There are some syllables between, I believe, but how many, is more than I can tell. There's a government in it, however, and a queen, and some Christian missionaries. Now, it strikes me that where there's a government, a queen, and Christian missionaries, there must be more or less of civilisation and safety, so I would advise that we make straight for the capital."

"Right you are, sir," said Hockins. "As I know nothin' whotsomever about the place, I'll take my sailin' orders from you, captain, an' steer a straight course for Anty-whatever-she-is-arivo, where I hope we'll arrive O!—'all alive O!' in the course o' time. What say you, Ebony?"

"I's agreeable; don't care much for nuffin when it don't trouble me. But I's gettin' awrful hungry, an' I don't see nuffin to eat in dis yer forest—not even fruit—dough it's pritty enough to look at."

The scenery through which they were passing at the time was indeed more than pretty. It was gorgeous, and would certainly have claimed more attention from the travellers had they been less anxious to advance, and, perhaps, less hungry.

By that time—near mid-day—they had got through the densest part of the woods, and were come to a part where occasional openings in the foliage lighted them up. They had also discovered a narrow track or footpath, which they gladly followed; for although by so doing they ran the risk of coming suddenly upon natives, who might be foes just as well as friends, the comparative ease of travelling was too great to be neglected. This path struck over hill and down dale in a somewhat dogged and straightforward manner, scorning to go round hillocks, save when too precipitous for un-winged animals. At times it wound in and out among trees of great beauty and variety, and of tropical aspect. Elsewhere it plunged into denser stretches of forest, where the profusion of vegetable life was extraordinary—here, a dense undergrowth of shrubs, tree-ferns, and dwarf-palms; there, trees of higher growth, and, shooting high above them all, the slender trunks of many varieties of palms, whose graceful crowns and feathery leaves were pictured vividly on the blue sky. Elsewhere, innumerable creeping plants interlaced the branches, producing

a wild and beautiful net-work, their tendrils crossing
in all directions, and producing a green twilight in
places. The whole was enriched by orchids, the
abundant pink and white wax-like flowers of which
contrasted well with other wild-flowers innumerable,
and with many large and gorgeous flowering trees.

Different species of bamboos gave quite a peculiar
aspect to the scenery in some places, and still
greater variety was secured by long pendant masses
of feathery grey moss and lichens. Some of the
trees were of enormous height; one palm, with a
straight stem, in particular, being estimated as not
less than a hundred feet high to the spot where the
leaves sprouted.

" 'Tis a perfect paradise !" exclaimed Mark, stopping suddenly and looking around with admiration.

" Yes, massa," murmured Ebony, with solemn
looks, " if dere was on'y a few wegibles—cooked !
Flowers is all bery well to look at, but we can't
heat him."

" Well, if we can't eat, we can, at all events,
sleep," returned Mark. " I believe it is usually
thought wise in tropical countries to cease work
and rest about noon, so, as I feel rather tired, I'll
have a snooze. What say you ?"

No objection being made, the party again climbed
into the branches of a low spreading tree, in order
to avoid snakes, scorpions, or any other noxious

creatures, though they knew not at the time whether such existed on the island. In less than five minutes they were sound asleep.

Awaking after about two hours' repose, they descended, wished for something to eat, sighed, put a bold heart on it, tightened their belts to suit diminishing waists, and continued their journey.

Perseverance is sure to be rewarded. If that is not a proverb, it ought to be! At all events the perseverance of our travellers was rewarded at this time by their coming suddenly out of the woods into a wide grassy plain on which was browsing a herd of wild cattle—at least they judged them to be wild from the fact of their being discovered in such a wild place, and resolved to treat them as wild because of the "wolves" inside of them, which clamoured so wildly for food.

"Beef!" exclaimed Hockins in some excitement, as he pointed to the animal nearest to them, which happened to be a black, sleek, fat young bull, with slender limbs and fierce eyes.

"Neber mind the wegibles, massa; shot 'im!" exclaimed Ebony in an excited whisper, as he turned his glaring eyeballs on his leader.

"Hush! don't speak," returned Mark, drawing quietly back into cover—for the animal had not observed them. "We must consult what is to be done, because, you know, we have lost our powder-flask, the two charges in my gun are all I have got, and these are only small shot—I have no bullets!"

Grave concern overspread the face of the sturdy seaman—blank dismay that of the sea-cook!

"Might as well blaze at the beast wi' sand," said Hockins.

"Or wid nuffin!" sighed Ebony.

"Nevertheless, I will try," said Mark, quickly. "We shall be starved to death at this rate. Yonder is a line of bushes that runs close out to the brute. I'll stalk it. When close I will make a dash at it, get as near as I can, clap the muzzle against its ribs if possible, and——well, we shall see! You two had better stop here and look on."

"No, massa," said the negro, firmly, "I go wid you. If you is to die, we die togidder!"

"What are you thinking of, Hockins?" asked the youth, observing that the seaman stood staring at the ground with knitted brows, as if in deep thought.

"I'll go with you too," he replied, drawing his cutlass and feeling its point with his finger. "You may need help. Heave a-head, sir."

Mark could not avoid smiling at the way in which this was said, although he was sufficiently impressed with the hopelessness, it might even be the danger, of the attempt he was about to make.

They found no difficulty in approaching to within

about thirty yards of the animal, being well concealed by the line of bushes before mentioned, but beyond that point there was no cover. Here therefore Mark cocked his gun and gathered himself up for a rush, and Hockins drew his cutlass. So agile was our young doctor that he actually reduced the thirty yards to ten before the astonished bull turned to fly. Another moment and the contents of both barrels were lodged in its flank. The effect was to produce a bellow of rage, a toss-up of the hindquarters, and a wild flourish of the tail, as the animal scurried away after the rest of the herd, which was in full flight.

Poor Breezy stopped at once, with a feeling of mingled disgust and despair. Ebony also stopped, and looked with wide sympathetic eyes in his leader's face, as though to say, " Well, massa, you's done your best."

But Hockins ran on with persistent vigour, although the creature was leaving him further behind at every stride.

"Absurd!" murmured Mark, as he gazed at him.

"No use wassomiver," said Ebony.

It did indeed seem as if the seaman's exertions would prove abortive, but something in the spirit of the wounded bull suddenly changed the aspect of affairs. Whether it was the stinging pain of the small shot in its flank, or the indignation in its breast that influenced it we cannot tell, but in a moment it wheeled round with a furious roar and charged its pursuer.

Hockins stopped at once, and his comrades fully expected to see him turn and run; but our seaman was made of better stuff than they gave him credit for, and the situation was not so new to him as they imagined. In the course of his voyaging to many lands, Hockins had been to a bull-fight in South America. He had seen with fascination and some surprise the risks run by the footmen in the arena; he had beheld with mingled anger and disgust the action of the picadors, who allowed their poor horses to be gored to death by the infuriated bulls; and he had watched with thrilling anxiety, not unmingled with admiration, the cool courage of the matadors, as they calmly stood up to the maddened and charging bulls and received them on the points of their swords, stepping lightly aside at the same moment so as to avoid the dangerous horns.

The seaman's purpose now was to act the part of a matador. He knew that he possessed coolness and nerve sufficient for the deed; he hoped that he had the skill; he felt that hunger could no longer remain unsatisfied; he feared that death by starvation might be the lot of himself and his companions, and he preferred to meet death in action—if meet it he must. All things considered, he resolved to face the bovine thunderbolt with unflinching front, like a true-blue British tar!

His coolness in the circumstances was evinced by the remarks muttered to himself in a growly tone as the bull approached.

"Three futt—that'll be enough. I don't rightly remember how near them mattydoors let him come before they putt their helms hard down an' let him go by, but I think three futt'll do."

This decision was barely reached when the bull was upon him with lowered head and erect tail. It was an awful rush, but Hockins stood like a rock with the cutlass pointed. At the pre-arranged moment he stepped to one side, but instead of letting the momentum of the animal do the work, he could not resist the impulse to drive the cutlass deeper into the bull's neck. The result was that, though he escaped the creature's horn by a very narrow shave, the cutlass was wrenched violently from his grasp, and he was sent head over heels upon the plain!

Seeing this, Mark and the negro ran to the rescue, the one howling like a maniac, the other clubbing his gun ; but their aid was not required, for the work of the amateur matador had been effectively done. After receiving the deadly thrust the bull plunged forward a few paces, and then fell dying upon the ground, while Hockins got up and began to feel himself all over to make sure that no bones were broken.

It need scarcely be told that they rejoiced greatly over their success, and that they cut off some of the flesh immediately, with which they returned to the forest to enjoy a much-needed meal.

"We must kindle a fire now," said Mark, stopping at an open space in the midst of a very secluded spot at the foot of a magnificent palm-tree. "You see I'm not prepared to act like a cannibal or Eskimo, and eat the meat raw."

"There won't be much fear now," said Hockins, "especially if we make the fire of dry wood an' keep it small. Just look at that, Doctor."

He held out his cutlass for inspection. It had been seriously bent in the recent encounter.

"Aint that a cryin' shame to the owners, now, to send us poor fellows to the eastern seas, where we may meet pirates any day, with tin cutlashes like that."

"You kin put him straight de next bull you kills," said Ebony, as he prepared some touchwood; "you've on'y got to stick 'im on the *left* side an' he'll twis' it all right. Now, massa, I's ready, bring de gun an' snap de flints ober dat."

While Hockins straightened his weapon between the branches of a tree, his comrades managed to capture a spark in a mass of dry combustibles, which soon burst into a flame. As the seaman had recommended, only the driest wood was used, and just enough of that to enable them to half-roast what food they required. Then they returned to the carcass of the bull, and cut off a large quantity of meat, using the cutlass as well as their clasp-knives in the operation.

"Cut the meat in thin slices," said Mark Breezy, when they began this work.

"Why you so 'ticklar, massa?" asked Ebony. "I's fond o' t'ick slices—w'en him's not too tough."

"Because then we can dry the meat in the sun or over a slow fire, and so be able to keep it longer without spoiling. We must spend the night here for the purpose, and perhaps part of to-morrow. —Why, Hockins, what are you about?"

"Makin' a pair o' shoes, sir; you see them old dancin' pumps as I left the ship with wouldn't hold out another day o' this rough travellin', so I'm makin' a noo pair of shoes when I've got the chance."

"They will be a primitive pair," observed Mark.

"If that means a good pair, you're right, sir. They are after the pattern first made by Adam for Eve—leas'wise it's supposed her first pair o' dancin' pumps was made this fashion. I'll make a sim'lar pair for you, sir, w'en your boots give out."

In case the reader should ever be reduced to

extremities in the matter of foot-gear we may explain the seaman's method.

Selecting what he believed to be the thickest part of the bull's hide, he cut off a small portion about eighteen inches square. Spreading this on the ground with the hair upwards, he planted his naked foot on it and marked the shape thereon. Then with his knife he cut away the hide all round the foot-mark at four inches or so from the outline of the foot. Next, he bored little holes all round the margin, through which he ran a line, or lace, also made of raw hide. Then, planting his foot again in the middle of the hide, he drew the line tight, causing the edges to rise all round the foot and almost cover it.

"There you are, sir," he said, stretching out his limb and admiring the contrivance; "rough-an'-ready, you see, but soon finished. It ain't recorded in ancient history what Eve said when Adam presented her wi' the little testimonial of his affection, but if I might ventur' a guess I should opine that she said 'puckery.'"

"Hm! Dey ain't a tight fit," observed Ebony. "I's ob opinion dat your corns are quite safe in 'em."

Having completed his shoemaking work, the ingenious seaman assisted his companions to prepare the dried meat, which they afterwards tied up

in three convenient little parcels to be slung on
their backs.

That night they found a more commodious tree
to sleep in.   Under the pleasant influence of a good
supper they enjoyed unbroken rest, and awoke the
following morning greatly refreshed.   They were
thus, both physically and mentally, prepared for the
events of that day, to which, as they afterwards had
a most important bearing on their fortunes in the
island, we will devote a separate chapter.

CHAPTER IV.

**THE DOCTOR FINDS UNEXPECTED WORK IN THE WILDERNESS, AND
A MYSTERIOUS STRANGER IS INTRODUCED.**

It has been said that the travellers—for we
cannot now appropriately style them fugitives—had
reached a more open country, and that Hockins's
fight with the wild bull had taken place on the
margin of a wide grassy plain.

This plain, however, was limited. In front of
them the scenery was undulating and beautifully
varied—almost parklike in its character, and only
in one direction—to the right—did it extend like a
sea of waving grass to the horizon. Behind them
lay the dense forest through which they had passed.
The forest also curved round to their left, and
stretched away on, apparently unbroken, to still
far-off mountains.

After they had breakfasted, packed their dried
meat, and sallied forth on the journey of another
day, they walked in silence until they reached the
edge of the plain, where there was room to walk
abreast.

"Now, comrades," said Mark Breezy, "we will go to the top of yon mound, see how the land lies, and hold a council of war."

"Just so, cap'n ; take our bearin's an' lay our course," assented Hockins.

They soon reached the spot, and found the view from it unexpectedly beautiful. The whole landscape was clothed with tropical verdure. Past the foot of the mound ran a considerable stream, which opened out into a series of lakelets in the hollows beyond, the waters of which seemed to be the home of considerable numbers of wild-fowl,—but there was no sign of the presence of man.

"Strange," said Mark, in a low voice, "that such a lovely scene should have been created a solitude, with no one to profit by or enjoy it."

"Well now, sir," remarked the sailor, "d'ee know that same thought has puzzled me now an' again ; for although my purfession is the sea, I've travelled a good bit on the land—specially in South America —and I've seen miles on miles o' splendid country, that made me think of Adam an' Eve in paradise, with never a soul, as you say, to make use of or enjoy it. I've often wondered what it was all made for !"

"Don't you tink," said Ebony, with his head a little on one side, and his earnest eyes betraying the sincerity of his nature, "don't you tink dat p'r'aps de ducks an' geese, an' sitch-like, makes use ob an' enjoys it? to say nuffin ob de beasts, hinsects, an' fishes."

"You may be right, Ebony," returned Hockins, with an approving nod; "we human bein's is apt to think too much of ourselves. Moreover, it has come into my mind that Great Britain was a solitood once—or much about it—an' it's anything but that now; so mayhap them lands will be swarmin' wi' towns an' villages some day or other. What d'ee think, Doctor?"

But the young doctor said nothing, for while his companions were thus indulging in speculations, he was anxiously considering what course they should pursue.

"You see, comrades," he said, turning to them abruptly, "if we go to the right and traverse this fine country we may very likely fall in with villages, but the villagers may be savages, like those we met on the coast. On the other hand, if we go to the left, we shall have to traverse the somewhat dark and difficult forests, but then we shall be making for the mountains and table-lands of the interior; and as the capital, Ant—Ant—"

"Anty-all-alive-O!" suggested Hockins.

"No, 's not dat. It ends wid 'arrive O!' w'ich is just what we wants."

"Well, whatever may be its name, I know that it

is in the centre of the island somewhere, and the centre of any land always means the mountains ; so I think we had better decide to go to the left, and—"

"Hallo! look yonder, sir," said Hockins, pointing towards a low cliff which rose in front of them not a quarter of a mile from the spot where they stood.

Turning in the direction indicated, they observed a man running swiftly, as if in pursuit of something. They could see that he was clothed, and that he carried several spears, from which they judged that he was a hunter. Coming to the foot of the cliff before mentioned, the man ascended the face of it with wonderful agility, and had almost gained the top, when a treacherous root or stone gave way, causing him to lose his hold and roll violently to the bottom.

"Poor fellow, he's killed!" cried Mark, running towards the fallen hunter, who lay on the ground motionless.

He was not killed, however, though stunned and bleeding profusely from a deep wound in the arm, caused by one of his own spears while in the act of falling. When the three strangers suddenly appeared the hunter grasped one of the spears and made a vigorous attempt to rise, evidently under the impression that he was about to be attacked; but the fall and the loss of blood were too much for him. He sank back with a groan, yet there was a look of quiet dignity about him which showed that he gave way to no craven spirit.

Our young doctor, kneeling down beside him, proceeded at once to staunch the wound and bind up the arm with his pocket-handkerchief. While he was thus engaged, Hockins brought some water from a neighbouring stream in a cup which he had extemporised out of a piece of bark, and applied it to the man's lips. Ebony stood by, with a look of profound pity on his face, ready for whatever might be required of him.

The hunter showed by the expression of his handsome brown features that he was grateful for these attentions. Yet, at the same time, there seemed to be something of perplexity, if not surprise, in his looks as he gazed on the white men's faces. But he did not utter a word. When the dressing of the arm was completed—of course in a most business-like manner—he again attempted to rise, but was so weak from loss of blood that he fell back fainting in the Doctor's arms.

"This is a most awkward business," said Mark, as he laid the man carefully on the ground, and put a bundle of grass under his head for a pillow. "It behoves us to push on our journey without delay, yet it will never do to leave him here alone, and we can't very well take him on with us. What *is* to be done?"

Both Hockins and the negro *looked* their incapacity to answer that question. Just then the answer came in the form they least expected, for a sound of many voices in clamorous talk suddenly broke on their ears. The speakers, whoever they might be, were still distant, and the formation of the ground prevented our travellers being seen by them.

"Savages!" exclaimed Mark and Hockins in the same breath.

"Hide!" cried Ebony, with a roll of his huge eyes, as he suited the action to the word, and leaped into the bushes. The others followed his example, and running about a hundred yards back into the woods, climbed into the branches of a lofty tree, from which outlook, well screened by leaves, they saw a band composed of some hundreds of natives walking smartly over the open plain. From the manner of their approach it was evident that they searched for some one, and as they made straight for the cliff where the wounded man lay, it seemed probable that they were following up his trail.

"We're done for," said Mark, in a tone of despair, as he noted this.

"Why d'ee think so, Doctor?" asked Hockins, who did not by any means seem to take such a gloomy view of their case.

"Don't you see? Savages can follow up people's trails almost as well as dogs. They'll easily trace us to the foot of this tree by our footprints, and then they 've only to look up !"

" That 's true.   I had forgotten that."

" Dere 's time to drop down yit, massa, and squati- late," suggested the negro, excitedly.

Mark shook his head.

" Might as well try to run from tigers as from savages," he returned, " unless you 've got a good start."

" But they aiu't all savages, sir," whispered Hock- ins, as the band drew nearer.   " Some o' the naked black fellows look savage enough, no doubt, but there 's a lot of 'em lightish brown in the skin, an' clothed in fine though queer garments.   They carry themselves, too, like gentlemen.   P'r'aps we 'd better go for'ard an' trust them."

" Trust to 'em, 'Ockins !" said Ebony with a decided shake of the head, " trust men wid *brown* faces ?   Nebber !"

The whispered conversation ceased at this point, for a loud shout of surprise mingled with alarm was raised as the band came to the foot of the cliff and found what appeared to be the dead body of the wounded man.   Evidently they were friends, for while some of them kneeled down beside the injured hunter to examine him, others gave way to gestures and exclamations of grief.

Presently the watchers observed that one of those

who kneeled beside the body looked up with a smile and a nod of satisfaction as he pointed to his chest.

" They've discovered that he's not dead," said Mark.

" Yes, massa, an' dey've diskivered de bandaged arm."

" Ay, an' it seems to puzzle 'em," added the seaman.

It did more than puzzle them. They had not observed it at first, because, just before running into the woods, Mark had covered it with a loose shawl —a sort of linen plaid—which the man had worn round his shoulders. When they removed this and saw the bandage which was wound round the limb in the most careful and perfect manner, they looked at each other in great surprise; then they looked solemn and spoke in low tones, glancing round now and then with saucer-like eyes, as if they expected to see something frightful.

" I do believe, Doctor," whispered the seaman, "that they think your work has been done by a goblin of some sort!"

It would indeed seem as if some such idea had entered the minds of the band, for instead of examining the ground for footprints and following them up—as was natural to have done—they silently constructed a litter of branches, covered it with some of their garments, and quietly bore the wounded and still unconscious man away in the direction of the plains.

With thankful hearts our travellers slid to the ground, and hurried off in the opposite direction towards the mountains.

That night they came to a deeply-shaded and rugged piece of ground in the heart of the forest where there were caverns of various sizes. Here the solitude seemed to be so profound that the fear of pursuit gradually left them, so they resolved to kindle a cheerful fire in one of the caves, cook a good supper, and enjoy themselves. Finding a cave that was small, dry, and well concealed, they soon had a bright fire blazing in it, round which they sat on a soft pile of branches—Mark and Hockins looking on with profound interest and expectation while the negro prepared supper.

"If I only had a quid o' baccy now," said Hockins, "I'd be as happy as a king."

"I have the advantage of you, friend, for I am as happy as a king without it," said the young doctor.

"Well, there's no denyin'," returned the seaman, "that you have the advantage o' me; but if I only had the baccy I'd enjoy my disadvantage. P'r'aps there's a bit left in some corner o'——"

He plunged his hands into each pocket in his garments, one after another, but without success until he came to the left breast-pocket of his coat.

When he had searched that to its deepest recesses he stopped and looked up with a beaming countenance.

"Ho! got 'im?" asked Ebony, with interest.

Hockins did not reply, but, slowly and tenderly, drew forth—not a quid, but—a little piece of brown wood about five or six inches long.

"A penny whistle!" exclaimed Mark.

"Speak with reverence, Doctor," returned the sailor, with a quiet smile, "it ain't a penny whistle, it's a flageolet. I stuck it here the last time I was amoosin' the crew o' the *Eastern Star* an' forgot I hadn't putt it away. Wait a bit, you shall hear."

Saying this Hockins put the tiny instrument to his lips, and drew from it sounds so sweet, so soft, so melodious and tuneful, that his companions seemed to listen in a trance of delight, with eyes as well as with ears!

"Splendid!" exclaimed Mark, enthusiastically, when the sailor ceased to play. "Why, Hockins, I had no idea you could play like that! Of course I knew that you possessed musical powers to some extent, for I have heard the tooting of your flageolet through the bulkheads when at sea; but two or three inches of plank don't improve sweet sounds, I suppose."

"Ho! massa, didn't I tell you t'ree or four times dat he play mos' awrful well?"

"True, Ebony, so you did; but I used to think your energetic praise was due to your enthusiastic disposition, and so paid no attention to your invitations to go for'ard an' listen. Well, I confess I was a loser. You must have played the instrument a long time, surely?"—turning to the seaman.

"Yes, ever since I was a small boy. My father played it before me, and taught me how to finger it. He was a splendid player. He used sometimes to go to the back of the door when we had a small blowout, an' astonish the company by playin' up unexpectedly. He was great at Scotch tunes—specially the slow ones, like this."

He put the little instrument to his lips again, and let it nestle, as it were, in his voluminous beard, as he drew from it the pathetic strains of "Wanderin' Willie," to the evidently intense enjoyment of Ebony, who regarded music as one of the chief joys of life—next, perhaps, to cooking!

But Mark and Ebony were not the only listeners to that sweet strain. Just outside the mouth of the cave there stood a man, who, to judge from the expression of his face, was as much affected by the music as the negro. Though he stood in such a position as to be effectually screened from the view of those within, a gleam of reflected light fell upon his figure, showing him to be a tall, handsome man in the prime of life. He was clothed in what may be styled a mixed European and native costume, and a gun on which he rested both hands seemed to indicate him a hunter.   He carried no other weapon, except a long knife in his girdle.   The mixed character of his garb extended also to his blood, for his skin, though dark and bronzed from exposure, was much lighter than that of most natives of the island, and his features were distinctly European. Quiet gravity was the chief characteristic of his countenance, and there was also an expression of profound sadness or pathos, which was probably caused by the music.

When Hockins finished his tune the three friends were almost petrified with astonishment—not un-mingled with alarm—as they beheld this man walk coolly into the cave, rest his gun on the side of it, and sit gravely down on the opposite side of the fire.

The first impulse of our three friends, of course, was to spring up, but the action of the man was so prompt, and, withal, so peaceful, that they were constrained to sit still.

"Don't be alarmed.   I come as a friend.   May I sit by your fire?"

He spoke in good English, though with a decidedly foreign accent.

"You are welcome, since you come as a friend," said Mark, "though I must add that you have taken us by surprise."

"Well now, stranger," said Hockins, putting his musical instrument in his pocket, "how are we to know that you *are* a friend—except by the cut o' your jib, which, I admit, looks honest enough, and your actions, which, we can't deny, are peaceable like?"

The seaman put this question with a half-per-plexed, half-amused air. The stranger received it without the slightest change in his grave aspect.

"You have no other means of knowing," he replied, "except by my 'jib' and my actions."

"Dat's a fact, anyhow," murmured Ebony.

"Who *are* you, and where do you come from?" asked Mark.

"I am an outlaw, and I come from the forest."

"That's plain-speakin', an' no mistake," said Hockins, with a laugh, "an' deserves as plain a return. We can't say exactly that *we* are outlaws, but we are out-an-outers, an' we're going through the forest to—to—Anty-all-alive-O! or some such name—the capital, you know—"

"Antananarivo," suggested the outlaw.

"That's it! That's the name-I couldn't recall," said Mark, quickly. "We are going there, if we can only find the way."

"I know the way," returned the outlaw, "and my reason for coming here is to offer to show it you."

"Indeed! But how came you to know our intentions, and what makes you take so much interest in us?" asked Mark, with a look of suspicion.

"My reason for being interested in you," returned the stranger, "is a matter with which you have nothing to do. How I came to know your intentions it is easy to explain, for I have followed you from the sea-coast step by step. I saw you escape from the savages, saw you frightened out of the cave by my friends the outlaws, who dwell in it, followed you while you traversed the forest, listened to your conversations, witnessed your exploit with the bull, and observed you when you helped and bandaged the wounded native."

It would be difficult to describe the looks or feelings with which the three friends received this information. Ebony's eyes alone would have taken at least half-an-hour of the pencil to portray.

"But—but—why?" stammered Mark.

"Never mind the why," continued the outlaw, with a pleasant look. "You see that I know all about you—at least since you landed—and I also know that you have been several times in unseen danger, from which I have shielded you. Now, you have arrived at a part of the forest which is swarming with brigands, into whose hands you are sure to fall unless I am with you. I therefore come to offer myself as your guide. Will you have me?"

"It seems to me," returned Mark, with something

of scorn in his tone, " that we have no choice, for you have us at your mercy—we cannot refuse. I suppose you are the brigand chief, and are guarding us for some sinister purpose of your own."

" I said not that I was a brigand," returned the stranger, quietly ; " I said I was an outlaw. What else I am, and my motives of action, I choose not to tell. You say truly—I have you in my power. That is one reason why I would befriend you, if you will trust me." The outlaw rose up as he spoke.

There was such an air of quiet dignity and evident sincerity in the man that Mark was strongly impressed. Rising promptly, he stretched his hand across the fire, saying, " We will trust you, friend, even though we were *not* in your power."

The outlaw grasped the youth's hand with a gratified look.

" Now," he added, as he took up his gun, " I will go. In the morning at daybreak I will return. Sleep well till then."

With something like a courtly salute, the mysterious stranger left them, and disappeared into the depths of the forest.

CHAPTER V.

THE OUTLAW'S FRIENDS.   THREATENED DANGER CURIOUSLY AVERTED.

As might be supposed, the unexpected appearance of the outlaw, as well as his sudden departure, tended somewhat to interfere with the sleep which he had wished the travellers at parting, and the night was far advanced before they grew tired of wondering who he could be, speculating as to where he came from, and commenting on his personal appearance. In short, at the close of their discourse, they came to the conclusion which was well embodied in the remark of Ebony, when he said, "It's my opinion, founded on obsarvashun, dat if we was to talk an tink de whole night long we would come no nearer de troot, so I'll turn in."

He did turn in accordingly, and, after exhausting the regions of conjecture, the powers of speculation, and the realms of fancy, Mark and Hockins followed his example.

One consequence of their mental dissipation was

that they slept rather beyond the hour of day-break, and the first thing that recalled the two white men to consciousness was the voice of their black comrade exclaiming :—

"Ho! hi! hallo! I smells a smell!"

They lifted their three heads simultaneously and beheld the outlaw sitting calmly beside the fire roasting steaks.

For the first time the mysterious stranger smiled —and it was a peculiarly sweet half-grave sort of attractive smile, as far removed from the fiendish grin of the stage bandit as night is from day.

"I knew you would be hungry, and guessed you would be sleepy," he said, in a deep musical voice, ' so I have prepared breakfast. Are you ready?"

"Ready!" repeated Hockins, rising with a mighty yawn, and stretching himself, as was his wont; "I just think we are. Leastwise *I* am. Good luck to ee Mister Outlaw, what have ee got there?"

"Beef, marrow-bones, and rice," replied the man. "You may call me Samuel if you like. It was my father's first name, but I'm best known among my friends as Ravoninohitriniony."

"Well, that *is* a jawbreaker!" exclaimed Hockins, with a laugh, as they all sat down to breakfast. "Ra-vo- what did ee say?"

"Better not try it till arter breakfast," suggested Ebony.

"Couldn't we shorten it a bit?" said Mark, beginning to consult a marrow-bone. "What say you to the first half—Ravonino?"

"As you please," replied the outlaw, who was already too much absorbed with steaks to look up.

"Not a bad notion," said Hockins. "Sam'l Ravonino—I've heerd wus; anyhow it's better than the entire complication—eh, Ebony?"

"Mush better," assented the negro; "dere's no use wotsomediver for de hitri—hitri-folderol-ony bit of it. Now, 'Ockins, fair play wid de marrow-bones. Hand me anoder."

"Is it far, Mr. Ravonino," asked Mark, "from here to the capital—to Antananarivo?"

"You cleared 'im that time, Doctor!" murmured Hockins, wiping his mouth with a bunch of grass which he carried as a substitute for a pocket handkerchief.

"Yes, it is a long way," said the outlaw; "many days' journey over mountain and plain."

"And are you going to guide us all the way there?"

"No, not all the way. You forget I am an outlaw. It would cost me my life if I were to appear in Antananarivo."

Mark was on the point of asking why, but, remembering the rebuff of the previous night, forbore to put questions relative to his new friend's

personal affairs. Indeed he soon found that it was
useless to do so, for whenever he approached the
subject Ravonino became so abstracted and deaf that
no reply could be drawn from him. As if to compen-
sate for this, however, the man was exceedingly communicative in regard to all other subjects, and there
was a quiet urbanity in his manner which rendered
his conversation exceedingly attractive. Moreover,
to the surprise of Mark, this mysterious stranger
gave evidence of a considerable amount of education.
He also gratified Hockins by his evident delight in
the flageolet, and his appreciation of nautical
stories and "lingo," while he quite won the heart of
Ebony by treating him with the same deference
which he accorded to his companions. In short,
each of our travellers congratulated himself not a
little on this pleasant acquisition to the party—the
only drawback to their satisfaction being their
inability to reconcile the existence of such good
qualities with the condition of an outlaw!

"However," remarked Hockins, after a long talk
with his comrades on this subject when Ravonino
was absent, "it's none of our business what he's bin
an' done to other people. What we've got to do
with is the way he behaves to *us*, d'ee see?"

"He's a trump," said Ebony, with a nod of
decision.

"I agree with you," said Mark; "and I only wish

he was a little more communicative about himself. However, we must take him as we find him, and try to win his confidence."

During the whole of that first day their guide conducted them through such intricate and evidently unfrequented parts of the forest that their advance was comparatively slow and toilsome, but, being young and strong and well-fed, they did not mind that. In fact Mark Breezy enjoyed it, for the wilder and more tangled the scenery was through which they forced their way, the more did it accord with the feelings of romance which filled him, and the thought of being guided through the woods too by an outlaw tended rather to increase his satisfaction.

"Are all the roads in your island as bad as these?" he asked, after plumping up to the knees in a quagmire, out of which he scrambled with difficulty.

"No, many of them are worse and some better," answered the guide; "but I keep away from them, because the Queen's soldiers and spies are hunting about the land just now."

"Oho!" thought Mark, "I begin to see; you are a rebel." Then, aloud, "Your country, then, is governed by a queen?"

"Misgoverned," returned Ravonino in a tone of bitterness, which, however, he evidently tried to restrain.

Fearing to tread again on forbidden ground, Mark forbore to put questions about the guide's objections to his queen, but simply asked her name, and if she had reigned long.

"Her name," said Ravonino, "is Ranavalona. She has reigned for twenty-seven years—twenty-seven long and weary years! I was a little boy when she usurped the throne. Now my sun has reached its meridian, yet she is still there, a blight upon the land. But God knows what is best. He cannot err."

This was the first reference that Ravonino had made to the Creator, and Mark was about to push his inquiries further, when a confused sound of voices was heard not far in advance of them.

Ravonino, who had been walking with an easy nonchalant air ahead of the party, on a very narrow footpath, suddenly stopped to listen with a look of anxiety. A moment later and he entered the bush that fringed the path and overhung it.

"Come," he said in a low voice, "follow me, close!"

Without a word of explanation he strode into the dense undergrowth, through which he went with the agility of a panther and the sinuosity of a serpent. The others, being, as we have said, very active and strong, kept close at his heels, though not without difficulty. Coming at last to a place where the shrubbery was so intertwined that it was impossible to see more than a yard or two in advance, they suddenly found themselves stopped by a sheer precipice. Only for a few seconds, however, was their progress arrested, while their guide turned to explain.

"There is another and an easier way to the place I am making for, but it is much longer and more exposed. I take for granted that you have strong arms and steady heads, but if not, speak out, for I would not lead you into danger."

"Lead on," said Mark, promptly, "wherever you go, we will follow."

With something like an amused twinkle of the eye, Ravonino began to climb up the face of the precipice, holding on to roots and rope-like creepers like a monkey.

"If this here sort o' cordage was only a bit more taut I wouldn't mind it so much," growled Hockins, as he lost his footing at one place, and swung off the face of the precipice,—holding on to a stout creeper, however, with seaman-like grip and coolness. He quickly caught hold of another creeper, and drew himself again into comparative safety. A minute later and they all stood on a ledge, high up on the face of the cliff, and close to what appeared to be the mouth of a cavern.

"Look there," said their guide, pushing aside the bushes which overhung the cliff in all directions.

They looked, and through the opening beheld a band of men moving in single file along the track they had just left. They were most of them nearly naked, with only short calico breeches which did not quite reach to their knees, but all had muskets on their shoulders and cross-belts on their dark bodies, one of which belts sustained apparently a cartridge-box, the other a bayonet. Their own thick hair was all the cap they wore, excepting two or three men of superior rank, who wore cloths wrapped in turban fashion on their heads, and a voluminous plaid-like garment on their shoulders. These carried swords instead of muskets.

"The soldiers of the Queen," said Ravonino, in answer to Mark Breezy's look. "They are out hunting."

"What do they hunt for?" asked Mark.

"Men and women."

"By which I suppose you mean rebels."

"No, they are not rebels; they are the queen's most loyal subjects!"

"But loyal subjects do not usually fly from their rulers," objected Mark.

"True, but loyal subjects sometimes fly from tyranny," returned the guide. "Come, I will introduce you to some fugitives from tyranny."

He turned as he spoke and led the way into the cave before mentioned. Profound darkness did not prevent his advancing with a firm unhesitating step. As he led Mark by the hand, Hockins and Ebony held on to him and to each other, and had no difficulty in following. Presently they came to a wooden obstruction which proved to be a door. Voices in conversation were heard on the other side of it. A knock from the guide produced sudden silence. Another knock drew from those within an exclamation of surprise, and next moment the heavy door swung open on creaking hinges.

"Yes, it *is* Ravoninohitriniony! I knew his knock. He is come!" exclaimed a girlish voice, as a pair of arms were seen dimly to encircle the guide's neck.

Of course the girl spoke in the native tongue, which was quite incomprehensible to our travellers, but if we are to enlighten our readers we must needs translate as we go along.

"My sister, Ra-Ruth," said the guide, presenting her to his new friends. "She was a lady in the palace of the queen once. Now she is an outlaw, like myself—has fled from tyranny, and, perhaps, death. All in this cave are in the same case— fugitives from our tyrant queen."

They reached the interior of the place as he spoke, and Ravonino, pointing to a bundle of dried ferns, bade his companions rest there until he had explained some private matters to the people.

Nothing loth—for they were all somewhat fatigued by their recent exertions—our travellers flung themselves on what proved to be a luxurious couch, and observed what went on around them.

Truly it was a strange scene, romantic enough even to satisfy the longings of Mark Breezy!

The cavern itself was a curious one, being in the form of a vast hall, with three smaller chambers opening out of it. The central hall seemed to have no roof, for although brightly lighted by several torches fixed to its rugged walls the upper part was lost in profound obscurity.

This strange abode was peopled by a considerable number of men and women—natives of the island—who from the variety in their costume, features, and complexion, evidently belonged to different tribes. Some were strong, tall, and rather harsh-featured, others were more slender in build and with refined countenances. A few were almost black, others of a light olive colour, and several made that approach to whiteness of skin which in England is known as brunette. All were more or less characterised by that quiet gentleness and gravity of demeanour which one is accustomed to associate with humbly borne misfortune.

It was evident from the appearance of the large chamber that its inhabitants were associated in groups or families, spaces being marked off by an arrangement of logs and household goods, etc., as if to indicate the habitation of each group, and, from certain indications in the smaller chambers, it was equally evident that these had been apportioned as the sleeping-places of the females. A larger space at the end of the cave, opposite to that on which Mark and his comrades reclined, seemed to be a general meeting-place.

To this spot it was that Ravonino went, leading his little sister Ra-Ruth by the hand, and followed by all the inmates of the place, who were eager to know what news he had brought. That the news was the reverse of good soon became evident, from the bowed heads and frequent sighs with which it was received.

Of course our travellers could make no use of their ears, but they made the best use of their eyes, and were deeply interested in the expressions and actions of the various members of the group who successively spoke after the guide had told his story. Poor little Ra-Ruth, whose age might have been about seventeen, was not one of the speakers. She was evidently a timid as well as a pretty little creature, for she clung to and nestled against her stout brother's arm while he was speaking, and hid

E

her face now and then in the masses of her luxuriant brown hair.

Close to her sat a young woman whose appearance and manner formed a striking contrast. She was much darker in complexion, but her features were of classical beauty and her air calm and self-possessed. When she had occasion to speak, she arose, displaying a tall elegantly-formed figure, which moved with queen-like dignity while she gesticulated with graceful animation, and frequently pointed upwards as if appealing to God. When she was speaking Ra-Ruth's timidity seemed to vanish, for she shook back her hair, and fixed her eyes on the other's face with a gaze that told of ardent love as well as admiration.

The next who spoke was a young man, who in face and figure so strongly resembled the last speaker, that it was impossible to resist the conclusion that they were brother and sister. There was the same tall commanding figure, of course on a larger scale, the same noble cast of feature and the same dignified mien. But in the man, more than in the woman, there was an air of gentle modesty which contrasted well with his powerful frame. He did not gesticulate much in speaking, and, judging from the brevity of his speech, he had not much to say, but what he said was listened to with profound respect by all.

After this youth, several others took part in the debate. Then they all stood up, and, to the surprise of their visitors, began to sing—very sweetly—an old familiar hymn !

"It minds me o' home," whispered Hockins, scarce able to restrain the tears that filled his eyes.

The hymn was nearly finished, when a rushing sound and a subdued cry were heard to issue from a dark passage, the mouth of which was close to the couch of our travellers. The singing ceased instantly. Next moment a man rushed into the chamber with labouring breath and flashing eyes. Springing towards Ravonino, he spoke several words eagerly, at the same time pointing in the direction of the passage just referred to.

"Lights out and silence !" cried the guide, authoritatively, in the native tongue.

Another moment and the cave was in total darkness, and a silence so profound reigned there that the three visitors could hardly persuade themselves the whole affair was not a strange dream. The voice of Ravonino, however, soon dispelled that idea.

"Be still !" whispered the guide, laying his hand on Mark's shoulder. "Our foes have discovered our retreat."

"There's a lot of stout fellows here," returned Mark, also in a whisper. "We will help you if you have to fight."

"We may not fight," replied Ravonino softly. "If it be God's will, we must die. Hush! They come."

Once more total silence prevailed in the cavern, and the sound of distant voices could be heard. In a few minutes a tiny light was seen at the end of the dark passage. It gradually increased in size, revealing a soldier who bore a torch. He advanced on tip-toe, and with slightly scared looks, into an outer cavern which formed a sort of vestibule to the large inner cave.

The soldier was brave, no doubt, and would have faced an army in the field, but he was extremely superstitious, and advanced with a palpitating heart, the torch held high above his head, and eyes glancing nervously from side to side. A crowd of comrades, similarly affected more or less, followed the torch-bearer and pushed him on.

"Nothing here," said the leading man, of course in Malagasy.

"Let us be gone, then," said one of his comrades.

"No," observed a third, who seemed bolder than the rest, "perhaps there is another cave beyond (pointing to the dark passage, through which, though unseen, Mark and his companions with the guide were gazing anxiously at their foes). "Give me the torch."

The soldier seized the light and advanced quickly towards the opening. Another minute and all must have been revealed. A feeling of despair took possession of Ravonino's breast and he gave vent to an involuntary sigh.

The sound reached the ear of the soldier with the torch and for a moment arrested him, but, thinking probably that the sound was in his imagination, he again advanced. The case was now desperate. Just then a gleam of light flashed into the mind of Hockins. Next moment, to the consternation of his comrades and the guide, a strain of the sweetest music floated softly in the air!

The soldiers stood still—spell-bound. It was not an unfamiliar air, for they had often heard the hated Christians sing it, but the sweet, liquid—we might almost say tiny—tones in which it was conveyed, were such as had never before reached their ears or even entered their imaginations. It was evident from their countenances that the soldiers were awe-stricken. The seaman noted this. He played only a few bars, and allowed the last notes of his flageolet to grow faint until they died away into absolute silence.

For a minute or two the soldiers stood rooted to the spot, gazing up into the roof of the cave as if expecting a renewal of the sounds. Then they looked solemnly at each other. Without uttering a word they turned slowly round, retreated on tip-toe as they came, and finally disappeared.

We need hardly say that the astonishment of the people in the cave at the mode of their deliverance from the threatened danger was intense.

When the torches were relighted the men and women assembled round Ravonino with looks little less solemn than those of the soldiers who had just taken their departure.

" Surely," said the handsome young man whom we have already introduced, " surely God has wrought a miracle and sent an angel's voice for our deliverance."

" Not so, Laihova," replied Ravonino, with a slight smile. " We are too apt to count everything that we fail to understand a miracle. God has indeed sent the deliverance, but through a natural channel."

" Yet we see not the channel, Ravoninohitriniony," said Laihova's queen-like sister, Ramatoa.

" True, Ramatoa. Nevertheless I can show it to you. Come, Hockins," he added in English, " clear up the mystery to them."

Thus bidden, our seaman at once drew forth the little instrument and began to play the hymn they had just been singing, with the air of which, as we have said, he chanced to be well acquainted.

It would be hard to say whether surprise or pleasure predominated in the breasts of his audience. At last the latter feeling prevailed, and the whole assembly joined in singing the last verse of the hymn, which appropriately terminated in "Praise ye the Lord."

"But our retreat is no longer safe," said Ravonino, when the last echo of their thanksgiving had died away. "We must change our abode—and that without delay. Get ready. By the first light of morning I will lead you to a new home. These soldiers will not return, but they will tell what they have seen, and others less timorous will come here to search for us."

Immediately the people set about collecting together and packing up what may be termed their household goods, leaving the guide and their visitors to enjoy supper and conversation in their own corner of the cave.

CHAPTER VI.

DURING the progress of supper, which consisted
of cold dried meat and rice, the quartette seated on
the ferns in the corner of the cave were unusually
silent. Mark Breezy and Ravonino continued to
eat for some time without speaking a word. Ebony,
although earnestly absorbed in victuals, rolled his
eyes about as he looked from time to time at his
companions with unwonted solemnity, and John
Hockins frowned at his food, and shook his shaggy
head with an air of dissatisfied perplexity.

"Ravonino," at length said the last, looking up,
and using his grass pocket-handkerchief, "it seems
to me, bein' a plain straight-for'ard sort o' seaman, that there's somethin' not exactly fair an'
above-board in all them proceedin's. Of course
it's not for me to say what a independent man
should do or say ; but don't you think that w'en a
man like you professes to be honest, an' asks other
men to trust him, he should at least explain *some* o'

the riddles that surround him? I'm a loyal man myself, an' I'll stand up for *my* Queen an' country, no matter what may be the circumstances in w'ich I'm placed; so that w'en I sees another man admittin' that he's a outlaw, an' finds the soldiers of *his* Queen a-huntin' all about the country arter him and his comrades—seems to me there's a screw loose somewheres."

"Dat's *my* sent'ments zactly," said the negro, with a decisive nod.

Mark took no notice of this speech, but silently continued his supper. For a few moments the guide did not speak or look up. Then, laying down his knife and clasping his hands over one of his knees, he looked earnestly into the seaman's face.

"You tell me you are loyal," he said.

Hockins nodded.

"If your queen," continued Ravonino, "were to tell you to give up the service of God and worship idols, would you do it?"

"Cer'nly not," replied the seaman, promptly, "for she has no right to rule over my soul. My duty to the King of Kings stands before my duty to the Queen of England."

Again the guide was silent for a few minutes. Then he said :—

"Hockins, by God's blessing you have saved the lives of all our party this day—at least it seemed so, for, another step, and that soldier would have discovered us if your little pipe had not stopped him. You are therefore entitled to expect some gratitude, and, from what I have seen of you and your comrades, I have reason to believe you will not betray us, even if you get the chance."

"Right you are, friend, I will never betray an honest man; an' I may speak for my comrades as well as self, for they're true-blue to the backbone—"

"Furder nor dat," interposed Ebony, "troo-bloo to de marrow!"

"Don't you shove in your oar till you're ordered, you nigger! Well, as I was a-sayin', we'll never betray honest men, but I give you fair warnin' if you're *not* honest, we'll have nothin' to do wi' your secrets, an' if our duty to God an' man requires us to go against you, we'll do it without flinchin'."

"So be it. I am satisfied," returned Ravonino, calmly. "I will tell you as much as I think you are entitled to know. It may have reached your ears, perhaps, that there has been terrible persecu-tion in this island for many years."

Here Mark Breezy took up the conversation.

"No," said he, with something of a deprecatory air, "we did not know it. For my part I am ashamed to say so; but I will say in excuse that the British empire is widely extended in every quarter of the globe, and her missions are so numerous that average men can scarcely hope to keep up with the details of all of the persecutions that occur. Rumours, indeed, I have heard of doings in Madagascar that vie with the persecutions of the Scottish Covenanters; but more than this I know not, though of course there are men connected with our Missionary Societies—and many people, no doubt, interested in missions—who know all about the persecutions in Madagascar. Is it in connection with this that you have been outlawed?"

"It is. Ranavalona, the blood-stained usurper, our present queen, is filled with such bitter hatred of Christianity that she has for many years persecuted the native Christians who have been taught by white missionaries from your land. Hundreds of men and women have been murdered by her orders because they refused to forsake Christ; others have been banished to regions so unhealthy that they have died, and many have been sold into slavery."

The eyes of the guide gleamed for a moment, and his stern countenance flushed as he thus referred to the sorrows of his people, but by a strong effort he controlled his feelings, and his countenance resumed its habitual quietude.

"My mother and my sister and I," he continued, "were sold into slavery. My mother was a native lady, high in station, and a member of the court of

King Radama the First, who was very favourable to
Missionaries. I was an infant at that time; my
little sister was not born. My father was an English
trader, skilled in many handicrafts, and a great
favourite with the king, who fostered the Christian
religion and helped those who came to teach us.
Our teachers learned our language; taught us the
love of God, and, through the power of the Holy
Spirit, brought many of us to the Saviour. But
they were persevering and wise as well as good.
Having learned our language—in which my father
helped them much—they taught us to read; translated many parts of the Word of God into our
tongue; sent home for presses and types, and had
these printed, as well as *The Pilgrim's Progress* and
other books.

" Peace, joy, and prosperity were spreading in our
land. Idol-worship and cruel customs were being
uprooted, and everything was going well when the
king died—whether a Christian or not, who can
tell? for, although favourable to, he never professed,
Christianity. 'The Lord knoweth them that are
His!' The rightful heir to the throne, according to
our customs, was Rakotobe—a good young man
who had been taught by the missionaries, and was
nephew to the king; but Ranavalona, one of the
king's wives, resolved to seize the opportunity. A
bold bad woman, with a powerful will and no

principle, she carried her point by reckless blood-shed. There were men at court as bad as herself who agreed to aid her. When she boldly claimed the throne, four loyal nobles asserted the claim of Rakotobe. They were instantly speared in the palace. The rightful heir was not present. Soldiers were sent to his residence to seize and kill him before he should hear of what was going on.

"Not content with shedding blood, the cruel monsters dug the poor youth's grave before his eyes. When they were thus engaged Rakotobe kneeled down to pray, and while he was in this position they speared him and cast him into his grave. Soon after the father and mother of Rako-tobe were murdered—the last being starved to death. The brother of Radama was destroyed in like manner. He lingered eight days in agony before death came to his relief. Then Rakotobe's grand-mother and other relations were slain by Ranava-lona's orders, and thus the murderess waded through blood to the throne of Madagascar!

"Think you," continued the guide, with a passing gleam of the anger which he strove to restrain, "think you that I owe allegiance to *such* a queen?"

"Truly ye do not," answered the seaman, stoutly. "My only wonder is that the people suffer her to reign."

Scarce heeding the reply the guide continued,

with suppressed excitement, "but she did not rest content. It was in the year 1829 that she usurped the throne. Since then she has persecuted the Christians for more than a quarter of a century, and at times blood has flowed like water in our land. Bad as she is, however, she would have been worse but for her love to her son. Ay, the woman whose heart is a stone to most people is soft towards the young prince Rakota, in spite of the fact that this youth is favourable to the Christians and has often stood between them and his mother.

" About nine years after the queen's coronation my little sister was born, and was secretly baptized —the name of Ruth being given to her. It is our custom to prefix Ra to many names—so she is Ra-Ruth. Look at her !" He pointed to a group not far off, where the delicate and graceful girl was busily assisting an elderly woman in her packing arrangements. "See you the lady beside her, with the grey hair and the sad worn face ? That is my mother. I have said she was high at the Court of Radama the First. She was young then. I was born the year that Radama died. Ranavalona was fond of her, though she loved not her Christianity, so she continued at the palace. The Queen also became very fond of my little sister when she began to grow to womanhood, but Ra-Ruth could not return the affection of one whose hands were stained so deeply with Christian blood. I was an officer in the palace at the time, but would gladly have left, only my doing so might have roused the queen's wrath against my father and mother.

"At last the missionaries were ordered to quit the capital. In 1849 a great persecution took place. The queen became furious because her people would not cease to love and serve Jesus. She ordered many men and women to be speared and burned and tossed over precipices, but all without avail, because 'greater is He who is for us than all who can be against us.'

"My father was away on a trading expedition at this time. One day in attempting to cross a lake he was drowned." The guide's voice deepened as he went on, "He was a good loving father to me. He taught me nearly all I know, and he was no mean scholar. He also sent me to the missionary schools. After his death the Queen hardened her heart against us; and as we refused to give up praying to God and singing His praise, we were cast out of the palace—my mother and sister and I, with several others, among whom were Laihova and his sister Ramatoa. We were sold into slavery in the public market.

"Our purchaser was cruel. He put us to the hardest menial work. We remained for several years with him. The health of my poor mother

and sister began to give way. Then he sold me to
another man, and we were separated. This was too
much, I suppose, for the English blood in me to
endure quietly. I made my escape. I went back
to my old owner, and, in the night, induced my
mother and sister to fly. Many persecuted Christians have fled since then and are now hiding in dens
and caves like hunted beasts. We soon found some
of these in the depths of the forests, and agreed to
band together. They made me their leader, and I
brought them here, where we have lived and wor-
shipped God in peace; but, as you have seen, we
are liable to be captured at any moment."

"And if captured," said Mark, "would the Queen
really put you to death?"

"I fear she would; nay, I am certain of it, because
one who recently escaped from Antananarivo has
just brought the news that the Queen has been
visited with a fresh burst of anger against the
Christians, has thrown many into prison and sent
out troops to scour the country in search of those
who have fled."

"But if that is so," said Hockins, earnestly,
"what's the use o' you riskin' your life by goin'
with us to Ant—Ant-all-alive-O! (I'll never git
that name into my head!). Why not just sketch us
out a rough chart o' the island on a bit o' bark, give
us the bearin's o' the capital, an' let us steer a

straight course for it. I 'll be bound that we 'll make our port easy enough."

"Yes, Hockins speaks wisely," added Mark. "It is very kind of you to take so much trouble for us, but there is no need to run such great risk on our account."

"You do not consider," replied Ravonino, "that it is more difficult for sailors to cross the wild forest than to find their way on the trackless sea, and you forget also that the way is long, that Madagascar is larger than Great Britain and Ireland put together. There are many tribes, too, some of which are not so hospitable as others. You could not avoid the dangers of this wilderness easily without a guide. Besides, I do not mean to enter the capital. I will merely guide you to within sight of it and then leave you. Fortunately you require no assistance from natives, not being encumbered with this world's goods."

"Das troo; ha, ha—a!" cried Ebony, opening his portentous mouth and shutting his eyes, "we 's got no luggidge."

"Well, we shall only be too glad of your company," said Mark, with some feeling, "and we thank you most heartily for your disinterested kindness."

"My conduct is not altogether disinterested," returned the guide. "The truth is, I had no intention at first of doing more than guiding you to the right

F

pass in the mountains, but since I have been with you my feelings have been modified, and the news which we have just received has—has filled me with anxiety, and raised in my mind the idea that —that I may even make use of you!"

"That's right," exclaimed Mark, heartily, "I'm glad if there is the smallest chance of our serving you in any way. In what way can we do so?"

For some moments the guide displayed a degree of hesitancy which his friends had not before noticed in him. Then he spoke, slowly—

"Well, the truth is, that I have a friend in the palace who is, I have been told, in great danger, owing to the wrath of Ranavalona. I thought that somehow, perhaps, you might give warning to this friend, and say that Samuel Ravoninohitriniony is in the neighbouring forest, and——"

Here the guide stopped short, and seemed to be in some perplexity. Mark Breezy, whose young and romantic spirit was deeply stirred by the prospect of adventure which his words had opened up, assured him with enthusiasm that whatever was possible for man to accomplish he might depend upon being at least vigorously attempted. To which assurance John Hockins begged to "putt the word ditto," and the negro fervently added, "Das so—me too!"

"But how are we to find your friend," asked

Mark, " seeing that we don't know and have never seen him ?"

" My friend is not a man, but a—a woman, a young girl," said Ravonino, with the slightest possible symptom of confusion, which opened the eyes of Mark instantly, and still further stirred his sympathies.

" Ravonino," he exclaimed, suddenly grasping the guide's hand, " treat me as a friend and trust me. You love this young girl! Is it not so? Nay, man, don't be angry with me. I can't help sympathising. Why, I know something of your—your —a—condition myself. The morning I left England, the very last person I said good-bye to was a fair young girl, with golden hair, and a rosebud mouth, and such lovely blue——"

" Das right, Massa," burst in Ebony, with a crow of admiration. " It doos my bery heart good to see a man as is proud ob his sweet'art. I 's got one too, bress you! but *she* ain't fair! No, she 's black as de kitchen chimbly, wid a bootiful flat nose, a mout' like a coal-scuttle, an' *such* eyes—oh !——"

" Hold your tongue, Ebony! Now, am I not right, Ravonino ?"

" You are right," answered the guide, gravely, yet without displeasure. " My Rafaravavy is in danger, and I must save her from this murderess at all hazards. It is right, however, to tell you that if you attempt to aid me you will encounter both difficulty and danger."

"Don't mention that, friend. No true man would shrink from either in a good cause," said Mark. "But when must we set out on this expedition?"

"By daybreak to-morrow. Our new hiding-place is on our way, so the change will not delay us; and from what the fugitives have told us, I hope— indeed I feel sure—that the Queen will do no further mischief for some weeks to come. But now, com- rades," said the guide, rising, "we must rest if we would work to-morrow. Follow me."

He led them into one of the side caves, when the whole of the people followed, as if by preconcerted arrangement. Here a much-soiled book in a leathern cover was produced. It was a portion of the Bible in the Malagasy language. A few verses were reverently read by the guide; a brief earnest prayer was offered by a very old man; a hymn was sung, and then the people dispersed to their several sections of the cave. Finally the lights were extinguished, and the place was left in silence and darkness profound.

CHAPTER VII.

DESCRIBES A MEEK MOTHER AND CROCODILE-SON. JOURNEY
RESUMED AND STRANGE TREATMENT OF THE KING
OF THE WATERS.

DAWN was still struggling to assert itself in the
far east, and the depths of the forest were still
shrouded in almost midnight gloom, when the strange
band of outlaws emerged from their cave, and, led
by Ravonino, went forth to search for a safer dwell-
ing-place in the still more inaccessible fastnesses of
the wilderness.

They had not much difficulty in finding a suitable
spot, for the particular region to which they had fled
from persecution was exceedingly wild and broken
in form, and abounded with concealed caverns
having outlets in several directions, so that pursuit
and discovery were alike difficult.

We may not delay here, however, to tell of their
wanderings. Like the Christians of other lands
and more ancient times, they were hunted like wild
beasts, though their only crime was a desire to
serve and worship God according to the dictates of

their consciences.   It is the old familiar story, and
comment is needless to those who understand it—

"Man's inhumanity to man
Makes countless thousands mourn."

There is only one other member of the party of
whom we will make mention just now, because she
appears again somewhat prominently in our tale.
This was a little elderly female who seemed utterly
destitute of the very common human attribute of
self-assertion, and in whose amiable, almost comical,
countenance, one expression seemed to overbear and
obliterate all others, namely that of gushing good-
will to man and beast! Those who did not know
Réni-Mamba thought her an amiable imbecile.
Those who knew her well loved her with peculiar
tenderness.   Her modesty and self-abnegation were
not, so far as any one knew, the result of principle.
She was too unassertive to lay claim to principle!
We are not sure that she understood the meaning
of principle.

Before Christianity in its doctrinal form reached
her she had only one source of discomfort in life, and
that was that in *everything* she failed! Failed to do
as much as she wanted to do for other people; failed
to express herself always as affectionately as she felt;
failed to avoid giving slight occasions of offence,
although she " never, *never* meant to do it !"   In short
she was, strange to say, a victim to self-condemnation.

When the Gospel of Jesus came to her, telling, as it does, that "God is Love," that Christ came to sweep away for ever the very sins that troubled her, and that His Holy Spirit would fight for and *in* her, so as to make her "more than conqueror," she caught it to her heart as the very thing she needed.

She did not indeed condemn herself less—nay, she rather condemned herself more than formerly— but the joy of being on the winning side, of knowing that all sin was pardoned for His sake, of feeling assured of progressive victory now and complete victory in the end, thoroughly scattered her old troubles to the winds.

Her very name was characteristic. It is a common and curious custom in Madagascar for parents sometimes to drop their own names and take the name of their eldest child with the word *raini*, "father of," or *réni*, "mother of," prefixed. Now this amiable little elderly woman had been married young, and it so happened that her husband was away on an expedition to the coast when the first and only son was born. One of the first things that the child did after opening its black eyes on this life was to open its uncommonly large mouth, with the intention, no doubt, of howling. But circumstances apparently induced it to change its mind, for it shut its mouth without howling.

The effect of the gape on the mother was to

remind her of one class of inhabitants of her native rivers—the crocodile—and cause her laughingly to style the child her "young crocodile." The Malagasy word for crocodile is *mamba*, and thus the child came by his name, with the usual prefix, Ra-Mamba. After a time his mother became so proud of her young crocodile that she dropped her own name entirely—congenially, as it were, obliterated herself—and ever after was known as Réni-Mamba, "mother of the crocodile."

At the time we write of, Mamba (we will drop the "Ra") was a stalwart handsome youth of over twenty, with no resemblance whatever to his namesake except a goodly-sized mouth and an amazing strength of appetite.

Need we say that his mother's gushing powers were expended upon him with the force of a Norwegian mill-race? It is gratifying to be able to add that the crocodile was keenly responsive!

The father of little Mamba—Andrianivo—had returned to the capital soon after his son's birth. He was a man in good position among the aristocracy of the land, and occupied a post of trust in the Queen's service. At that time the first great persecution of the Christians had begun. It was known that Andrianivo favoured the Christians. On the question being put to him, he frankly admitted that he was one of them. He was therefore despoiled of all he possessed, and banished into perpetual exile and slavery. He was sent in chains to a pestilential part of the island, with the intention that toil and disease should end his life. So secretly and promptly was he spirited away that no one could tell the precise locality to which he had been banished. His heart-broken wife and child were also sold, but were taken to a more healthy region, where the child grew and became a stout boy; his little mother, meanwhile, acting the part of a meek and faithful slave. She would probably have lived and died in this condition had not her stout son, when he grew up, resolved to become free. His mother had taught him what she knew of the Christian religion. From Ravonino he learned more, and heard of the escaped Christians who found a refuge in forests and mountains. Finally he persuaded his mother to run away with him, and thus it came about that we find them with the band of which Ravonino was leader—Laihova being lieutenant of the band.

An occasion for the display of his affectionate nature was afforded to Mamba on the morning we write of. Active as a kitten, though middle-aged, Réni-Mamba was skipping from rock to rock in a very rugged part of their route, when, her foot slipping, she fell and sprained her ankle badly.

Mamba was close to her.

"Mother!" he exclaimed, hurrying forward and raising her carefully, "why jump about like the squirrel? Are you hurt?"

"My son, help me to rise."

Gently the youth lifted her, and set her on her feet, whereupon she sank down again with a little shriek, and looked up with an expression of mingled humour and pain.

"My leg, I think, is broken!" said Réni (for the sake of brevity we will drop the "Mamba").

"Surely not, mother; it has been too tough and strong to break ever since I knew it."

Mamba spoke encouragingly; nevertheless, he examined the limb with anxious care. Being ignorant of surgery his examination was not of much use, but, fortunately, just then Mark Breezy, who had lingered behind to gather some plants, arrived on the scene. He found the injury to be a bad sprain, and did the best he could for the poor woman in the circumstances.

"Now, we must carry her," he said to the guide, "for she won't be able to walk for many days."

On this being translated, Mamba gathered his mother up as if she had been a bundle of clothes, or a baby, and marched away with her.

"Stop, stop!" cried Ravonino, "you can't carry her more than a few miles on such ground as I shall soon lead you over. We must arrange for her a *filanzana*."

The guide here referred to the sort of palanquin used by travellers in a country where there were no roads.   It consisted of a shallow, oblong basket, with light wooden framework, filled in with plaited strips of sheepskin, and hung between two light poles or bamboos.   As several such machines were used by some of the party to carry their few household necessaries, one of them was at once emptied and Réni put therein by her affectionate son.   Four stout young men put the ends of the poles on their shoulders, and the party once more advanced, Mamba walking by the side of the *filanzana* to be ready to assist in cases of difficulty or danger, and to relieve the bearers occasionally.

That afternoon they arrived at their new abode— a large, dry cavern—the entrance to which was not only well concealed on the face of a cliff in the heart of a dense jungle, but so difficult of access that a mere handful of men might easily have maintained it against a host.

Here Ravonino made no further delay than was necessary to see the party fairly settled.   Then he left them, but not before receiving many an earnest and affectionate message to friends and kindred of the fugitives still at the capital, but who had, as yet, managed to elude the vigilance and escape the malignity of Queen Ranavalona and her spies. Some of the women even wept as they bade the guide farewell, saying that they felt sure he would at last fall a victim to the relentless fury of the Queen, and that they should see his face no more.

With these the guide gently remonstrated.

"Think you not," he said, "that God is as able to protect me in Antananarivo as here in the wilderness? I go because I think that duty calls me. I expect no miracle in my behalf. I will take all possible precautions. Farewell."

Once more our three travellers found themselves advancing rapidly in single file through the forest, with the guide in advance. Before the sinking sun compelled them to encamp under the trees that night they had put many miles between them and the hiding-place of the outlawed Christians.

Next day, as they were about to resume their journey, Ravonino told them that about noon they would come to a large river on the other side of which there was a village where they could spend the night, for the people and their chief were friendly.

"Are they Christians?" asked Mark.

"No—at least the most of them are not, though there may be a few secret converts among them; for this hot persecution at the capital has scattered the Christians far and wide through the land, so that the knowledge of the blessed Gospel spreads. Thus our God makes the wrath of man to praise Him. The remainder of wrath He has promised to restrain. If He wills it otherwise, are we not prepared to die at His bidding? Many of our people have died already under the bloody reign of Ranavalona the usurper. How many more shall perish, who can tell?"

"But how do it come about," asked Hockins, "that this here chief is friendly?"

"Because I had occasion to render him good service at one time, and he is grateful."

"Good! Das allers de right way," remarked Ebony, with an approving nod. "W'en a man's grateful he's safe—you's sure ob 'im. Is dat de ribber you refur to jes' now?"

He pointed to an opening among the trees ahead, through which the sheen of water glittering in the sunlight could be seen.

Before the guide could reply a loud shout startled them, and next moment they were surrounded by half-naked savages, who brandished their spears threateningly.

Quick as lightning, according to a pre-arranged plan in case of sudden attack, Mark, Hockins, and the negro stood back-to-back, facing in all directions —the first with his gun advanced, the seaman pointing his cutlass at the foe, and Ebony levelling a spear with which he had provided himself. Little

would their courage have availed them, however,
if Ravonino had not been there, for a flight of spears
would have ended their resistance in a moment.

"Voalavo, your chief, is my friend," said the
guide, calmly, without putting himself in an attitude of defence, or showing the slightest symptom
of alarm. "Is Voalavo with you?"

"Voalavo comes," they replied, at once lowering
their weapons and pointing in the direction of the
river, whence proceeded sounds as of the lowing of
cattle.

"We have been to visit our enemies," said one of
the party, who, from his tones and bearing, appeared
to be a leader. "We have smitten them, and we
have brought away their cattle."

As he spoke another native was seen approaching.
He was a large burly jovial-looking man, somewhere about forty years of age, armed with a spear
and enveloped in the native *lamba*, a garment
used much in the same way as the Scottish plaid,
which it resembled in form, though of much lighter
material. The ornamentation of this garment proclaimed the wearer a person of distinction, and
the evident satisfaction that beamed on his broad
jovial countenance when he recognised and greeted
Ravonino showed that it was Voalavo himself—
the chief of the village they were approaching.

'I'm sorry to see," said the guide, after the first

few words of salutation, "that my friend still delights in war and robbery."

"Don't be sorry, friend, don't be sorry," returned the chief with a hearty laugh, as he gave the other a slap on the shoulder. "Sorrow does no good. It only puts water in the eyes and makes them red. Look at me—just returned from 'war and robbery,' and as happy as a squirrel. If a man does not delight in war and robbery, what is there in the world to delight in? If *I* am not sorry why should *you* be? If you can't help it—then laugh at it and try to enjoy your sorrow. That's the way *I* do. It suits me. I grow fat on it!"

He certainly did grow fat—if not on laughing at sorrow, certainly on something else—and his followers, although respectfully silent, showed by their smiling faces that they sympathised with their chief's hilarious mood.

"But where did you fall in with the white men?" asked Voalavo, turning suddenly towards Mark and Hockins, who stood listening with interest and curiosity to the rapid flow of his unintelligible talk. "Such pale flowers do not grow in *our* forests!"

In a few words Ravonino explained the history of our adventurers as far as he knew it, and the chief, on learning that they were his friend's friends, bade them welcome, and shook hands heartily in the European fashion—a mode of expressing friendship which had probably been learned from the missionaries, who, after spending many years in Madagascar, had, about the time we write of, been all banished from the island.

"Come now," cried the chief, "the rice will soon be ready—*that* won't make you sorry, Ravonino, will it?—and we have yet to cross the river with the cattle in the face of the hungry crocodiles—which wont make *them* sorry! Come."

Turning impulsively, in the brusque careless manner which characterised him, Voalavo led the way to the banks of the river—a considerable stream—where the cattle were assembled and guarded by a band of over a hundred warriors.

"Cattle seem to be plentiful in these parts," said Mark to the guide as they walked along.

"They are numerous everywhere in Madagascar. In truth a large part of our exports to the Mauritius and elsewhere consists of cattle.—Look! the chief was right when he said the crocodiles would not be sorry to see the cattle crossing."

He pointed to a ripple on the water caused by the ugly snout of one of the creatures referred to. It seemed by the activity of its movements to be already anticipating a feast.

"Crocodiles," continued the guide, "are numerous in many of our lakes and rivers, and dangerous too, though they are naturally timid and can be easily frightened away. I remember a curious instance of this kind happening on the east coast, where a European trader was cleverly imposed on—deceived, or, what you call ——"

"Humbugged," suggested Hockins.

"Well, yes—humbugged! He was a big ignorant fellow, this trader; strong and energetic enough, but full of conceit—thought he knew almost everything, but in reality knew next to nothing, yet self-willed and obstinate enough to—to— You know the sort of man?"

"Yes, yes; a stoopid cockscomb," said Hockins. "I know the breed well—lots of 'em everywhere."

"Jus' so—a born idjit; go on, massa," said Ebony, who was always charmed at the prospect of a story or anecdote.

"Well, this trader," continued the guide, "was on his way from Antananarivo to the coast with cattle for exportation, and one day they came to a place where they had to cross a narrow part of a lake. The natives of that place advised him not to venture without trying the effect of their *ody*, or charms, on the crocodiles. These they said, and believed, would protect the cattle in crossing. But the trader scouted the idea, and, laughing at their superstitions, gave orders to drive the bullocks into the water. He quickly repented his obstinacy, for no sooner were they in than the crocodiles seized nine of them and dragged them down. 'Oh! bring the *ody*—work the *ody*—quick!' cried the anxious man, fearing lest all the cattle should be seized. The *ody* was worked instantly, and to his astonishment, as well as the triumph of the natives, the rest of the cattle crossed in safety. Even those that had been nearly drowned escaped and passed over."

"But how was dat?" asked Ebony, with a perplexed air. "If de *ody* was nuffin, how could it do suffin?"

"Simply enough," returned the guide. "The charm consisted merely in noise. The natives, in canoes and on both sides of the lake, shouted furiously and beat the water with branches of trees, so that the poor crocodiles were scared away. See —there is something of the same sort going to be performed just now."

Previous to this process, however, the chief Voalavo went through a singular ceremony to propitiate the crocodiles. The Malagasy, like the ancient Egyptians, regard the crocodile with superstitious veneration. They esteem him the king of the waters, and to dispute his right to reign would, they believe, expose them to his vengeance. Hence they seldom kill crocodiles, and rather avoid whatever is likely to provoke them. It is their custom also, sometimes to make solemn speeches and vows to the crocodiles when about to cross rivers.

Voalavo, who was unusually reckless, free-and-easy, and regardless in ordinary affairs, was nevertheless remarkably superstitious. Before giving orders to cross the river, therefore, he advanced to the water's edge and mumbled incantations or made vows in a low tone for nearly half-an-hour. Then, elevating his voice, so as to be heard across the river, he continued, addressing the crocodiles :—

"Now, I pray you, good mamba, to do me no injury, and particularly to spare my cattle, for you do not know what trouble I have had to get them. No doubt you know how anxious I and my people are to eat them, for you have much of the same desire; but I beseech you to exercise self-denial. You don't know how pleasant that will make you feel! Remember that I have never done your royal race any injury—never waged war with you or killed you. On the contrary I have always held you in the highest veneration. If you do not remember this, but forget it, I and my whole race and all my relatives will declare war and fight against you for evermore! So be good and do what I tell you!"

"Now, my men," he cried, turning round, "drive in the cattle, work the *ody*, and make all the dogs bark!"

In the midst of an indescribable hubbub the herds

were then driven into the river, and the men—some in canoes and some on both banks—enacted the very scene which Ravonino had described.   In a few minutes the whole herd was got over in safety.

Half-an-hour later and our travellers were seated in the chief's house regaling themselves with beef-steaks and marrow-bones, chickens and rice.

CHAPTER VIII.

A FRIEND APPEARS UNEXPECTEDLY, AND OUR TRAVELLERS SPEND
A DISTURBED NIGHT.

WHATEVER ethereal persons may say to the contrary, there can be no doubt whatever that the consumption of food is an intellectual treat, inasmuch
as it sets the body free from the cravings of appetite,
and by stimulating those nervous influences which
convey vigour and vitality to the brain, not only
becomes the direct cause of physical gratification, but
induces that state of mind which is most favourable
to the development of the interesting creations of
fancy and the brilliant coruscations of imagination.

We might pursue this subject further did time
and space permit; but our objection to "skipping"
is so great, that we shrink from giving the reader
even a shadow of excuse for doing so.   Moreover we
dread the assault of the hypercritical reader, who
will infallibly object that it is not "the consumption
of food," but the resulting mental effect which is the
"intellectual treat."   As if we did not know that!
"But," we would retort with scorn, "can any cause be

separated from its effect without bringing about, so
to speak, the condition of nonentity ?"

Passing to the subject which gave rise to these erra-
tic thoughts, we have to relate that the whole party,
entertainers and entertained, did ample justice to the
rice, beef, chicken and marrow-bones, after which
Hockins wafted the natives to the seventh heaven of
delight and wonder by means of his flageolet.   It
was very late that night before they retired to rest.
It was later still before they went to sleep.

The native village at which our travellers had
arrived was a rude, poor-looking place, inhabited by
a brave and warlike tribe, who depended more for
defence on their personal prowess and the difficulties
presented by their forests, than upon ditches or
ramparts.   The village was, however, surrounded by
a fence of trees growing so close together that it
would have been almost impossible to carry the
place by assault if resolutely defended from within.

The huts were roughly constructed of bamboos,
plastered with clay and lined with matting,—also
with the large leaves of the " traveller's tree," and
thatched with rushes.

The chief's hut, in which the white guests were
feasted, was of course larger and somewhat better in
construction than the others.   Its floor, composed of
hard-beaten clay, was covered with matting, clean
pieces of which were spread for the visitors to squat

upon, for there were no chairs, stools, or tables. In the north-west corner was the hearth—a square of between two and three feet, with a few large stones for supporting the cooking utensils, but without chimney of any kind. Smoke was allowed to find an exit as it best could by crevices in the roof and by a small window or hole in the north gable. A few cooking-pots, earthen jars, rice-baskets, some knives, a wooden chest, and several spears, completed the furniture.

Against the northern roof-post hung a small bottle-shaped basket, which contained the household *sampey*, or god, or charm. In Madagascar this usually consists of a meaningless stone; sometimes a chip of wood, the leaf of a tree, or a flower, and this is what the natives pray to and profess to trust in!

Our travellers found, after supper was over, that they were not to sleep in the chief's house, for they were led to that of a head man of the village, and told they were to rest with him. This man was old, and seemed to have no wife or family, for the only person at home at the time, besides himself, was an old woman, perhaps his sister, who looked after the household. He was a hospitable old man, however, and made them heartily welcome to their beds of matting in the north end of the hut. Unfortunately the south end of it was usually occupied by pigs and poultry. These were expelled for the occasion, but they insisted several times on returning to their own abode, being unable, apparently, to believe that their expulsion was really intended! As there were several openings in the hut, the difficulty of excluding the animals was great, for when expelled at one hole, amid remonstrative shrieks and screams, they quickly re-entered at another with defiant grunts and cacklings.

By stopping up the holes, however, the enemy was finally overcome. Then the old man, having retired to his corner, and the sister having departed, Mark Breezy, John Hockins, James Ginger, and Ravonino drew round the fire, heaped-on fresh logs, lay down at full length on their mats, and prepared to enjoy that sleepy chat which not unfrequently precedes, sometimes even postpones, repose.

"That was a curious speech that Voalavo made to the crocodile, Ravonino," said Mark. "Do you really think he believed it did any good?"

"Yes, truly, he believed it. This is a land of charms and superstition. Voalavo is of too honest and straightforward a nature to practise what he does not believe in."

"Does *you* b'lieve in churms an' soopistition?" asked Ebony, with expectant eyes.

"What need to ax that, you stoopid nigger?" said Hockins; "don't you know he's a Christian?"

"Das true, 'Ockins. I goed an' forgot."

" But tell me, Ravonino, are de crokindiles awrful rampageous when dey're roused ? "

" Yes, they are pretty bad," said the guide, clearing his throat, for he was fond of expatiating on the wonders and beauties of his native land! " And although they look sluggish enough when sprawling on mud-banks, half-asleep in the sun, you would be surprised to see them go after fish, which is their principal food.   Their favourite haunts are the deep rugged banks of a river or lake overhung with trees, where they can hide themselves and watch for prey. It is not only in water that they are dangerous. They fasten their teeth, if they get the chance, on any animal that comes to the river to drink. They sometimes get hold of bullocks when drinking, and often do so when the cattle are swimming across. They are unnaturally ferocious, too, for they will devour their own young."

" Oh ! de brutes ! " exclaimed Ebony, poking the fire with a bit of stick savagely.   " Don't de mudders fight for de young uns ? "

" Not they.   The mothers lay their eggs in the sand and leave them to look after themselves.   The others are sly, and——"

" Dat's de fadders, brudders, an' unkles ob de eggs, you mean ? "

" Yes, that's what I mean.   The old he-crocodiles watch where the eggs are laid, an' when it's about time for them to break an' let the young ones out, these monsters go into the water at the edge and wait. When the baby-crocodiles get out of prison they make straight for the water, where the old villains are ready to receive an' devour them. Sometimes the young ones are stupid when they are born, they take the wrong road and escape their relations' teeth only to get to the rice-grounds and fall into the hands of the natives. Many of the eggs, too, are destroyed, before they are hatched, by vultures and other birds, as well as by serpents. Men also gather them by hundreds, boil them and dry them in the sun to preserve them for use or sale."

" The miserable young things seem to have a poor chance of life then," said Mark, sleepily.

" Das so, massa. I 'd rader be a nigger dan a crokindile."

Hockins said nothing, being sound asleep.

" What makes that rattling among the cooking-pots ? " asked Mark, looking round lazily.

" Rats," replied the guide. " Didn't you see them running along the roof when you came in ? "

" No, I didn't."

" Look up now, then, and you 'll see them on the beams."

Mark and Ebony both looked up, and beheld a row of rats on the beam overhead—their bead-like eyes glittering as they gazed over one side of the beam, and their long tails just showing on the other.

"Das funny," said the negro, who was in sympathy with the whole brute creation!

Mark thought it very much the reverse of funny, but held his peace.

"Dar's a ole grey un, massa, right ober 'Ockins's head—a tremenjous big un.   Don't you see 'im wid a griggy young un beside 'im?"

Whether the griggy young one was also larky we cannot tell, but while the negro was speaking it executed a flourish (whether intentional or otherwise who can say?) which knocked the big grey rat off the beam, and caused it to fall with a heavy flop on Hockins's face.   Three others fell off in their anxiety to observe the result.

Hockins leapt up with an indignant roar, and the rats leaped among the pots and pans with a horrified squeak, while Ebony and the others looked on with excruciating enjoyment.

The scurrying of many little feet among the household implements told that the grey rat's friends were numerous though unseen, and the angry grunting of pigs proved that other slumbers had been broken. Of course the whole party were thoroughly awakened by this incident, but they took it good-humouredly, and, after replenishing the fire, lay down again, and resolutely shut their eyes and ears.

Slumber was once more stealing over them, when a noise at the door of the hut awakened them. Next moment they started up, for two warriors of the tribe entered with a prisoner between them.

"We caught this man entering our village," said one of the warriors, fiercely, to the guide; "we would have taken him to our chief, but he says that you are his friend—yet I think he lies."

"He speaks the truth," returned Ravonino, calmly. "He is my friend. Doubtless he has good reasons for coming here. Leave him with us, we will guard him till morning."

The warriors at once released their prisoner and retired, while the man stepping forward into clearer light revealed the handsome countenance of Laihova.

"Sit down, my brother," said Ravonino to the youth, in tones of unusual tenderness, "and let me know what brings you here so unexpectedly."

"I come to offer my service," replied the youth, with a modest air. "You have told me that you go to Antananarivo to rescue Rafaravavy. Your face is known to every one in the town. If you enter it, your death will be certain."

"But I do not intend to enter it," said Ravonino, "these my white friends will aid me."

"The white men may be wise and brave, but they know not how to aid you. I am not so well known

in the town.   I will venture into it and will show
them where to go and what to do."

The guide shook his head and was silent for some
moments.   He seemed uncertain how to act.

"What says Laihova?" asked Mark Breezy at this
point, for the conversation having been conducted
in the native tongue they as yet understood nothing.

The guide briefly explained, and then turned to
the young man.

" But how can you think of leaving your friends in
the cave, Laihova?   They may require your strong
arm; and my sister is —— "

"It was my friends who advised me to leave
them," said the youth, quickly, "and Ra-Ruth bade
me go.   Besides, have we not entered into the Covenant of Blood?"

" Well, you may come with us.   After all, Ra-
Ruth is right."

" What does he mean by the Covenant of Blood?"
asked Mark when the guide explained what had
just been said.

" It means that he and I are united by one of the
closest ties that bind the men of this island.   No
doubt you will think it a strange alliance, nevertheless it is a true and a strong bond of brotherhood.
It is meant to unite two people in sacred friendship,
so that ever afterwards they feel bound to help and
defend each other.   When two persons agree to form

this bond, a meeting is arranged for the performance of the ceremony and taking the vow. Some gunpowder and a ball are brought, with a little ginger, a spear, and two particular kinds of grass. A fowl is also used. Its head is nearly cut off, and it is left to bleed during the ceremony. Then a long vow of mutual friendship, assistance, and defence is pronounced. After this each man drinks a few drops of the other's blood. To obtain it they make a small cut in the skin of the centre of the bosom, which they call 'the mouth of the heart.'"

"And did you go through this ceremony with Laihova ?" asked Mark.

"I did, many years ago, when we were little more than boys. He saved my life by jumping into a deep pool in a lake and rescuing me from the crocodiles. I had fallen in off the steep bank. I could not swim, and he could. After that we made the alliance of brotherhood. Laihova was not a Christian at that time. Since then God has made use of me to rescue him from a more awful death than that which threatened me. Laihova is grateful, and, knowing that I run much risk in going near the capital, has come, as you see, to help me."

"Not a bad style of brotherhood that," said Hockins, with a tremendous yawn. "Eh, Ebony ? What d'ee think of you an' me goin' in for the same sort o' thing ?"

"P'r'aps," answered Ebony, with a responsive yawn which threw that of Hockins quite into the shade, "p'r'aps black blood mightn't agree wid your stummick. But I say, Massa Breezy, don' you tink it a'most time we was goin' to sleep?"

As the night was far spent—or, rather, the morning far advanced—by that time, the whole party willingly assented. Laihova was supplied with a separate mat, the embers of the wood-fire were drawn together, and they all lay down once more to make the most of what remained of the period of repose. But circumstances were against them.

True, being tired and healthy men, they dropped off at once with the facility of infants, and during a quarter of an hour or so, while the fire continued to emit an occasional flicker, all went well; but when the last vestige of flame died away, the rats again came out with bead-like eyes and cautious tread. Gradually they became bolder. Impunity never fails to encourage presumption. In short they soon began to hold a sort of carnival. The pots and pans became, as it were, musical, to the evident distress of the slumbering seaman—especially when the large grey rat fairly overturned a small rice-jar, which in its fall removed several props from other utensils and caused a serious clatter. Still the wearied men slept through it all, until the enemy took to scampering over their bodies. Then the enraged Ebony, being partially awakened, made a fierce grasp at one of the foe, and caught Hockins by the ear. Of course the result was a howl, and a sleepy request from Mark, to " Stop that noise!"

But even that incident failed to arouse them thoroughly, though it filled the rats with temporary horror, and caused them to flee.

The last word reminds us that there were others there that night, besides rats, to disturb the sleepers' dreams—but we merely make a suggestive hint at that!

Soon the rats returned in greater force and more demonstrative hilarity than ever. They evidently went in for a game of hide-and-seek round and over the slumberers, causing the sleepy growls of John Hockins to resemble the fitful mutterings of distant thunder.

Thus they went on until the grey dawn of morning appeared. Then an extremely large cock, in the south-east corner of the hut, feeling that it had enjoyed a sufficiently good night's rest, flapped its ungainly wings, stretched out its neck, and gave vent to a clarion-crow which ——

" Brute!" exclaimed Hockins, not even giving us time to finish the sentence!

He said no other word, but seizing a piece of wood, sent it forth with such true and effective aim, that he cleared not only the cock, but all his wives off their perch, and sent them in cackling consternation out of the hut by the nearest hole in the wall.

After that the much-tried party slumbered in peace until the sun was high.

CHAPTER IX.

A JOVIAL CHIEF, AND NEW EXPERIENCES OF VARIOUS KINDS.

THE friendly hospitality of the chief of this village was found to be likely to cause delay, for he would not hear of his visitors departing until they had been feasted and entertained with games and hunting.

As they were completely in his power there was nothing for it but to submit with the best grace possible, although Ravonino was naturally anxious to push on.

"You see it won't do to look as if we were indifferent to his hospitality," said the guide. "He would be greatly offended, for you must know that the Malagasy pride themselves on their hospitality. Come, we will go and have a look at the neighbouring woods while they are preparing breakfast for us, and I will tell you a story about the late King Radama."

"Was that the good king you told us about who did so much for the missionaries, though he wasn't a Christian himself?" asked Hockins, as they all passed through the enclosure of the village and entered the woods.

"Yes, the same," replied the guide, "though whether he was a Christian or not I cannot tell. I judge no man. He made no profession of Christianity, but he was kind to the missionaries—very different from Ranavalona."

"Das de oosurper, what you call 'er?" said Ebony.

"Just so," returned the guide. "Well, as I was saying, our people are very hospitable. Everywhere, almost, throughout the country, when a traveller enters a village, a present is usually brought to him of rice, poultry, or fruit, or whatever they have on hand. You'll find out that for yourselves as you go along—"

"A bery proper state ob tings," remarked Ebony.

"And whatever house you come to," continued Ravonino, "the owner will invite you politely to enter, and make you welcome. Of course there are greedy and surly people here and there, but these are an exception to the rule. Well, on one occasion King Radama heard of some people of that sort. You must know that our chiefs have always required that they should be entertained on the best the people could provide. It is an old custom. Well, Radama made a law that all the provisions and other kinds of property should belong to the people, but all the houses in the country should belong to the sovereign; and he ordered the inhabitants to furnish lodgings to his servants and soldiers wherever they went. In order to make sure that his orders were obeyed the King soon after went in disguise to a village some distance off, and towards evening entered a peasant's house and asked to be taken in for the night.

"The heads of the family did not refuse, but rendered their hospitality in such a way as showed that he was not welcome. Next day he went to another house. There he was kindly welcomed, civilly treated, and the best they had in the house was set before him. In the morning when taking leave he made himself known, no less to the surprise than consternation of the family, and he left, assuring them that their hospitality should not be forgotten. The King kept his word, for he afterwards sent his officers to the village with a stern reproof to his first entertainer and a handsome present to the other."

Just as the guide finished his anecdote a resplendent butterfly of enormous size rose from the bushes, and Mark, to whom it was quite a new specimen, bounded after it, but failed to effect a capture.

"Neber mind, massa," said the sympathetic Ebony, " you 'll hab better luck nix' time—p'r'aps!"

"Besides," added the guide, "there are plenty

more where that came from, for we have got into a
good region for insects."

"Seems to me," said Hockins, "it's a good region
for everything.   Look at that now,"—he pointed to
an object in front of him. "I would say that was
a spider if it warn't as big as a bird, and hadn't set
up a fishin'-net for a web!"

Although not strictly correct, the seaman's description had a foundation in truth, for some of the
spiders of Madagascar are enormous, and their webs
so thick that it requires a considerable effort to
break them.   Moreover they are said to be poisonous, and the bite of some even deadly.

The contemplation of those creatures, however,
had to be cut short at that time, as they did not
dare to risk keeping Voalavo waiting breakfast for
them.

"We are going to stick pigs and hunt wild cattle,"
said the jovial chief, with his mouth full of chicken
and rice, when they arrived.   "We will show the
white men some fun."

On this being translated Ebony hoped that the
black man was included in the white, and Mark
asked if the hunting-ground was far off.

"A long way," said the chief, "we shan't reach it
till night.   But that's no matter, for night is our
time to hunt."

He said this with a twinkle in his eye, for he

saw well enough that his guests were impatient to be gone.

"But," continued he, on observing that they did not seem cheered by the prospect, "our road to the hunting-plain lies on your way to Antananarivo, so you won't lose time."

As he spoke he opened a small box containing a brown sort of dust, of which he put as much as he possibly could between the teeth of his lower jaw and the lip.

"What in all the world is he doin'?" asked Hockins of the guide in a low tone.

"He is taking snuff."

"I always s'posed," remarked Ebony, "dat snuff was tooken by de nose!"

"So it is, they tell me, in England; but we have a different fashion here, as you see, and quite as foolish."

"You don't mean that it's tobacco he treats in that way?" exclaimed Mark.

"Not pure tobacco, but tobacco mixed with other things—something like the cheap cigars which you English are said to smoke!" replied Ravonino with something of a humorous twinkle in his eyes. "But we don't smoke. We only snuff. In making our snuff we first dry the tobacco leaves and grind them to powder. Then to this we add the ashes of the leaves of a sweet-smelling herb, the mixture being twice as much tobacco as ashes; a small quantity of potash or salt is added, and then it is considered fit for use."

"Don't your people smoke at all?" asked Hockins.

"Not much, and never tobacco—except those on the coast who have been corrupted by Europeans. Some of us used to smoke *rongona,* a kind of hemp. It is a powerful stimulant, and used to be taken by warriors before going out to battle, because it drove them nearly mad, and so fitted them for their bloody work. Government has lately forbidden its use—but it is still used in secret."

"They've got baccy, an' don't smoke!" murmured Hockins to himself in a kind of meditative surprise, as though he had just been told that the natives possessed food and did not eat.

"But *you* don't smoke?" remarked the guide.

"That's 'cause I hain't got baccy nor pipe. You give me pipe and baccy an' I'll smoke you into fits in no time."

"Do you feel the want of it much?"

"Not much. At first I did, most awful, but now I'm gettin' over it."

The guide was silent. He might have remarked, "Yet now, if you had the chance, you would enslave yourself *again !*" but, not being of an argumentative turn of mind, he merely shook his head and changed the subject. It was well, for Hockins was

one of those people who, " if convinced against their
will, remain of the same opinion still."

After breakfast, while the young men of the tribe
armed themselves and made preparation for the
expedition, Ravonino took his friends through the
village, the inhabitants of which were evidently as
deeply interested in seeing the white men as the
latter were in seeing the brown ; for each were
objects of curiosity to the other.

During the stroll our friends saw the weaving of
the *lamba*—the large plaid-like garment of hempen
cloth worn extensively in the island. The looms
were rude and simple, but the fabrics produced
were wonderfully good in appearance and texture,
some being made of a kind of coarse silk. Many of
them were ornamented, and rendered very heavy
with immense quantities of small leaden beads
fastened to the garment either in straight or curved
rows, the lead having been procured from traders at
the coast, and the beads having been manufactured
by themselves. These natives wore but little
clothing—merely a cloth round the loins, and
sometimes a jacket made of coarse material. The
lamba is usually worn over the shoulders in the
cool of the morning, but at the time we write of
most of the men who used the garment had bound
it tightly round their waists.

Our travellers were made acquainted at this

time with a game which interested them greatly—especially arousing the enthusiasm of the negro. It was a kicking game, played by some of the more active among the young men, who, having got ready for the field quickly, were waiting for their slower companions. The chief peculiarity of the game consisted in the mode of kicking, namely backwards, in the horse or donkey fashion. The guide explained that the name of the game, when literally translated, was, "striking blue with the sole of the foot!" It is a desperate game, and when played, as it frequently is, by hundreds of active and powerful young men, the results are sometimes sprained ankles, broken legs, etc.

"Oh! das de game for me!" cried the enthusiastic Ebony, who could hardly be restrained from joining. "De sole ob my foot's awrful broad, an' I could strike black as well as blue. Do let me try, massa!"

Fortunately, perhaps, for our negro, the chief came out of his hut at that moment and gave the signal for the hunters to advance, thus bringing the game and Ebony's aspirations to an abrupt end. The young men at once fell to the rear, and the whole party sallied forth into the forest.

It was magnificent weather, with just cloud enough to prevent the sun being overpoweringly hot, and the tract of country over which they passed was surpassingly beautiful. To Mark Breezy it seemed as if all the winged insects in the island had come forth to welcome him. There were butter-flies of various sizes and brilliant colours flitting to and fro among the wild-flowers, besides dragon-flies, grasshoppers of exquisite beauty, spiders with coats of gold and silver, caterpillars half-a-foot long in gorgeous array of black, scarlet, and yellow, and many other creatures which we may not pause to describe here, though Mark and the guide frequently paused to look at them, insomuch that they were often left a considerable way behind. One of the butterflies which Mark caught at that time was very beautiful, and a slow flier. It actually measured eight inches across the extended wings.

Of larger animals they saw none; and it may be as well to remark here that there are no large car-nivora in Madagascar—no lions, tigers, leopards panthers, or creatures of that sort—nothing larger than a wild-cat and a wolf being known. Neither are there elephants, giraffes, rhinoceroses, hippopotami, antelope, nor deer; the only large animals being two species of ox, and the wild-boar, goats and sheep, and crocodiles. There are also huge bats, an animal of the monkey tribe called the lemur, hedgehogs, and rabbits.

The lemurs are very pretty little things, and, being gentle affectionate creatures, are sometimes tamed and kept as pets.

The scenery, we have said, was beautiful. At

one turn of the road in particular a landscape of such beauty appeared suddenly before them that Mark was arrested as if spell-bound; it was such a gorgeous combination of luxuriant foliage—ferns and palms and bamboos, interlaced with creepers, and enlivened by streams which brawled and tumbled in picturesque cascades, over which hundreds of butterflies sported in the sunshine. From the height of land on which they stood a wide, well-watered plain was seen to extend far below them. It was hemmed in on either side by wooded hills and backed by the interior highlands. Far down the hillside their companions could be seen wending their way through the tangled shrubbery, just in rear of the native hunters, led by their energetic chief Voalavo. As the men carried spears, the points of which glittered in the sun, the party had quite a martial aspect.

To our young student the whole scene was enchanting. It had the effect of subduing and solemnising his feelings in a way which he had never before experienced. The earnest, religious cast of his companion's spirit also tended not a little to deepen this feeling and induce him for the first time in his life to understand that "nature's God" was in very truth present with him.

"Is not the hand of the Master here?" said Ravonino, after a long silence.

"Truly, my friend, it is," replied the young man, "and your remark puts me to shame. For, many a time, through the microscope and the human frame and the surrounding world, might I have seen this Master-hand everywhere—if my eyes had been open."

The guide turned on Mark an earnest, inquiring look.

"Friend," he said, impressively, "if this be so, you are now very specially awakened to the Truth. If you have passed through and seen so much without recognising God in his creatures, you have been brought for the first time to know yourself. Turn now—now—to the Saviour, and you will henceforth see a glory in all things that you never saw before. Turn, my friend—for 'now is the accepted time.'"

Ravonino spoke with such an earnest look and tone that the youth could not doubt the sincerity of his belief in the Saviour whom he so affectionately held up to his view.

"Ravonino, I believe you are right. God help me to turn!"

"He *has* helped you already," said the guide. "That prayer, *if true*, never yet came from an un-renewed heart."

As he spoke a shout from those further down the hill-side stopped the conversation and obliged the friends to resume the descent.

"That is the plain, I am told," said Ravonino, "where they expect to find wild cattle, and where we shall have to encamp, no doubt, till night enables us to hunt."

"Not a very cheerful time to go sporting," said Mark.

"They do not count it sport," remarked his comrade, gravely. "They are short of meat, and hunt for food."

A few minutes later and the party was encamped in the thick woods that bordered the plain.

CHAPTER X.

TELLS OF A GRAND HUNT AND OTHER THINGS.

WHILE the party of hunters awaited the approach of night (for the wild cattle feed chiefly at night) they kept as quiet as possible. The scouts had brought news that a large herd was feeding on a part of the plain which was not far distant, although concealed from view by the formation of the land.

Still thinking of the recent conversation which he had had with the guide, Mark Breezy retired a little from the rest of the party and flung himself on the ground under a tree to rest and meditate.

He was not left long, however, in solitude, for Hockins and Ebony soon discovered his retreat. Each of these worthies was armed with a spear.

"Hallo, Doctor," exclaimed the former, as he came up, "are you not supplied with a weapon?"

"Yes, I am," replied Mark, pointing to a native spear which lay at his side, "but I think I won't use it."

"Why not, massa?" asked Ebony.

"Because I don't yet know how to go about this style of hunting, and if I were to attempt anything I might spoil the sport. I intend merely to look on."

"Right you are, sir," remarked the sailor. P'r'aps it'll be as well for all of us to keep in the background."

"Pooh!" ejaculated Ebony, turning up his nose —a needless action, as it was well turned up already—"pooh! I not keep in de background! You're all wrong. W'en you knows nuffin, jest you wait till you knows suffin—ebber so little—an' den go at 'im."

"That's just what I said I should do, Ebony. I will merely look on at first."

"But how long does you prepose to look on, massa? Ain't five or six minits enuff? Dis is what I's a-gwine to do. I'll foller close on de chief—what you call 'im?—Vollyvo—an' w'en I sees him stick one hox, das nuff for me. I den go at 'im on my own hook, an' stick away right an' left!"

"I'll give you a wide berth, then, for it's as like as not that you'll stick some o' the hunters in the dark," said Hockins, rising, for just then there was a stir in the camp as if preparation was being made to go out.

A few minutes later and Laihova came to them with the news that he had heard the chief say they were getting ready, as it was necessary to make a long round through the woods to get well to leeward of the cattle.

This process of getting ready consisted in every man stripping and washing himself all over in order to get rid of the smell of the smoke of their huts. Even the guests were obliged to conform to the custom. Then they set off in profound silence, every man being armed with a couple of spears, excepting the guests, who were allowed only one spear each, it being feared that if they carried two they might chance to rattle them together and thus alarm the game, for the kind of cattle they were about to attack are exceedingly active and suspicious —always on the alert, continually snuffing and snorting at the bare idea, as it were, of an approaching enemy. Unlike the tame cattle of the island, these animals have no hump, but strongly resemble the ordinary cattle of England, save that their horns are shorter and their bellowings deeper. They are, however, very savage, and when wounded or annoyed are apt to attack their enemies with terrible ferocity.

To Mark Breezy and his companions the expedition proved to be full of excitement, for, apart from the novelty of the situation and uncertainty as to what lay before them or was expected of them, the extreme darkness of the night, and the quick silent stealthy motion of the almost invisible hunters, filled their minds with—if we may say so—awfully pleasurable anticipations!

The whole band followed their chief in single file, and as he was intimately familiar with the topography of the region, the only anxiety of each man was to tread carefully in his footsteps.

As for Ebony, his whole soul and spirit were in the enterprise, as well as his black body, and the varying expression of his mobile features would have charmed the heart of a physiognomist, had such a man been there with light enough to enable him to see. As there was no physiognomist, and no light, the reader must fall back on imagination.

Intent on carrying out his pre-arranged plans, our negro walked close behind the chief—so close indeed, that he inadvertently brought his spear down rather heavily on the left shoulder of that fiery person, for which he received a buffet on the ear, and an order to keep further back. In other circumstances the plucky spirit of Ebony would have been roused to indignation—perhaps to retaliation; but a sense of justice was strong in that negro's breast. Overwhelmed with shame at his clumsiness, and eager to rectify the error—yet not daring to speak, for silence had been strictly enjoined—he raised the spear over his shoulder and turned the point backwards, thereby bringing it down on the head of the man in the rear.

Doubly shocked at this, he raised his weapon to

the perpendicular, and knocked some tropical bird violently off the lower branches of a tree. It fluttered screeching to the ground, and bounced angrily into the bushes.

The whole band of hunters came to a sudden and breathless halt, but no word was uttered. In a few moments the chief resumed his silent march, and the ghostly column moved on—Ebony, greatly subdued but by no means crushed, keeping his weapon at such a slope as would prevent its doing damage to birds above or men below.

Thus they proceeded for nearly an hour, at the end of which time they could hear the wild cattle roaring and bellowing not far off.

When the hunters had got completely to leeward, and were beginning to draw quite near to the feeding-ground, they advanced with increased caution, and some of the men began to pull the tops of the grass with their hands, as they went, in order to mimic as nearly as possible the noise made by an ox grazing.

The instant this sound reached the ears of the cattle they became absolutely silent, neither bellowing nor feeding! It was evident that they were listening with the utmost attention. Understanding this, the hunters stood quite still, without a whisper, but a few of those who were adepts at the art continued their imitation of cropping the grass. After listening for a time the animals appeared to arrive at the conclusion that it was a false alarm, for they re-commenced feeding, and the hunters continued their stealthy approach.

Soon they came to the thinly scattered shrubbery which marked the termination of the woods and the beginning of the plain. And now, profoundly dark though the night was, they could faintly perceive the forms of their game looming black against the dark sky beyond—themselves being quite invisible, however, owing to their background of forest.

Nearer and nearer the men moved, still cropping the grass as they advanced, until they fairly got up to the herd, and were less liable to disturb them, for, being almost invisible, they were, no doubt, mistaken for members of the family !

As the hunters now scattered, Ebony had some difficulty in keeping close enough to the chief to observe his movements. Voalavo himself was too intent upon his work to think of anything else, or to care who was near him.

Gradually he approached close enough to an animal to thrust his spear deep into its side. It sprang from the ground and made a noise as if hurt by the horn of a comrade, but this is so common an event that the rest of the cattle were in no way disturbed by it.

The chief saw by the staggering of the animal

that it was mortally wounded, and that there was no need to follow it up, as it could be easily tracked and found in daylight. He therefore turned to attack another animal that was close at hand.

"Now den," said Ebony to himself mentally, "your time's come. Go at 'im!"

Lowering his weapon to the charge, he glanced round and observed the indistinct form of an animal on his right. It was apparently a little one.

"Weal is as good as beef," thought Ebony, as he made a silent but furious rush, scarcely able to restrain a shout of anticipated victory.

The spear-point missed the animal, just grazing its back, and went deep into the ground, while the negro plunged with crushing violence on the back of John Hockins, who had been trying to approach his game à *la* Red Indian!

To say that poor Ebony was filled with horror, as well as shame and self-abhorrence, is but a feeble statement.

"Don't speak, you black monster!" whispered the seaman in his ear, as he seized him by the throat.

The rush of apology which had sprung from Ebony's heart was checked abruptly at the lips.

Hockins released him, picked up his spear, and resumed his creeping way. By this time several of the hunters had dealt silent death around them, but still the herd failed to take alarm!

Being left alone Ebony's courage returned, and with it his enthusiasm.

"Come," he muttered, mentally, as he drew the spear from the ground, "'Ockins not killed yet. Das one good job. No use to cry for not'ing. You try again, Ginjah. Better luck nixt time."

Greatly encouraged by these thoughts he advanced on tip-toe—spear at the charge—eyes glancing sharply all round. Suddenly a tall form seemed to rise up right in front of him. The negro's heart leaped violently. He was on the point of charging when a doubt assailed him. The creature before him, though scarce distinguishable from the surrounding gloom, was not long-bodied like an ox. He could perceive that clearly. It was tall like a man—very tall. Perhaps it was Mark Breezy? The recent mistake made him think anything possible!

"Is dat you, massa?" he whispered, in anxious alarm.

A furious bellow was the reply, followed by a still more furious charge. Ebony had forgotten that an ox "end on" and head up is tall and not long!

Happily, in stepping back he tripped, and the animal went right over him. But the alarm had been given, and a sudden thundering of feet told that the entire herd had taken to flight, while the shouting and cries of the hunters, added to the confused roaring, showed that there was now no need for concealment.

When the muster-roll was called it was found that nobody was missing or hurt, though several had to tell of narrow escapes, especially John Hockins, whose account of Ebony's exploit formed, at the feast that followed, subject of interesting converse and much comment during the brief intervals of relaxation between beef-steaks and marrow-bones.

Daylight revealed the fact that somewhere between thirty and forty animals had been killed outright, besides a dozen or so which, having been fatally wounded, were afterwards followed up and some of them secured.

But daylight also brought a large party of men from a distant village with a pressing invitation to Voalavo and his men to pay them a visit, and a possibly disinterested offer to assist him in the consumption of the cattle which he had slain; for it chanced that several young men of this village were encamped in the woods that night near the spot where the hunters attacked the cattle. Knowing full well what was being done, these youths hurried home to tell what was going on. The head-man of the village was on good terms with Voalavo at the time, besides being a distant relative. Hence the message and the invitation.

As our happy-go-lucky chief was out in what may be termed a larky state of mind, and had nothing particular to do, he accepted the invitation. The meat was slung to bamboo poles, hoisted on the shoulders of his men, and away they went over the plains to pay this visit. Happily the village lay on the way to the capital, so that the guide and his party could still accompany them without losing ground.

The plain over which they passed was a very wide one, seeming to extend to the very base of the distant mountains of the interior, but our travellers were mistaken in their ideas about it. The plain was itself part of the mountain region into which they had already advanced, but by so gradual an ascent that they had scarcely perceived the rise in the land—a deception which was increased somewhat by the frequent descents they had to make when passing over ridges.

On the way Hockins pushed up alongside of Ravonino, who was walking beside Mark.

"Ravvy," said the seaman (for to this had he at last curtailed the guide's name), "where do these fellows fall in wi' the iron to make their spearheads and other things?"

"In the earth," answered the guide.

"What! D'ee mean to say that you manufacture your own iron in them parts?"

"Of course we do. Think you that no people can work in iron except the British ? We have plenty iron ore of good quality in the island. One of our mountains is so full of ore that we call it the iron mountain. It is named in our language the mountain of Ambohimiangavo."

" An' how d'ee work the ore o' this Am—Ambo—bo—bominable-avo mountain ? " asked the sailor.

"We smelt it, of course. We break the lumps of ore into smallish bits and spread them on charcoal, layer and layer about, in a hollow in the ground. This is covered over with a top-dressing of stone and clay. Then we set it on fire and keep the blast going with wooden bellows, till the metal is melted and runs in a mass to the bottom of the hole. This we break into smaller pieces, purify them with more fire, and run them into bars convenient for use. Our bellows," continued the guide, " are not like yours, with two boards and leather between. The rats would soon make short work with these. They are two cylinders formed from the trunk of a tree, with a piston in each, packed with coarse cloth, and having valves. An old musket-barrel carries the air to the furnace, and, by pumping them time about, the blow is kept going continuously."

" Why, how do *you* come to know so much about valves, pistons, cylinders, and such like ? " asked Mark.

"You forget that my father was an Englishman," returned the guide, "and, besides being a trader, was a sort of Jack-of-all-trades. He taught me many things about which the kinsfolk of my mother know very little. You must not suppose that because some of us are only half-civilised we can do nothing neatly or well. Many of our men are skilful workers in metal, and we owe much of our power in that way to English missionaries, who brought Christian mechanics to the capital. There is hardly anything in the shape of wrought ironwork that we cannot execute if we have a model or pattern. We can work also in copper and brass. But it is not only in metals that we can work fairly well—indeed *very* well, if we are to take the word of some of your own countrymen who have seen and judged our work—we are also pretty good at pottery and cabinet-making. As you have seen, we can weave good cloth of cotton and silk, and some of our ingenious men have even tried their hands at clock-making and musical instruments."

"From what you say, Madagascar will soon become a great country, I should think," said Mark, somewhat amused as well as interested by the evident enthusiasm of the guide.

Ravonino shook his head. "My country might become great," he returned, "but there are some things much against her. The system of forced service to the government instead of taxes is one. This tends to repress ingenuity, for the cleverer and more ingenious a man is the more will be demanded of him, both by the government and his own feudal superior. Then the love of strong drink is too common among us; and last, as well as most serious, great multitudes of our people have no regard at all for their Maker."

"Why, Ravonino," said Mark, with something of a smile, "from the way you speak of 'our' people and 'my' country, I fear you think more of your Malagasy than your English extraction."

For a few moments the guide was silent. At length he said, slowly, "England has indeed done us a service that we can never repay. She has sent us the blessed Gospel of Jesus Christ. She is also the land of my father, and I reverence my father. He was very kind and good to me. But this is the land of my *mother !* I am a man of Madagascar."

It was evident from the expressive features of Ebony, who had joined them, that he heartily approved of this maternal preference, but the gravity of the guide's countenance, no less than his pathetic tones, prevented his giving the usual candid vent to his ever-ready opinion.

Towards the afternoon the party arrived at the native village, where grand preparations for festivities had been made. It was evident also that some parts of the festive libations had been taken in advance, for the head-man had reached the solemnised point of intoxication, and some of his young men the owlish condition.

In some parts of this island of Madagascar, as in other parts of the world, the people reduced themselves to great poverty through strong drink. Though they had abundance of rice, and much beef, which latter was salted for exportation, they sold so much of their food for arrack—imported by traders from Mauritius and Bourbon—that little was left for the bare maintenance of life, and they, with their families, were often compelled to subsist on roots. They did not understand "moderate drinking"! Intoxication was the rule until the arrack was done. The wise King Radama I. attempted to check the consumption of ardent spirits by imposing a heavy duty on them, but his efforts were only partially successful.

The tribe to which our travellers were at this time introduced had just succeeded in obtaining a quantity of the coarse and fiery spirits of the traders. Their native visitors being quite ready to assist in the consumption thereof, there was every prospect of a disgusting exhibition of savagery that night.

"Don't you think we might escape this feast?" said Mark to the guide, after the ceremony of introduction was over, " by urging the importance of our business at Antananarivo ?"

" Not easily. Voalavo is one of those determined and hearty men who insist on all their friends enjoying themselves as they themselves do. To-morrow we may persuade him to let us go. Besides, I do not object to stay, for I intend to preach them a sermon on ungodliness and intemperance in the middle of the feast."

Mark could scarcely forbear smiling at what he deemed the originality of the guide's intention, as well as the quiet decision with which he stated it.

" Don't you think," he said, " that this way of bearding the lion in his den may rouse the people to anger ? "

" I know not—I think not ; but it is my business to be instant in season and out of season," replied Ravonino, simply.

Mark said no more. He felt that he had to do with a Christian of a somewhat peculiar type, and thereafter he looked forward with not a little curiosity and some anxiety to the promised sermon. He was doomed, like the reader, to disappointment in this matter, for that night had not yet run into morning when an event occurred which modified and hastened the proceedings of himself and his friends considerably.

CHAPTER XI.

AN UNINVITED GUEST APPEARS WITH NEWS THAT DEMANDS INSTANT ACTION.

THE villagers and their guests were still in the midst of the feast, and the arrack had not yet begun to stimulate their imaginations, so that the deeds of their ancestors—which formed the chief subject of conversation—were still being recounted with some regard to modesty and truth, when Voalavo said to the assemblage, with a beaming countenance, that he had a treat in store for them.

"You are all fond of music," he said. "Who does not know that the Malagasy are good singers? The songs you have already sung have delighted my ears, and the clapping of your hands has been in the best of time; but you shall soon have music such as the idols would enjoy, I have no doubt, when in a merry mood."

The chief uttered the last sentence with an air of good-natured contempt, for he was what we may style an unbeliever in all gods—not an uncommon state of mind in men of superior intelligence when they think seriously of the debasing absurdities of idolatry.

"Now, my friend," he said, turning to John Hockins, with an air and tone of command, " let them hear the little pipe on which you—you—tootle-ootle."

Hockins had much ado to keep his gravity as he drew out the flageolet, and every eye was instantly fixed on him in glaring expectancy.

It need hardly be said that the effect of the sweet instrument was very powerful, and it is probable that the party of admirers might have taxed the seaman's powers of performance to the uttermost, if they had not been suddenly interrupted by the entrance of a tall wild-looking man, who was evidently in a state of tremendous excitement.

He wore the usual cloth round the loins, and the *lamba*, which was thrown like a Scottish chieftain's plaid over his left shoulder—but these garments bore evidence of rough usage and hard travel. The man was not a stranger, for, as he suddenly stood panting vehemently in the midst of the party, with his long arms outstretched, Voalavo addressed him in tones of surprise.

"Razafil!" he exclaimed. "Glad are we to see the Bard of Imarina. Your coming is well-timed. We are feasting, and singing, and story-telling. Words from the poet will be welcome."

Notwithstanding the friendly reception thus accorded to the Bard of Imarina, it was evident that the words were thrown away upon him, for he continued for some time to glare and pant, while perspiration rolled down his face, and it became clear to every one that something was wrong with him. At last he spoke in a kind of low singing tone which harmonised with his appearance—

> " Vain man ! Observ'st thou not the dead ?
> The morning warmth from them has fled,
> Their mid-day joy and toil are o'er,
> Though near, they meet fond friends no more."

He paused and looked wildly yet tremblingly round, as if in search of some one, but took no notice of his friends, many of whom were present at the gathering. Then he continued in the same strain—

> " A gate of entrance to the tomb we see,
> .But a departure thence there ne'er shall be.
> 　The living waves his signal high,
> 　But where 's the loved one's fond reply ?
> 　Ah ! where are those thus doomed to die ?

> " Vain man ! observ'st thou not the dead ?
> No more their homeward path they tread.
> The freeman lost may ransom'd be,
> By silver's magic power set free ;
> But, once the deadly haud has laid them low ;
> No voice can move them, for they cease to know.
> 　Regardless of our love they lie ;
> 　Unknown the friends that o'er them sigh ;
> 　Oh ! where are those thus doom'd to die ? "

Again the poor man paused, and gasped as if some terrible agony were rending his bosom, yet no tear moistened his eyes, from which there seemed to gleam the wild light of insanity. His appearance and words had sunk like a pall upon the festive party, but no one spoke or moved. It was as if they were spell-bound. Once more the poet spoke, and this time in tones of deepest pathos—

"Vain man ! why groan ye for the dead ?
  To be with Jesus they have fled,
  With shattered limbs—'mid scorching flame,
  They sang the praises of His name ;
  Now, joy unspeakable, they tread the shore
  Whence ransom'd sinners shall depart no more.
    But ah ! while mangled corpses lie,
    Our trembling, riven hearts *will* cry—
    ' Why, why were those thus doom'd to die ?' "

The man ceased; his arms fell listlessly by his side, and his chin sank on his breast.

"I fear much," whispered Ravonino to Mark, "that I understand but too well what he means."

Without waiting for a reply the guide rose. Going up to Razafil he laid his hand gently on his arm, and said—

"My brother !"

The bard looked at him earnestly for a few seconds, then, grasped him by the wrist as with a grip of iron.

"Ravoninohitriniony," he said, fiercely, "my

little one is dead! She is gone! They took her—
a mere child—they tortured her, but she would not
yield. Hear what I say. You knew her well—
the soft one; the tender one, who was always so
pliable, so unselfish, so easily led,—she *would not*
yield! They led her to the place of execution;
they tied her to a stake and kindled the fire about
her beautiful limbs,—my little child, Raniva! I saw
the skin upon her flesh blacken and crack and blaze
But she sang! sang loud and clear! I would have
rushed into the fire to her but they held me back—
four strong men held me! When she was consumed
they led me away to the torture—but I burst from
them—escaped—I know not how—I care not! for
my little one is lost!—lost!—— "

"Nay, Razafil—not lost!" said Ravonino, in a
quiet but firm tone, for he saw the gleam increasing
in the poor father's eyes. "Did you not say just
now that she is singing with joy unspeakable the
praises of His name?"

The words were fitly spoken. The father's agonised soul was quieted, but as quietness partly returned to him, a new expression appeared on his
countenance.

"Listen," he said, still holding the guide's wrist
in his powerful grasp. "I go to my poor wife.
She is safe in the cave with Reni-Mamba—"

"Not in the cave you think of," interrupted the

guide, explaining the change of abode which had been recently made by the Christian fugitives.

"No matter," returned the bard, "I know all the caves, and can find the one she has gone to. But now I must warn you—warn all of you who are Christians," he added, with emphasis, looking round upon the natives, "if there be any such among you—that Queen Ranavalona has got one of her bad fits again. She has ordered that no one is to sing or pray to Jesus, or to read the Word of God, on pain of imprisonment, death, or being sold into slavery. Many have been sold already, and some have died. Things would have been even worse, for the English missionary has left Antananarivo, but Prince Rakota remains our friend. Still, he cannot save every one. He could not save my Raniva! Now," he added, turning to the guide abruptly, as if anxious to keep his mind from dwelling on his terrible bereavement, "you must go to Antananarivo with all haste if you would save Rafaravavy, for she is in great danger."

The bard had touched a cord in Ravonino's breast which vibrated sensitively.

"She has not confessed? She is not in prison?" he asked, quickly, with emotion which was too powerful to be entirely suppressed.

"As to confessing," returned Razafil, "there is no need for her to do that, for it is well known that she is a Christian ; but the queen is fond of her and wishes to spare her. Nevertheless, she is so exceeding mad against us just now, that there is no saying when her forbearance may come to an end. If you would save Rafaravavy, you must get her out of the palace without delay."

The guide did not reply for a few seconds. It was evident, from the knitted brows and the pallor of his countenance, that he was endeavouring to make up his mind to some course of action. Suddenly the frown passed from his brow, his countenance became perfectly calm, and his eyes closed.

"He is speaking with God," whispered Laihova to one who sat near him.

Laihova may have been right. If so, the prayer was a very brief one, for the guide turned almost immediately to Voalavo and explained that in the circumstances it was absolutely necessary for him and his comrades to depart at once for the capital.

The chief, being a sympathetic as well as a hilarious soul, made no objection, but rather urged him to make haste.

Ravonino then turned to his white companions, who could, of course, only guess at the meaning of all that had been said, and explained to them the whole matter. They rose at once, and, having no preparations to make, professed to be ready to start there and then.

Now, while they were yet speaking, the festive party received another surprise, or alarm, which was even more exciting than the previous one.

A young man suddenly burst into the village with the announcement that a body of the Queen's soldiers were close at hand. They had been sent off in pursuit of Razafil, with directions to scour the country, and bring in as many Christian fugitives as possible, and he—the young man—being a fast runner, had been sent in advance by some friends of the bard to warn him of his danger.

"I would not try to avoid them if I stood alone," said Razafil, softly. "Should *I* shrink from dying for Jesus, after seeing my Raniva go to Him in a chariot of fire? But I stand not alone. My wife claims my support, and my little boy."

While he was speaking, it was seen that a few of the hunters, as well as one or two inhabitants of the village, rose quietly and left the place. These were either professing or suspected Christians, who were anxious to make their escape from the danger that threatened.

After bidding Voalavo farewell, the guide and his friends left the village and struck into the woods. They were accompanied by the bard a short distance, until a point was reached where their routes diverged, and here, after a few words of brotherly sympathy and counsel from Ravonino, the bereaved man went on his solitary way, and the others directed their course towards the capital.

"Poor man," said Ebony, who looked over his shoulder with profound sorrow in his earnest eyes as long as the tall figure of the bard was in sight, "I's most awrful sorry for 'im. Why don't dey hang Randalvalona, or shot 'er?"

"History teaches that it's not always so easy as one might think to get rid of objectionable queens in that way," said Mark.

"Hm! I'd teach history suffin diff'rent if I had my way," returned the negro.

"But surely the great men around her might have some sort o' power to clap a stopper on 'er?" said Hockins.

"They have some power, but not much," returned the guide, "for Ranavalona is a passionate, self-willed, cruel woman; and when such a woman happens to be a despotic queen, nothing short of a revolution, or her death, can save the country. She usurped the throne in 1829, we have now reached 1857, so she has been reigning more than twenty-seven years, and a bitter reign it has been. There have been many persecutions of the Christians since it began. Hundreds have been slain; thousands have been sold into slavery; many more have been banished to pestilential districts, where disease has laid them low. God grant that this mad fit may not be the forerunner of another burst of cruelty."

"But do you really think," said Mark, "that Rafaravavy is in great danger? Did not the bard say that she is a favourite with the queen?"

"That is some security, but not much, for Ranavalona is changeable as well as cruel. But my dear one is in the hands of God. No harm can come to her unless He permits. Nevertheless, our God works not by miracles but by means, therefore it is my business, having the opportunity given me, to hasten to her rescue."

"And it is mine to help you," said Mark, an impulse of youthful enthusiasm and sympathy swelling his heart as his mind suddenly reverted to the morning when he left England, and said his last good-bye to the fair one with the golden hair and the rosebud mouth and "such lovely blue eyes!" "But how," he continued, "shall we best aid you in this matter?"

"That question I cannot answer immediately. When we draw near to the capital and hear what is going on I shall be able to form a plan. What we have to do just now is to travel fast. You are strong stout men, all of you. Do you think you can walk fast and far with little rest or sleep, and without breaking down?"

"I think so," answered Mark, modestly.

"I's cock-sure ob it," said Ebony, "if we's allowed lots o' grub."

"I'm not quite so sure," said Hockins; "you must remember I've only got sea-legs on—but I'll try."

And he did try, and so did the others; with such success, too, that before the sun set that evening they had penetrated into the very heart of the mountain range which runs through the centre of the island.

There had not been much conversation on the way, for hill-climbing all day at top-speed is not compatible with small talk. Besides, the obvious anxiety of Ravonino rendered his companions less inclined than usual to engage in desultory remarks. Nevertheless there were occasions—during momentary halts to recover breath, or when clear bubbling springs tempted them to drink—when the prolonged silence was broken.

"Putty stiff work dis hill-climbin', massa," said Ebony, during one of these brief halts, as he wiped the perspiration from his sable brow with the back of his hand. "Lucky I's used to it."

"Used to it?" repeated Mark.

"Yes. Di'n't I tell you I was born an' raised among de Andes in Sout' Ameriky?"

"To be sure, I forgot that, but there must be a considerable difference between the two mountain ranges."

"Das troo, massa, but de diff'rence don't make much diff'rence to de legs. You see, wild rugged ground much de same wheder de mountains rise a few t'ousand foot, like dese, or poke der snow-topped heads troo de clouds right away up into de blue sky, like de Andes. Rugged ground is rugged ground, an' hard on de legs all de same, an' dis am rugged 'nuff even for 'Ockins!"

The negro opened his huge mouth in an amiable laugh at his companion, who had taken advantage of the brief halt to give a hearty rub to his colossal limbs.

"Rugged enough it is, no doubt," said the sailor, gravely, "an' it makes my sea-legs raither stiffish. But never you fear, Ebony; they're tough, an' will last as long as yours, anyhow."

"You's right, 'Ockins. Dey'll last *longer* dan mine by eight or ten hinches—if not more."

"Your jokes are small, Ebony, which is more than can be said for your mouth. Shut it, man, or some of us 'll go tumblin' into it by accident."

While these two were indulging their little pleasantries, the guide and his friend Laihova had gone to the top of a neighbouring bluff to consult as to the best route to adopt in the present troubled state of the country.

The view from the commanding height on which they stood was indeed marked by a rugged grandeur

which might have done credit even to the giant
Andes themselves, and offered a variety of routes,
or rather obstructions to routes, which might well
perplex men who were eager to cross country
swiftly.

The point which they had reached, and much of
the range they had crossed, was formed of basalt in
various stages of decomposition ; but in the country
before them, for several miles in advance, huge
masses of granite and fragments of quartz indicated
a change in the nature of the prevailing rock.   The
position of these masses, as well as their size, gave
a wild Titanic aspect to much of the scenery.

Many enormous stones projected out of the ground
at various angles.   One of these stood out horizon-
tally to the distance of between twenty and thirty
feet, forming a cave under it, in which it was evident,
from sundry suggestive appearances, that wayfarers
were accustomed to lodge.   The neighbourhood of
this cave formed one of the most romantic and
picturesque scenes they had yet seen.   It was a
dark narrow vale, in many places not less than five
hundred feet deep, with a considerable stream at
the bottom, which brawled among detached and
shattered rocks, or was partly lost to view in its
meanderings among the beautiful green shrubs which
clothed its banks.   Various kinds of birds twittered
among the bushes, and wherever water expanded

in the form of pond or lakelet numerous waterfowl sported on the surface.

"A glorious prospect!" exclaimed Mark, as he joined the guide and his friend, "and a splendid place, I should think, for fugitives from persecution."

He pointed, as he spoke, to the scene on his right, where masses of rock varying from thirty to fifty feet in length projected from the side of the ravine. On the top of these rested other masses in a position that seemed to threaten destruction to all who ventured beneath them.

"The caves of this region," said the guide, "have served to shelter the Christians many a time. It looks as if God had provided these blocks of granite for this very purpose, for the caverns which extend beneath them are dark and intricate, having many entrances, and being lighted in some places by openings between the blocks, while in other places they are profoundly dark and of unknown extent. See also, if you look at the stream below, they form a splendid bridge. At this distance they do not seem large, but some of these blocks are not less than a hundred feet long. This whole region is infested by robbers, but the recent act of the Queen in sending troops out to scour the country for fugitive Christians seems to have driven them away. But if they had been here we should have had little to fear, for robbers are not usually fond of attacking even small parties of men who are well able to defend themselves; besides, they do not injure the outlawed Christians much. Perhaps they have a sort of fellow-feeling for us!"

At this point Laihova spoke a few words to the guide in the native tongue. The latter nodded approval, and turning to Mark, said—

"We have been consulting about our route. There are two roads—one rugged, round-about, and safe, which would take us a longer time, however, to reach the capital than the other, which is the regular beaten path, through the villages. But this latter way lays us open to the danger of meeting with soldiers, and of my being captured along with my friend Laihova. There would be no danger to you and your friends, for you are strangers."

"Ravonino," said Mark, quickly, "do what is best for rescuing Rafaravavy. We have no will but yours. We will follow wherever you choose to lead."

A quiet look of satisfaction played on the guide's features as he turned to his friend.

"What says Laihova? The Englishmen are willing to do whatever we wish."

"Let us go by the villages. Let us push on by night as well as by day," said Laihova. "Time flies! Ranavalona is mad! Rafaravavy is in danger!"

It was finally arranged that, at this place, which was considerably to the south of Antananarivo, they should diverge to the right, so as to avoid certain points of danger, and arrive ultimately at the eastern side of the capital.

Having settled this point, the three men rejoined their comrades, who were still conversing amicably beside the spring. Thereafter they all descended into the valley by a steep and rugged pathway.

CHAPTER XII.

A NARROW ESCAPE AND THREATENING CLOUDS.

THEIR progress after leaving the spot described in the last chapter was not so rapid as could have been desired by anxious men, for it was absolutely necessary to proceed with extreme caution.

Not only were the Queen's troops out in various directions, but many of her spies had been seen prowling about, like the evil one they served, seeking whom they could devour. Of this the travellers were made aware at the first villages they came to; and as Ravonino had formerly been well known at the capital, it became necessary for him not only to disguise himself, but to keep as much as possible out of sight.

Disguising himself was not very difficult, owing to the fact that when he lived in Antananarivo he had, like his father, worn a bushy beard. This had made him a marked man. for the Malagasy, as a rule, have little beard, and what little they possess is usually pulled out by the roots. Since he became a fugitive the guide had shaved closely. This of

itself went a long way to change his appearance;
but when, in addition, he had modified the arrangement of his hair, and stained his face of a darker
hue, he had made himself almost unrecognisable, even
by his best friends. His chief difficulty was with
his voice, which had a mellow sweetness in it that
resisted modification. However, by keeping silence,
or speaking low, he hoped to escape recognition until
he should reach the vicinity of the capital, where he
had friends who would gladly receive and conceal
him, even at the risk of their lives.

As to the great object that lay nearest his heart,
he hoped to manage that through his friend Laihova,
without himself entering the capital.

Our travellers soon reached the inhabited part
of the country, where, being surrounded by men
and women going about, as well as journeying
towards the Antananarivo market with provisions,
etc., they ceased to attract much attention. Of
course the Englishmen were subjects of curiosity—
sometimes of inquiry,—but as Laihova reported that
they were men who had been cast on the southern
coast of the island and whom he was guiding to the
capital, suspicion was not aroused.

Laihova at this point became leader of the party,
in order to enable the guide more easily to fall into
the background; and he was all the more fitted
for the position in that he had acquired a smattering

of English from his friend Ravonino, and could both understand much of what was said to him and also make himself pretty well understood by his white friends.

This part of the journey was by no means without adventure, sometimes of a kind that filled them with anxiety.

One evening they approached a small hamlet, or group of cottages, where they learned, among other things, that two of the Queen's spies were at that moment in the neighbourhood, searching for two ladies of the Court who had fled because Ranavalona had threatened them with imprisonment.

"Are they young?" asked Ravonino, forgetting his caution in his anxiety.

"I know not," replied the man who had informed them of the fact. "I think some one told me they were not young—but I forget."

The guide said no more. He regretted having said so much, for the man glanced at him suspiciously.

Affecting an air of unconcern he turned away and bade his comrades follow.

"Come," he said, when out of earshot of the man, "we must pass through this village quickly, for we know not in what house the spies may have taken up their quarters."

"But, don' you tink," suggested Ebony, "dat we

five could wallop any oder five men in de univarse,
to say not'ing ob two spies ?"

A grim smile was all the reply that the guide
gave him, as he walked quickly along the path that
led out of the hamlet.

" I have a friend," he said to Mark, " who lives in
a solitary cottage half-a-mile further on. He is rich,
and, I think, a Christian man—but secretly, for fear
of the Queen. We will call at his house in passing."

As he spoke, they approached a large house by
the roadside, the owner of which, a brown old
gentleman, was enjoying himself with his wife and
family in front of it.

" Is that your friend ?" asked Mark.

"No; he lives in the house just beyond. We
shall see it on clearing this group of trees."

The track which they were following led close
past the large house above referred to, necessitating
compliance with a custom of the country, which
greatly surprised, and not a little amused, the
Englishmen.

We have spoken of the residence as a house,
because it belonged to one owner, but it would be
more correct to call it a farm-steading, or a group
of buildings. Except among the very poorest
people, a Malagasy family has usually two or three
houses in its enclosure—frequently more, for young
married people often live beside their parents, and

some houses are appropriated to slaves, while others are used as kitchens, etc., the whole being surrounded by a wall of clay.   Where a house is near the public road they have usually a little square platform, called the *fijerèna*, in an angle of the wall, or at the gate, with steps leading up to it.   Here the family sits, when the work of the day is over, to watch— and, doubtless, to criticise—the passers-by; also to do the polite according to Malagasy ideas, for it must be told that these people are very courteous.   Even the poorest have a natural dignity and ease of manner about them.

As our travellers approached the house they were observed with much interest by the brown old gentleman and his comfortable-looking wife, and his pretty little light-brown daughter, and a very uncomfortable-looking elderly female with her head tied up, who were all squatted on the *fijerèna*.

When within hearing Laihova stopped, and said in the politest tone and manner possible—

"Will you allow me to pass, sir?"

"Pray proceed, sir," replied the old gentleman, with a gracious smile.

This interchange of civilities was entirely formal, and stood in the place of the Englishman's opening remarks on the weather, to which a Malagasy would as soon think of referring, in this connection, as he would to the hatching of crocodiles' eggs.

Then followed the conventional inquiry, "How are you?   How is it with you?" which politenesses, in a number of variations unknown to Western speech, would have been continued, in ordinary circumstances, until the passers-by were beyond the range of hearing; but the appearance of the Englishmen induced the brown old gentleman on this occasion to beg the travellers to stop and accept his hospitality.   This they declined to do, with many expressions of regret, on the ground that their business at the capital was urgent.

"It would have gratified me much," said the old gentleman, "to have entertained you.   But you are all well, I hope?"

"Yes, we are very well," answered Laihova; "and how do *you* feel?"

"I feel as well as possible.   And is it well with *you?*"

"It is well with us.   But it does not seem to be well with the lady," returned Laihova, glancing at the uncomfortable female with her head tied up.

"No, it is not well with her.   She has toothache on the north side of her head.   Farewell," said the brown old gentleman, re-squatting on the *fijerèna*, as the travellers moved on; "may you live," he shouted after them, when nearly out of earshot, "and reach old age."

Great was the amusement of our travellers at all

this, especially when Ravonino explained about the toothache. "You must know," he said, "that almost all the houses in the central provinces of the island are built with their length running north and south, or nearly so, and the people use the points of the compass in describing the position of things. Thus, if they tell a slave to look for a thing in the house, they will say, Look in the north, south, east, or west corner, or side; and they apply this rule to the person also. I once heard the member of a mission from England told by his host that some rice was sticking to his moustache. The missionary wiped the wrong side. 'No,' said the host, 'it is on the *southern* side of your moustache.'"

"Do you know," said Mark Breezy, "that is not so strange to me as you might suppose; for I was once told by a friend who lived in the Scottish Highlands, that an old woman there actually said to her that she had toothache on the east side of her head!"

Further comment on this point was arrested by their coming suddenly in sight of the house where the guide's friend dwelt.

"You had better stay here at the edge of this wood, while I go forward alone," said the guide; "because although the man is kind, and has always professed to be my friend, I am not quite sure of him. It is well to be cautious. If I wave my hand to you, come up to the house, all will be well. If things don't seem favourable I will return to you—but keep close; don't show yourselves needlessly. You see, my friend is an officer of the palace. If friendly he can be very useful to us, if unfriendly he can be dangerous."

"But why run risk by going near him at all?" asked Mark.

"We *must* run risk when life and death are in the balance," replied the guide, shortly.

Concealed by the bushes, the travellers watched their companion as he went up to the house. Before he reached it a man opened the door and stepped out. Suddenly this man seemed to burst into a furious passion. He grasped Ravonino by the throat, almost threw him on his back, and, seizing a stick, began to belabour him violently, while two other men appeared at the door of the house, and, from their inordinate laughter, seemed fully to enjoy the scene.

"Hi!" exclaimed Ebony in shrill falsetto, as he jumped up in blazing wrath, intending to rush to the rescue, but Hockins grasped his woolly head and pulled him back.

"Obey orders, you black grampus! D'ee think he's a babby as can't take care of himself? Didn't he tell us to keep close?"

Great as had been the surprise of the watchers

at this sudden and unprovoked assault, it was as nothing compared with their astonishment when they saw their guide fairly turn tail and run towards them, closely followed by the furious man, who continued to thrash him all the time.

As Ravonino drew near, the angry man seemed to have exhausted himself, for he fell behind, and finally stopped. The guide ran on at full speed until he reached the wood, but did not even then slacken his speed. As he ran past his friends, however, he exclaimed in a sharp, stern voice—

"Follow me!"

Laihova obeyed with the unquestioning readiness of a faithful hound. The others followed suit with the open eyes of perplexity and amazement!

Reaching a sequestered dell in a few minutes, Ravonino suddenly stopped and turned round with a calm air of satisfaction.

"Well, dis am de most awrful supprise I'se had since my mudder give me my fust wollopin'."

The expression on the negro's face rendered the remark needless.

"It was well done," said the guide, seating himself on the trunk of a fallen tree.

"A'most too well done!" returned Hockins, with a touch of sarcasm.

"Do you know," continued the guide gravely, "I've had a narrow escape? The two men you saw laughing at the door are the very men we have been trying to avoid,—the Queen's spies,—whom I have long known, and who would certainly have discovered me in spite of my shaved and stained face if we had come to talk to each other in the same room. Luckily my friend is smart as well as true. He knew my voice at once. To have talked with me, or warned me, or let me enter his house, would have been fatal. His only resource lay in thrashing me off his premises—as you have seen. How he will explain matters to the spies I know not, but I can trust him for that."

"Das most awrful clebber!" exclaimed Ebony, his every feature broadening with delight at the success of the ruse.

"But what are we to do now?" asked Mark.

"Wait till he comes here. He told me to wait."

"What! Told you?"

"Ay—you don't suppose he let his tongue lie idle while he was using his stick. Of course I was myself taken aback at first when he seized me by the throat, but two or three muttered words in the midst of his anger opened my eyes, and I ran at once. All the way as he ran after and belaboured me he was giving me important information in furious tones! The spies are only staying with him for a short rest. When they are gone he will come and find us here."

"He's a born actor," said Hockins.

"True—and he acted some of his blows heavier than I could have wished, in his anxiety to impress his information on me!" said the guide.

"What is his name?" asked Mark.

"Fisatra. He is named after a great chief who lived in this district not long ago.—But here he comes to speak for himself."

At that moment a tall, fine-looking man, of very dark complexion, and clad in the ample folds of a beautiful lamba, approached them. His whole countenance was wrinkled with the lines of fun, and his brilliant teeth glistened as he smilingly held out his hand to the Englishmen, and asked them to accept his hospitality.

As they passed into the house they saw two slave-girls pounding rice in a large wooden mortar, with two enormous wooden pestles, while the savoury steam that arose from some invisible kitchen served to put a finer edge on their already sharpened appetites.

When the mats were spread, and the feast was being enjoyed, Ravonino asked the host how he had got rid of the spies, and how he managed to explain his conduct without raising their suspicions.

"Nothing easier," said Fisatra, while his broad shoulders heaved with an inward chuckle. "You know that I used to be feared in the palace in days

gone bye because of my violent nature, and the way
in which I used to knock about the furniture and
make the household slaves—sometimes the household troops—scurry when I was in a rage. Yet I'm
sure you know very well (he looked sheepishly
innocent here) that I never was an angry man—at
least not a cruel one. But that's all changed. I
am one of *your* set now, though no one suspects it.
Since I met Mr. Ellis —— "

"Is Mr. Ellis here just now?" interrupted
Ravonino, anxiously.

"Not now," answered Fisatra; "he departed some
weeks ago, but I believe has not yet left the coast.
And now there is no check on the Queen's violence.
Well, as I was about to say, I took to the old habit
in pretence, as you have seen, and when I returned
from thrashing you I went storming through the
house, kicking about the pots and pans, and foaming
at the mouth in such a way that I not only stopped
the spies laughing, but put them in fear of their
lives."

Again the fun-wrinkles corrugated the visage of
Fisatra, and his mighty shoulders heaved with
internal explosions.

"After I had calmed down a bit," he continued,
"the spies ventured to ask timidly if that was a
great enemy that I had beaten. This set me into a
worse passion than ever. 'Enemy?' I shouted

'no—no—not an enemy—he—he's a—a——' but I got no further than that, for I didn't know what to say, and I wouldn't lie, so I took to foaming and stamping again ! At last I said 'Don't speak to me about him—excuse me, my friends; I can't stand it —and—and the rice is nearly ready. You must be hungry!' I said this with a look and tone as if another fit was coming on. They excused themselves. 'No,' they said, 'we are not hungry, and we have yet far to go this day before the sun descends. The Queen's orders will not wait.' And off they went, glad to get out of my way. Truly, if it is sinful to get in a rage, it is useful sometimes to act it! So now, my friends, eat—eat—while you have the chance, and fear not the return of the spies!"

"Tell me," said the guide, anxiously, "are you sure that Rafaravavy is still safe ?"

"She is still safe—but no one knows how long that may be, for she is fearless, and utters the forbidden prayers even in the presence of the Queen. If it had not been for the love that Ranavalona bears her, she would have been tossed from the 'rock of hurling' long ago."

"Faithful, even unto death," said the guide, with a look and tone in which pathos and triumph were strangely blended.

"She has not yet been tried to that extent, but if she is, God will enable her to stand firm," said

Fisatra, whose grave child-like sincerity, when talking of religious subjects, was not less impulsively honest and natural than were the outbursts of his fun when another humour stirred his feelings.

The "rock" to which he alluded was a frightful precipice at one side of the city from which criminals were usually hurled—a spot which is hallowed by the blood of many Christian martyrs who perished there during the long reign of that tyrant queen Ranavalona.

"Has then the queen forbidden the Christians to pray?" asked Ravonino.

"Have you not heard?—but of course you have not, being an outlaw and having only just returned. Recently a very bad fit has come over the Queen. You know that for some years past there have been a few French people living in Antananarivo, who by their knowledge and skill in mechanics and mercantile matters have made themselves useful to our government. These men lately tried to dethrone the Queen, on pretence of delivering the country from her cruelties, and establishing a 'French Protectorate.' They gained over some of our chief men, collected in one of their houses a large quantity of weapons and ammunition, and had even fixed the night when the palace was to be invaded, the Queen seized, and the Protectorate set up. Fortunately the plot came to my knowledge. I say fortunately, because a bad queen is better than a French Protectorate, for the first will die, but the latter might never end! Well, I at once informed the Queen, who had the conspirators seized and banished from the country for ever. Among them were a Roman Catholic lady and two Jesuits. The anger of the Queen was of course very great, and she has had, as I have said, a very bad fit against the Christians; for, as these unprincipled conspirators have the name though none of the reality of Christians, she naturally mixed us all up together— and I know not what the end will be, but I have much fear, because the Queen is very angry."

"Has she done nothing yet?" asked Ravonino.

"Nothing—except threaten and fume. But when the black cloud is overhead, and muttering thunder is heard, one knows too well what to expect— especially when one has been exposed to the storm in former years."

"The sun is shining behind the black cloud and it will break through when the Master wills," said Laihova, joining in the conversation for the first time that evening, and looking earnestly at his friend Ravonino, as if the words were meant for his ear alone—as indeed they were.

"Thanks, thanks, my friend, for the comforting words," said Ravonino, "and I take shame to myself that my faith is so weak."

"You will spend the night with me?" said their host to the guide.

"No, Fisatra, I dare not delay. Even now I may be too late. I will journey all night."

Ravonino rose quickly and prepared to go. The others followed his example, and soon the party was proceeding rapidly along the high-road towards the capital, under a cloudless sky and a galaxy of twinkling stars.

CHAPTER XIII.

ARRIVAL AT THE CAPITAL—QUEEN RANAVALONA'S TROUBLES AND PERPLEXITIES.

TOWARDS sunrise on the following morning our travellers, on passing out of a rather dense piece of plantation which crowned the brow of a low hill, came in sight of the capital—Antananarivo. It was still in the far distance, with many a ricefield and garden between, but distinctly visible, for it occupies the summit and slopes of a considerable hill.

"Here, then, through the goodness of God, we have reached the end of our journey," said Ravonino, halting, "and I must remain behind, while you, my friends, push on to the city. Fain would I go with you, but that would ruin all, for I am a known and marked man. Laihova will now guide you, and tell you what to do. I have just one word for you at parting. Be peaceful, do not take offence. Interfere not with our customs. Use not the fist, and commit your way to God."

The guide looked so pointedly at Ebony while

he spoke that that sable comrade could not help noticing it.

"What you looks so hard at me for, hey?" demanded the negro.

"Because you are somewhat hot-tempered and apt to get people into scrapes," answered Ravonino, with a slight twinkle in his eye.

"*Me* 'ot-tempered!" exclaimed Ebony, in surprise, with an appealing glance at his comrades. "I'd knock you down, Ravonino, for sayin' dat, only it would be like as if what you say's true! Ob all de niggers on 'art' I's de meekest, quietest—jest like a babby; why, my moder always said so, an' surely *she* ought to know!"

"No doubt she knew, whatever she said," observed Hockins, with a laugh.

"We will be careful," said Mark. "But are your people, then, so particular, that we should require this caution?"

"Well, they are not very different from other people," replied the guide, "and if things had been as usual I should have had no fear; but when Queen Ranavalona has one of her bad fits, there's no saying what she may do. Her banishing the Europeans is a bad sign. I would that I had not brought you here, but there is no help for it now. We have been seen by many people. The news will spread to the town, and if you did not soon appear you would be suspected as spies, and the country would be scoured in search of you. No, there is nothing for it now but a bold face and an honest purpose."

"Humph!" ejaculated Ebony, "you's a fine feller to talk 'bout bold faces an' honest purpusses, w'en you're goin' to steal a young ooman out ob de pallis, fro' under de bery nose ob de queen!"

"To help Rafaravavy to escape of her own free will is not theft," replied the guide, gravely. "When we are persecuted in one city Scripture advises us to flee to another."

"Das true, Ravonino. No offence meant. Gib us your flipper, old boy!"

Grasping the guide's hand, the negro shook it warmly, and at the same time vowed that he would be most "awrful careful," and that he would bring Rafaravavy to his feet, dead or alive, though he should have to fight the whole town single-handed to effect his object.

It was a Thursday evening when they stood thus conversing. They had kept count of the days because of the guide's quiet but firm determination to rest in camp on the Sabbath—a plan which, although they had no very strong principle on the subject, commended itself to the rest of the party because of the pleasant effect of the day's rest on both soul and body, for it afforded opportunity to have long and earnest talks with Ravonino about the former days of persecution, as well as quiet strolls, alone or in couples, and—it must be admitted—occasional slumbers in the cool shade of bush or tree!

"I have purposely contrived," said the guide, "that, by walking all night, you shall arrive early to-morrow —Friday—because it is market-day in the town, and you will be less noticed as well as more amused by what you see than if you were to arrive on any other day. Go, and God go with you! I shall be found in the cave that Laihova knows of. Farewell."

He turned, with a wave of his hand, as he spoke, and re-entered the bush, while the others, taking the most direct route to Antananarivo, descended into the open country. Soon they were involved in the crowds which were passing along all the roads leading to the city. The people were either taking their goods for sale or going to make purchases— mayhap to meet friends or kindred.

All night Laihova led his friends at a smart pace. Next day, as the first object of our travellers was to get into the town without attracting attention, they kept in the thick of the throng all the way up to the market-place. Of course the people nearest them took special note of the two Englishmen, and some were inquisitive, but, by telling the simple facts regarding their arrival in Madagascar, Laihova removed any unpleasant suspicions that might have arisen regarding them.

The crowds increased as they advanced, and the numbers were still further augmented, as well as diversified, by the Hova army, which they came upon exercising on a plain just below the city. Ascending the sides of the steep hill on which Antananarivo stands, they obtained a magnificent view of the animated scene, which conveyed the impression rather of a grand holiday than an ordinary market-day. This, no doubt, was largely owing to the operations of the soldiers, whose manœuvres Hockins watched with a critical eye, for his father, having been a soldier, had made him intimately acquainted with the drill as practised in the British army at that period.

"Why, I do believe the fellers are speakin' English!" he said, in some surprise.

"Not wonder much, for Ingleesh drill'd um," said Laihova, who, since they parted from Ravonino, had begun to use his broken English to the best of his power. It must be said that that power was not great, even at the best.

He explained to his friends that Radama the First —that wise king who had been so fond of the English, and had done so much to aid the missionaries, abolish the slave-trade, and civilise his people—had, among other changes, remodelled his army after the British pattern, and had obtained the services of non-commissioned officers from the Mauritius to drill his troops. These organised them into divisions, brigades, regiments, companies, etc., and as they found no native words suitable to express military evolutions, they introduced their own English words of command, which have remained in use ever since.

By means of this army of Hova troops, and the flint-lock weapon known familiarly as 'Brown Bess,' Radama succeeded in subduing all the native chiefs of Madagascar, with only a few exceptions, and thus became the recognised king of an island considerably larger than Great Britain. Being an enlightened and well-disposed monarch, he made good use of the power thus acquired. It was only after his death in 1828 that a retrograde movement set in, as we have said, under the wicked Queen Ranavalona.

It is one of the misfortunes of our fallen condition that rectitude in any course, however good, cannot long be maintained—at least in reasonable perfection. The army which had enabled Radama to pursue on the whole a beneficent course, ere long began to make its creator know its power. Feeling his dependence on it, Radama adopted the unwise policy of increasing the military influence, and weakening that of the civil officials, the heads of the people, and other functionaries whose position was derived from ancient political arrangements. Public offices of honour and importance were given to military officers rather than to civilians, and this unfair exaltation of the military over the civilian class led, as it always does, to tyranny and injustice.

The system of service was in itself a gross form of injustice to the people, for, although the theory of service does not at first sight appear unjust, the practice of it was very much so. More than the half—perhaps nearly two-thirds—of the whole effective male population of the central province were enrolled either as officers or privates. These received no pay, except an occasional gift of a lamba, and about a week's rice during the year! The soldiers were indeed freed from money taxes in consideration of their service, but this was small compensation for the hardships that it entailed. Although the drills at ordinary times did not occur more frequently than for a day or two every fort-night, much time was taken up in passing to and from the exercises, especially in the case of those who lived at a distance, and thus found it almost im-possible to cultivate their own rice-fields. Frequently, also, the officers would not allow the men to return home without a money bribe. In short, the private soldier was little better than a slave—in some cases worse—while the officers of the highest rank possessed unreasonable power.

Military rank was founded on a system which led to some absurdities. It was reckoned by numbers, commencing with *one honour* for the private, *two honours* for the corporal, three for the sergeant, and so on up to thirteen for a field-marshal of the higher rank—a few having sixteen honours! Those thus highly *honoured* were not numerous; but the number of officers of lower grade was much greater in proportion to privates, than in the British army. Indeed from a third to a fourth of the army was composed of officers, so that "ta Phairshon," with his excess of pipers over fighting men, would not have appeared very outrageous in the eyes of the Malagasy troops!

These officers had an eye to profitable business when not on service. It is stated by the missionaries that when engaged in building their churches and schools they sometimes found they had a field-marshal for a foreman, a colonel for mason or carpenter, a major for bricklayer, and so on! Above the thirteenth rank the numbers were very few, and of the sixteenth there were not above half-a-dozen.

Good, stout, courageous fellows were the men whom John Hockins and his comrades saw that day manœuvring below them on the plain of Imahamasina; men who, although by no means comparable to European troops in precision of movement, understood their work nevertheless, and would have proved themselves formidable opponents to deal with in war. Laihova further informed them that the first man who organised the force was a Sergeant Brady, who began his work in the year 1816, carried it on for many years, and rose to the rank of major-general in the service of King Radama. After General Brady's death, the native officers continued the work on the same lines.

But in costume and appearance these soldiers were what is familiarly known as "a queer lot!" The uniform of the rank and file consisted of a tunic and trousers of white material, with a narrow-brimmed straw hat painted white, cross-belts and cartouche-box—by no means an unbecoming dress. But it was worn only at drills and reviews and state ceremonies. At other times, when on duty, soldiers went about almost naked, and the contrast of their dirty-white cross-belts with their brown breasts was curious, to say the least, while their straw hats and slovenly gait suggested anything but soldierly bearing.

The variety of dress indulged in, however, by the crowd of officers was outrageous as well as mirth-provoking.

"Why it seems to me," said Mark, "that every officer may put on what seemeth right in his own eyes! I see old regimental red coats and pantaloons; hats and shakos that must have been worn a hundred years ago. I even see what looks at this distance like naval uniforms and cocked hats, and no two of them seem to be dressed alike."

Mark looked inquiringly at Laihova as he spoke, but that dignified native merely smiled, and made a slight inclination of his head, as if to say, "Just so, that's the way we do it here!"

"Why do they let civilians mix wi' them?" asked Hockins, pointing to a particular part of the field.

"To keep 'em cibil, I s'pose," suggested Ebony.

"Where?" asked Laihova, with a puzzled look.

"There—don't you see 'em? Fellers all in black —with bell-toppers—beavers—chimney-pots on— I don't know what you call 'em here."

"Them be officers too," said Laihova.

And this was true, for the higher grades of officers usually appeared at drill in a full suit of black cloth, with the common black silk hat doing duty as a helmet, and contrasting oddly enough with the rough home-made scabbardless sword, which was carried naked in the hand.

On some occasions, as our travellers afterwards learned, these regiments turned out in every variety of costume, with coats, hats, vests, and trousers, of all colours and patterns—as if they had been got up by an extensive dealer in old clothes. This passion for variety even extended to the officers of the palace, with whom, however, the material was of the best as well as gayest—for they were all gorgeously clad in blue and scarlet cloth, and velvet, with gold and silver lace, embroidery, feathers, etc.,—but what nation, even in the so-called civilised world, is free from barbarism in this respect?

One pair of eyes beheld this review on that Friday with something of fiendish satisfaction. These belonged to no less a personage than Queen Ranavalona herself. High up on the balcony of her palace she sat under the shade of a scarlet umbrella.

That very day she had had an angry interview with her Prime Minister, Rainiharo, in reference to her only child Prince Rakota, who was a young man of mild gentle disposition, as kind to the Christians as his mother was cruel and unjust. Indeed it was believed that he himself was among the Christians, for he dared openly to defend them before his mother, and often protected them secretly from her violence. Rainiharo, the Prime Minister, on the contrary, was their bitter foe, and in his interview with the Queen above mentioned, had ventured to accuse the prince of aiding in the protection of those who practised the proscribed religion.

The one redeeming point in the character of Ranavalona was her love for this son. When asked to punish the prince for his conduct, she would say in tones of tenderness that seldom issued from her lips, " Is he not my son—my only son?" Alas! she had little pity for the son or daughter of any one else, whether "only" or otherwise!

The dress of Ranavalona, as she sat in her balcony under her scarlet umbrella observing the troops, was gorgeous, but the greater part of it was hidden under the voluminous folds of the scarlet lamba of finest English broad-cloth with which her person was enveloped. Here and there, however, portions of a rich silk dress of European manufacture could be seen, as well as various gold and silver rings, bracelets, chains, charms, and ornaments of ivory. Scarlet being the royal colour, only the Sovereign is entitled to wear the scarlet lamba or use the scarlet umbrella. The Queen's lamba was ornamented heavily with gold lace. Her head was not much decorated, but her hair was anointed with that hideous horror of the sick-room, castor-oil! the odour of which, however, was disguised, or rather mixed, with a leaf which smelt like nutmeg.

" I will submit to this no longer," said the Queen, with a stern frown. " Have I not said it ? Is the will of Ranavalona to be thwarted ?"

This remark was, in the conversation above mentioned, made to the Prime Minister, a stern old man, dressed in a scarlet coat with huge gold epaulettes, and profusely braided with gold lace, blue pantaloons, also gold-laced, and a magnificent brazen-sheathed sword. He stood at the Queen's elbow with a perplexed expression of countenance, being the bearer of news about the effect of which he felt uncertain. But Rainiharo was a bold man as well as a bad one.

"Your will, madam, is sure to be thwarted," he replied, "as long as you suffer Prince Rakota to act as he pleases. Your son is a Christian. He prays with the Christians and encourages them in this new doctrine. We are lost if your Majesty does not stop the prince in his strange self-willed ways."

"But," repeated the Queen, "he is my son—my only, my beloved son! Let him do what he pleases. If he wishes to be a Christian, let him—he is my beloved son!"

"But, madam," urged Rainiharo, who hated Rakota, "if your son resists your will what becomes of the Government? I know that Rakota ——"

"Cease to speak to me of Rakota," interrupted the Queen, impatiently. "He is my son, I tell you. I love him. Let him alone—he will not disobey me."

"Prince Ramonja, it is said, has also joined the Christians," continued the minister, with a slightly cynical expression.

"Is this true?" demanded Ranavalona, fiercely, while she seemed to grind her teeth in wrath.

"I have reason to believe it."

"Let inquiry be made, and if it proves to be true,"

said the Queen, sternly, " let Ramonja be deprived of
all his military honours, reduce him to the ranks,
and fine him heavily."

" But he is your own nephew, madam," returned
the Minister, simply, yet with a touch of sarcasm in
his tone.

" It matters not.   It is of our mercy that he does
not die, as many others have died before him.   Let
my orders be obeyed if Ramonja is guilty.   Let him
be a warning to others in the palace, for it has come
to my ears that some of our courtiers are hankering
after this religion that seems to have turned my
people mad.   Indeed it is said that some related to
yourself are among them."

She looked pointedly at Rainiharo as she spoke,
and the prime minister winced, for he had lately
discovered that his own son was among the number
of the " praying people."   Recovering himself in a
moment, however, he merely said that he was not
aware of any of his kindred having fallen away from
the customs of their ancestors.

" I hope not," returned the Queen, darkly, " for
degradation and slavery, if not death, await them if
they do.   Go.   Let a proclamation be made to-day
in the market-place.   Let my people and the army
know that I have resolved to extinguish Christianity.
Tell those officers who have become Christians, or
have taken any part in religious teaching, that they

shall lose their honours. They have transgressed my laws and deserve death, but through the supplications of the people of Imérina their lives are spared. But their honours, I say, shall be thrown into the river and carried over the cataract of Ifarahantsana, for they are trying to change the customs of our ancestors. Of some, half the honours shall be thrown into the river. Of others, one-third of their honours shall be thrown in, and some shall lose all their honours; the precise number shall be in proportion to their offences. Moreover," continued the angry woman, as she worked herself into a state of great wrath, "there must be no more praying; no more psalm-singing among my people; no more——"

She stopped suddenly and listened, while the veins in her neck and forehead seemed to swell almost to bursting, for at that moment the clear notes of a sweet female voice came from some distant part of the palace and broke softly on her ear. There was no mistaking the nature of the music, for the Queen had long been familiar with the music of the psalms in which the "praying people" were wont to sing praise to the name of Jesus.

"Who sings?" she asked, with a fierce look at Rainiharo.

The prime minister again gave vent to a very slight touch of sarcasm as he replied, "I think it is Rafaravavy."

This time the queen noted the tone, and sharply ordered her minister to be gone and do her bidding.

Now, Rafaravavy was a lady of the palace, as we have said, and a great favourite with her royal mistress, but the queen's affection for the girl had been severely tested since the latter showed symptoms of a leaning towards the Christian religion. It is probable that Ranavalona would have cared little as to what her favourite thought about Christianity if she had only kept quiet, but Rafaravavy was one of those earnest straightforward souls who are prone to act in accordance with their conscientious beliefs without regard to consequences. She did not indeed go about endeavouring to proselytise the household, for she was naturally timid, soft-hearted, and meek, but she made no attempt to conceal her opinions and her sympathy with the persecuted Christians. She had even gone the length of interceding for them once or twice when she found her mistress in an amiable mood, but the explosion of wrath which resulted warned her not to presume again in that way.

For some time Ranavalona sat brooding over the mystery of that religion, which, notwithstanding all her power and cruelty, she had, after so many years of tyranny, been unable to suppress. Then she sent for Rafaravavy.

The girl, who in a few minutes entered her

presence, was possessed of no ordinary beauty. Her delicate features and oval face were much lighter in complexion than those of the other ladies of the court, resembling rather those of a Spanish brunette than a Hova beauty. Her eyes were large, soft, and lustrous; her nose was straight and thin, and her mouth small, with an expression of habitual gravity which made her smile, when it came, all the more attractive. Little wonder that poor Ravonino had lost his heart to her, for, besides beauty of countenance, the girl was endowed with a sylph-like form, a sprightly disposition, and the sweet grace of humility.

"You have disobeyed me, Rafaravavy," said the Queen as she entered.

"Forgive me!" answered the girl in a low musical voice. "I did not think my song of praise would reach your ear. It was meant only for my God and Saviour."

"Is your God then deaf, that you must sing so loud?" asked the Queen, sharply.

"He is not deaf, blessed be His name!" exclaimed the maiden, with enthusiasm, "neither is His arm shortened that it cannot save. Oh! if you —— "

"Stop!" cried the angry Queen, "you have presumed to talk to me thus too often. You deserve to die for singing psalms. Have you given up praying since I forbade it?"

There was that in the voice of Ranavalona which alarmed the girl, and caused her to tremble as she replied, with some hesitation, that she still prayed.

Instead of giving way to another burst of passion the Queen adopted a bantering tone, and said—

"Come, Rafaravavy, tell me what you pray for."

"I pray for the pardon of my sins."

"Is that all? Surely you pray for something more than that. Something nice that you want very much."

"Yes," continued the girl, becoming somewhat pale, yet praying silently for courage even while she spoke. "Yes, I pray for the pardon of—of *your* sins, and—"

"Go on! Why do you stop?"

"And that your eyes may be opened that you may 'see the King in His beauty,' and be drawn to Him by the cords of love, so that you may cease to persecute the Christians and learn to join with them in praising the name of Jesus who redeemed us from destruction, and is ready and willing to save us from our sins."

While Rafaravavy was speaking Ranavalona put her hand over her eyes. When the former ceased, she did not remove the hand, but said, in a tone which the poor girl could not quite understand—

"Go! Enough. Leave me!"

As Rafaravavy left the balcony, a prepossessing

youth of delicate form and gentle mien emerged upon it by another door.

"Mother," he said, earnestly, "do, *do* give me leave to recall your proclamation. I have just heard of it from Rainiharo. Believe me, many of the nobles are not so good—I mean so guilty!—as you think. And the poor Christians—why should they not pray and sing? It is all that you have left to them, for they no longer dare to worship together in the churches."

"No, Rakota, I will not recall it. Your constant pleading worries me. It is enough to say that the people shall be examined—by the tangena ordeal if necessary—and they shall be punished according to their deserts. Is that all that you come here for, my son?"

It was evident from her tone that Ranavalona relented a little, though her words were firmly spoken.

"I came also to tell you," said the prince, "that the Europeans whom your spies brought news of some time ago have arrived. They are even now in the market-place. By my orders the guards have let them pass without question."

"Always interfering, Rakota!" said the Queen, angrily. "Why were they not seized and guarded till I should find time to speak with them?"

"Because, mother, that would scarcely be a civil way of receiving strangers."

" Strangers ! Spies you should have said. Have you forgotten the ungrateful Frenchmen who so lately tried to overturn my government ? "

" But these are not Frenchmen. They are English," said the prince, " and I will answer for them being good and true men."

" No doubt English are better than French—at least I hate them less ; but they are all pale-faced liars and Christians, and none of them shall remain in my land. But how can *you* tell, boy, that they are good and true men ? Have you had speech with them ? "

" Not I," returned the prince. " I have only seen them as they entered the town, but that was enough. One glance satisfied me of their being true men. When the sun rises it needs not much wisdom to know that there is heat and light. An honest face is like the sun. You cannot fail to know it."

" Go, foolish boy. You are too confident. I will not tolerate Europeans. These men shall be arrested. Hence, and send hither an officer."

Finding that the Queen was not in a temper to be trifled with, Rakota wisely made no reply, but bowed and went his way. In delivering the message to the officer, however, he whispered such words to him as secured a little delay in the execution of the royal commands.

CHAPTER XIV.

THE PRIME MINISTER LAYS DEEP PLANS—SO DOES HIS NEPHEW—THE
GREAT MARKET-PLACE—A FRIEND IN DEADLY PERIL, AND OUR
THREE HEROES COME TO GRIEF.

RETURNING to his own quarters in the palace, and chafing to find that some one had informed the Queen about his son's defection, Rainiharo encountered a favourite nephew, named Soa, who had also, unknown to his uncle, given up idolatry, and, like Prince Ramonja, been led to embrace the Gospel through the instrumentality of Prince Rakota.

"Well met, Soa," said the premier, "I have a proclamation to make which will bring sorrow to the hearts of some of these hated Christians."

He paused a moment, as if in thought, and Soa, a fine-looking young man of pleasant countenance and agile frame, seemed about to reply, but checked himself.

"Now, my boy," resumed the old man, "I have a piece of work for you to do. You have heard of the arrival of the Englishmen?"

"Yes, uncle."

"Well, I have reason to believe that they have been led hither by that son of a thunderbolt, Ravoninohitriniony, and that he is even now in hiding in the neighbourhood. At the gate you will find one of our spies who will conduct you to the cavern in which he lies concealed. Of course I could have him seized at once if I chose, but I have a deeper game to play, and want to make Ravoninohitriniony an unwitting instrument. It seems that more of the people in the palace are Christians than I knew of. It has come to my ears that some of these intend going stealthily to the cave to meet Ravoninohitriniony, for they are fond of this son of a wild boar, and probably hope to have news by him of their banished kindred."

Lest it should be supposed that we are putting flippant expressions into the mouth of Rainiharo, we may explain that the Malagasy define an ungrateful man as the "son of a thunderbolt," and sometimes as the "offspring of a wild boar," because—so they say—the young of the wild boar, when running by the side of its dam, continually gets in advance and turns round to bite her. The ingratitude of which our friend Ravonino was supposed to be guilty, consisted in his having forsaken the idols of the country and renounced the favour of the Queen by becoming a Christian, preferring, like Moses, to suffer affliction with the banished people of God.

"No doubt," continued the premier, "they will be praying and psalm-singing. Now, knowing your detestation of these Christians, I have resolved to send you to their meeting *as a Christian*. You are wise enough to know how to act when among them. Take note of the men and women you see there, whether high or low ; make out a list of them, and bring it to me. Death and chains shall be their portion, for I am fully more determined than the Queen is to stamp out this religion. Go, and do as I bid ye as quickly as you can."

For a few seconds the youth stood perplexed and irresolute. Then he said, suddenly, " Yes, uncle, I will go, according to your bidding, *as a Christian !*" and hastily left the room.

Meanwhile Mark Breezy and his companions, led by Laihova, followed the throng of country-folk to the market-place. They had passed the guard at the gate by means of that potent talisman, silver, before which few gates are permanently closed. If the party had sought to pass with any pomp or circumstance, or if they had carried merchandise along with them, they could not have passed so easily ; but Laihova had only to bestow some bits of silver on the guard and the way was at once clear. They might have passed without it, however, had they known of Rakota's interference in their favour.

We speak of " bits " of silver advisedly, for the Malagasy take the simplest and most literal way of making small change; they clip their dollars into little pieces of various sizes, and therewith transact the business that in other lands is settled with pence. As these clippings are not very accurate, however, they weigh the pieces, and for this purpose every one carries about with him a tiny pair of scales in his waist-cloth. These dollars were all foreign coins, for the Malagasy at that time had (and we believe still have) no native coinage. All silver that comes to their net is considered good fish. The standard coin is the Spanish dollar, but one will find every variety of European and American money in circulation among them. The method of clipping and weighing the small change might be thought somewhat cumbrous in European markets, for the dollar is cut up into eight *sikàjy* (each about six-pence); the sikàjy into nine *èranambàtra*, and each èranambàtra into ten *vàry-venty*, each of which last is about the weight of a plump grain of rice. Four weights, marked with a government stamp, are used in weighing the money. These weights are equal, respectively, to about a half-a-dollar, a quarter-dollar, sixpence, and fourpence. Other amounts are obtained by varying these in the opposite scales and adding grains of rice. But all this forms no diffi-culty in Madagascar. Like most Easterns the natives there dearly love to haggle and prolong a bargain—as our travellers found to their amusement that day; for not only were the principals vociferous in their disputations, but the bystanders entered into the spirit of the thing and volunteered their opinions!

Profound was the interest of the white men in this market, and deep was the absorption of Ebony, for that amiable negro had a faculty of totally forgetting himself and absolutely projecting himself into the shoes of other people, thus identifying himself with their interests—a faculty which cost him many anxious, indignant, pathetic, and hilarious moments.

"Das a most 'straor'nary sight," he said, looking round with glistening eyes and expanded lips at the crowds of people who pressed along the road leading to Zomà, the great market-place.

"By the way they stare at you, Ebony," said Hockins, "they evidently think *you* something 'straor'nary!"

"Not at all, 'Ockins. You's wrong, as usual," retorted the negro. " Dey quite used to black mans, but I tink dis de fust time dat some ob dem hab saw a man wid a face like putty."

There was indeed some ground for the negro's remark, for the people crowded round our heroes and gazed at them with undisguised interest.

The market-place was well suited to give some

idea of the various types of countenance among
the different tribes from distant parts of the island,
also for making acquaintance with the products of
the country and the manufactures of the people.
It was a sort of museum and centre of commerce
combined, with all the varied incidents, comical,
semi-tragic, and otherwise, for which markets in
general are more or less famed.

Here were to be seen great heaps of earthenware
of red clay—pans for cooking rice, water-jars, bottles,
and dishes of all sorts, as well as English crockery,
especially that with the old willow-pattern design!
There were great varieties of straw hats, beautifully
made of rice and other straw.   Elsewhere might be
seen iron-work of native manufacture, some of it
displaying considerable taste and skilful workman-
ship.   There were also beds, with well-turned posts,
made of a wood like mahogany, and the mattresses
for these were stuffed with down from a certain
flower, which made soft and comfortable couches.
Lambas of many kinds were also to be seen, from
those of coarse ròfia cloth to those of finer and more
ornamental material—though the finest silk lambas
and the more expensive European goods were not
often exposed for sale there, but were to be had at
the houses of the traders and manufacturers.   One
part of the market was devoted to wood for the
rafters and framework of houses, another to the sale

of vegetables and fruits—among which were sweet potatoes, manioc, beans, maize, peaches, bananas, mangoes, pine-apples, oranges, lemons, pumpkins, melons, grapes, Cape gooseberries, mulberries, guavas, pomegranates, and many others, besides bread-fruit and rice—which last is the staple food of the people.

"Oh! I say, 'Ockins," whispered Ebony at this point, "my mout 's a-waterin'."

"Well, mine 's somethin' in the same way," returned the seaman, "but we haven't a rap to buy with."

Whether Laihova overheard the whisper or not we cannot tell, but he stopped at that moment, purchased a large quantity of the tempting fruit, and handed it, without a word, to his friends, who received it with becoming gratitude.

"You 's a trump, Hovey," said the negro, as he put a whole peach into his capacious mouth.

"Ditto," said Hockins, performing the same feat with a banana.

"Do I hear music?" said Mark Breezy.

"An' don't I smell rum?" remarked Hockins.

"An' doesn't I hear cackling?" inquired Ebony.

By way of answer to all three, Laihova turned round the corner of a stall, when the party reached a spot which was devoted to the sale of native rum, or "toaka"—a coarse fiery spirit made from sugarcane, and sold at a very low price. Here a native musician was discovered twanging a native guitar, either as an accompaniment to the cackling of hundreds of fowls and the gobbling of innumerable turkeys, or as a desperate effort to beat these creatures at their own game of noise.

On inquiry Mark found that fowls were sold at from fourpence to eightpence a-piece; geese and turkeys from a shilling to eighteenpence. Also that beef and vegetables were proportionally cheap.

"It seems to me," remarked Hockins, as they moved slowly along, enjoying the fruit and the scene, "that this here island is a sort of paradise."

Before many minutes were over the seaman had reason to change his views considerably on this point, for their guide led them to a spot where the slave-market was held. The sights they witnessed there were such as filled the hearts of the white men with deep sorrow and indignation, while it drew tears from the eyes of the sympathetic negro. For the men and women and children were no mere criminals who might in some sense be deserving of their fate —though such there were also amongst them,—but many of the men were guilty of political offences only, and not a few, both of men and women, were martyrs, who, because they had left the faith of their fathers and become followers of Jesus Christ, were sold into temporary—in some cases perpetual— slavery, with their wives and families.

At sight of these unfortunates Laihova was evidently much affected, though he made strenuous efforts to conceal his feelings.

"You are grieved, I see," said Mark, in a tone of profound sympathy which touched his guide's heart.

"Grieved! Yes—verily," said Laihova, whose broken English was much interlarded with Scriptural words and expressions, "for does I not see my friends there? But com. They must not know me. It is danger. Com."

He led them quickly away from the slave-market, and as they walked along he explained that some of the poor slaves whom they had just seen thus publicly exposed for sale were among the nobles of the land—not only in regard to human rank, but in right of that patent which man can neither give nor take away,—an upright regenerated soul. He further explained, as best he could, that slaves in his land were derived from three or four different sources—namely, captives taken in war; persons condemned to slavery for crime, for political offences, and for religious opinions; people who had been sold for debt, and the descendants of all of these.

They had gradually quitted the market while thus engaged in conversation, and were ascending one of the steeper parts of the city, when their attention was attracted by a shouting not far off.

Presently they observed a number of men and boys running in and out amongst the houses and the low walls which surrounded them, as if in chase of something. Soon a man was seen to dart along the road they were following. As he drew near they observed that he stumbled as he ran, yet forced the pace and panted violently—like one running for his life. A few moments more and the crowd was close at his heels, pelting him with stones and yelling like wild beasts. The fugitive turned up a narrow lane between high walls close to where our party stood. He was closely followed by the crowd.

At this point some of the pursuers stopped as if from exhaustion.

"What has he done?" said Laihova to one of these.

"He has been stealing in the market by cutting a lamba."

It is the practice to carry money tied up in a corner of the lamba, and thieves, by cutting off this corner, sometimes manage to secure the money.

A great cry arose just then, and some of the pursuers came running back.

"He is down," said one. "He is dead!" said another.

Now our friend Hockins was one of those men who have at all times an irresistible tendency to take the part of the weak against the strong, without much regard to the cause of battle! He instantly, without a word, ran off at full speed to the rescue. Ebony ran after him from sympathy. Mark Breezy followed from the natural desire to keep by his comrades, and back them up, while Laihova followed—no doubt from good-fellowship!

They soon came upon the poor man, who was completely naked, bruised and bleeding, and surrounded by a crowd of youths, who were deliberately stoning him as if he were a dangerous animal or a mad dog.

With a roar like a lion Hockins went at them. He tripped up some half-dozen big boys, flattened still more the flat noses of some of the men, stretching them flat on their backs, and then, standing astride the fallen man, flourished his enormous fists, and invited the entire population of Antananarivo to "come on!"

The population refused the invitation and retired.

Ebony was not slow to follow suit, with this variation, that instead of roaring he yelled, and instead of bestriding the fallen man, he gave sudden chase hither and thither, with powerful effect, rendering the rout complete.

Meanwhile Mark attended to the injured man, who seemed to be dead. Turning him over on his back he discovered, to his inexpressible amazement, that he was no other than their old friend Mamba

—the crocodile—whom they had left with his mother and the others in the cave many days before.

"How is it possible," he exclaimed, while dressing his wounds, "that he can have arrived at the same time with us, for we started before him and have travelled fast?"

Laihova explained that Mamba was one of the fleetest men in the island, and that he could easily have passed them though starting later than they did. But why he had come, and why he had passed instead of overtaking and travelling with them, he could not even guess.

As most of poor Mamba's wounds were bruises, and the few cuts were not deep, his four friends raised him and carried him quickly into a neighbouring house, the door of which was immediately shut. Laihova explained that it was the house of a personal friend of his own, who was also a Christian, but secretly, for fear of the Queen.

Here Mamba was sufficiently brought round by Mark's ministrations to be able to sit up and answer questions, but at first he seemed disinclined to speak, and then gave evasive replies.

"Why this secrecy, my friend?" asked Laihova, in the native language.

"If I could answer," said Mamba, "there would be no secrecy."

"True, and I would not pry into your secrets,"

returned Laihova, "but we would help you if we can."

"You cannot help me," returned Mamba, in a somewhat sad tone. "I have business in hand which requires haste. I have tried to keep clear of you to prevent delay, and to avoid mixing myself up in your dangers, for you are in danger here. I would not have come near the town at all, but I required to make a purchase in the market, and hoped to do so without being recognised. Unfortunately an old enemy saw me. He fell on the device of cutting off the corner of his own lamba, and then, raising the cry of thief, pretended that I had done it. I ran. You know my speed of foot. I trusted to that instead of trusting to my God. They surrounded me. You know the end."

While Mamba was yet speaking a loud knocking was heard at the door, and a stern voice demanded admittance.

On hearing it Mamba leaped from the couch on which he had been laid as if nothing were the matter with him. He glanced hastily round. The owner of the house seemed to divine his wishes, for he pointed to a small window which opened into what appeared to be a court at the back of the dwelling. The window was merely a square opening, which appeared scarcely wide enough to let a man's shoulders pass, but Mamba did not hesitate.

To the amazement of Mark and his friends he took
what is familiarly known as a " header " through the
window — *à la* harlequin — and disappeared. To
the still greater amazement of Mark and his friends,
Laihova instantly followed suit, without a word of
explanation!   Indeed there was no time for that.
A moment after the owner of the dwelling opened
the door with a very submissive look and admitted
a band of armed men.

The leader of the band, from his dress and
bearing, was evidently a man of position.   He
carried in his hand a large spear highly ornamented
with silver.   This weapon—as Mark afterwards
learned—was an official spear with the Queen's
name engraven on it.   The bearer of it, as well as
the spear itself, was named " Tsitialainga," which
means " Hater of Lies."

Turning to the owner of the house, the Hater of
Lies sternly asked some questions of him ; but as he
spoke in the native tongue he was unintelligible to
our travellers, whose spirits were not cheered by the
scowling looks of the armed men.   Whatever the
question was, the answer appeared to be unsatis-
factory, for the Hater of Lies immediately turned to
his men, and pointing with the silver spear to the
three strangers, gave them a command.

Instantly they sprang upon Mark and his
companions, and seized them.   Both Hockins and

Ebony were for a moment paralysed by surprise; then, their impulsive souls being stirred by a sudden gush of indignation, they gathered themselves up for a mighty burst which would certainly have resulted in disaster of some sort if Mark had not recovered presence of mind in time.

"Submit!—submit!" he shouted in a loud voice of authority. Then, in a sharp but lower tone, "It is our only chance! *Don't* resist!"

With feelings of something like despair the two men obeyed. A few minutes more and they were bound, led through the streets surrounded by a guard, which alone protected them from death at the hands of the angry populace. Then they were cast into a dark prison, loaded with chains, and left to their reflections.

CHAPTER XV.

THE SPIES AND THE SECRET MEETING—THE PRIME MINISTER FOILED BY THE PRINCE.

THE sun was setting, the air was balmy, the face
of nature was beautiful, the insects and birds were
buzzing, humming, and chirping happily, as if there
were no such things as care and sorrow in the wide
world, when Soa, the prime minister's nephew, with
his guide, approached the forest in which was the
cavern where the persecuted Christians had arranged
to hold their secret meeting.

"I am to go as a Christian!" thought Soa, as he
walked on swiftly and in silence, "as a Christian
hypocrite and spy!"

The young man's countenance relaxed into something like a smile as he thought thus; then it
became solemnised as he offered the silent prayer,
"Lord, enable me to do the work honestly and
well."

The way was long, but the youth's limbs were
strong and agile, so that night had not long over-

spread the land when he reached the end of his journey. The night was unusually dark—well adapted for deeds of secrecy and crime. If it had been lighter the two spies would have seen a number of men and women, and even children, hurrying along stealthily in the same direction with themselves. They observed only two or three of these, however, who chanced to fall in their way. They loomed up suddenly like spectres out of the surrounding darkness and as quickly melted into it again. Soa paid no attention to these apparitions, neither did he utter a word to his companion during the journey.

Most of the way he kept a pace or two in advance of his guide, but when they reached the more intricate and broken grounds of the forest, he fell behind and suffered the other to lead.

At last the path wound so much among broken rocks and over steep knolls that their progress became very slow—all the more so that the overshadowing trees rendered the darkness profound. Sometimes they had to clamber up steep places on hands and knees.

Suddenly they were arrested by what seemed to them a faint cry or wail. Listening intently, they perceived that the sounds were musical.

"The Christians are singing," said the spy in a tone which, low though it was, betrayed a touch of contempt. "They hold their meeting in a cave on the other side of this mound."

"Remain here, then, till I return to you," said Soa. "They know you to be a spy. They will not suppose that *I* have come in such a capacity."

The man gave vent to a slight laugh at the supposed joke and sat down, while the courtier advanced alone.

On the other side of the mound the sounds which had reached the listeners' ears as a wail now swelled upon the young man as a well-known hymn in which he had many times joined. A feeling of joy, almost amounting to triumph, filled his heart as he stood there listening. While he listened he observed several indistinct forms glide past him and enter the cave. He crept after them.

A strange sight met his eyes. The cave was so large and high that the single torch which burned in it merely lighted up a portion of the wall against which it was fixed. Even in the immediate neighbourhood of the torch things were more or less indistinct, while all else was shrouded in darkness profound. Here more than a hundred dusky figures were assembled—those furthest from the light melting, as it were, into the darkness, and leaving the imagination to people illimitable space with similar beings.

Soa slipped in, and sat down on a jutting rock

near the entrance just as the hymn was closing. Few people observed him. Immediately after, an old man who sat nearest the light rose to pray. Beside him stood our friend Ravonino. On the other side sat a young man with a remarkably intelligent countenance.

With intense earnestness and great simplicity the old man prayed, in the name of Jesus, that the Holy Spirit might bless their meeting and deliver them from the power of their enemies. He also prayed with much emphasis that their enemies might be turned into Christian friends—at which petition a loud "Amen" arose from the worshippers.

"Now Totosy will speak," said the old man, after a brief pause, turning to the young man with the intelligent countenance. "Let the Word be brought forth."

"Stop!" cried a man, rising in the midst of the crowd, "it may not be safe to bring out the Word just now."

"Why not, my son?" asked the old man. "Are not all here to-night our friends?"

"I think not," returned the man. "As I came along I saw one of the Queen's spies, who is well known to me. He was walking with the nephew of our deadly foe Rainiharo, and Soa himself sits *there !*"

He turned as he spoke, and pointed straight at Soa, who rose at once and advanced to the front.

" My friends," he said, in a gentle voice, "the last speaker is right. I am here, and I was led here by one of the Queen's spies. But the spy is not here. He awaits me outside. Let two of your young men guard the entrance of the cave so that our conference may not be overheard."

Two stalwart youths rose at once and hurried to the outside of this primitive meeting-house, where they mounted guard.

"I have been sent," continued Soa, " by my uncle, with orders to enter your meeting '*as a Christian*,' take note of your names, and report them to him ! "

There was a tendency on the part of some to shrink into the background on hearing this.

" Now," continued Soa, "I have come to obey only part of his orders. I have come, *as a Christian*, to warn you of the dangers that surround you. The Queen is exceeding mad against you. It will be your wisest course to refrain from meeting together just now, and rest content with worshipping in your own homes. But let not this distress you, my friends. The God whom we love is able to turn darkness into light and to make crooked things straight. Neither let it break up our meeting just now. We are safe at present. Let us get out the Word and enjoy the worship of our Saviour while we may."

There were murmurs of assent and satisfaction at the close of this brief address, and one of the young men, with grave—almost mysterious—looks, took up a small spade and went towards that part of the wall where Ravonino sat. The latter rose to let the young men get at a particular spot, which was marked on the wall with a small—almost imperceptible—red square. Here, after turning up a few spadefuls of earth, he struck upon a stone. Lifting it, he disclosed a hole about a foot square. The old man who presided at the meeting thrust his hands into this hole and gently lifted out a thick volume, which he laid reverently upon a flat rock that formed a sort of natural table in front of him.

This was "the Word" to which reference had been made—an old, much-soiled and worn Malagasy Bible, which had been buried there, so that, whatever might become of its Christian owners, it might escape being found and condemned to the flames, as so many of its fellows had been.

It was a curious Bible this, in more respects than one. In Madagascar the Bible was printed first in sections by the natives, under the superintendence of the missionaries; these sections got scattered, for teaching purposes, and various editions of different sizes were printed at different times. The original owner—if we may not call him fabricator—of the

Bible, now referred to as having been dug up in the cave, must, in his desire to possess the Word of God complete, have been at considerable pains to secure every fragment and leaf that came in his way, and then had them all bound together. A clasp of leather and a European hook-and-eye fastened the edges. The different portions, of course, did not fit exactly, and some of the verses necessarily overlapped. Nevertheless, a nearly complete and substantial Bible was the result of his labours.[1]

Taking up the treasured book with great care, the young man before mentioned by the name of Totosy opened it and selected a text. "Fear not, little flock, it is your Father's good pleasure to give you the kingdom."

From this he preached an admirable sermon, full of hope and consolation to men and women situated as his companions were at that time, and holding up Jesus not only as the deliverer of the world from sin but from fear of physical death. Strengthening of this sort, truly, was much needed, for during the previous persecutions of 1837 and 1849 Queen

---

[1] A Bible of the kind here described may now be seen in the Museum of the British and Foreign Bible Society, 146 Queen Victoria Street, London, just as it was dug up out of the earth, where it had been buried by Christian natives who probably perished in the persecutions. The New Testament bears the date of 1830, the Old Testament that of 1835.

Ranavalona had given terrible evidence of her fierce and relentless nature, so that Christians were now well aware of what they had to expect if another cruel fit came upon her.

The sermon finished, another hymn was sung, followed by a prayer, after which, before finally breaking up and dispersing, the worshippers collected in various groups; and exclamations of surprise, joy, and fervent thanksgiving were heard, now and again, when friends who had parted as enemies on account of religious differences unexpectedly met as brothers in the Lord.

It has ever been a result of persecution that the persecuted cause has made progress—naturally so, for trial and suffering winnow out the chaff and leave the good seed to flourish with increased vigour. Few false professors attended those midnight meetings, which were so full of joy and danger, and none of these ever got the length of Ranavalona's fiery stakes or the fearful "rock of hurling."

For fully a quarter of a century (from 1836 to 1861) did the persecution of the native Christians last in Madagascar. During most of that dark period Queen Ranavalona I. endeavoured, by cruel prohibitive laws, torture, and death, to stamp out the love of Christ from her dominions. Through most of that period she tried to prevent her people from

meeting for worship, praying to God in the name of
Christ, or reading the Scriptures or any other
Christian book, and those who disobeyed her did
so at the risk of losing property, liberty, or life.
Nevertheless, in spite of this, worship was kept up
in secret—in secluded villages, in recesses of the
forest, in caves, even in rice-holes; the Word was
read, faithful natives preached, and Baptism and
the Lord's Supper were continuously observed.
Small portions of Scripture—even leaves—were
carefully treasured and passed from hand to hand
until "these calamities" were past; and now, at the
present time, the Church in Madagascar is ten
times stronger than ever it was before!

Of course active persecution was not maintained
throughout the whole period of twenty-five years.
The volcano smouldered at times. For brief periods
it almost seemed as if about to become extinct, but
at intervals it burst forth with renewed violence.
At the time of which we write (1857) there were
mutterings of the volcano, and portents in the air
which filled the persecuted ones, and those who
loved them, with grave anxiety.

In a dark corner of the cavern Soa and Ravonino
stood apart, after the service was over, and conversed
in subdued tones.

"Do you think the lives of my comrades are in
danger?" asked the latter, anxiously.

"It is difficult to answer that," replied Soa.
"The Queen fears to offend the English by putting
European subjects to death; but she is in a savage
mood just now, and your friends have intermeddled
with matters that they would have been wise to let
alone. Banishment is more likely to be their fate,
but that will be almost equal to death.

"How so?" asked Ravonino.

"Because Ranavalona will probably treat them as
she treated the Europeans who lately tried to over-
throw her government. She sent them down to the
coast with orders to their conductors to keep them
so long on the way—especially on the unhealthy
fever-stricken parts of the route—that sickness
might have time to kill them."

"And was the plan successful?"

"Not quite, for the white people turned out to be
tough. They managed to get away from our island
alive, but in a state of health, I believe, that will
very likely prevent them from ever wishing to
return!"

"I have much love for these men," said Ravonino,
after a pause. "You have influence with Rainiharo.
Can you not befriend them?"

"I shall have little influence now with my uncle,"
returned Soa, sadly, "for I am a Christian, and he
will soon discover that. But I will help them if I
can—for your sake."

"And Rafaravavy," said Ravonino, in a lower voice, "do you think she can be induced to fly? If she were brought to me here, I should have little difficulty in taking her to a place of safety."

"The difficulties in your way are greater than you suppose," said Soa.   "The Queen's spies and soldiers are out all over the land.   Even now, were it not that I am your friend and brother in Jesus, you would have been caught here as in a trap.   Besides, there is the greater difficulty that Rafaravavy is filled with fidelity to her royal mistress, and pities her so much that she will not leave her.   You know that she openly confesses Christ in the palace, yet so great is the Queen's regard for her that she will not listen to my uncle, who would gladly see her tossed over the 'rock of hurling.'   I had converse with her the other day, and I see that she even hopes to be the instrument of the Queen's conversion to Christianity."

"God bless her!" exclaimed Ravonino, fervently.

"Amen!" returned Soa, "and I doubt not that the blessing will come, though it may not come in the way we hope.   It is no easy matter to say 'Thy will be done' when we are suffering."

"Prince Rakota has done much for the Christians in time past," urged poor Ravonino, who felt that all hope of delivering the girl he loved, at the present time, from the dangers that surrounded her was gradually slipping away from him; "surely he can and will protect her."

"I fear he has not the power," answered Soa. "He has interfered in behalf of the Christians so often of late that the Queen is losing patience; and you know that if she once gives way to her cruel rage, the life of Rakota himself is not safe. But, you may trust me, my friend; I will do my best to move him to aid you—and your friends also."

Most of the people had left the cave while these two were conversing, with the understanding that they were not to return, as it was no longer a safe retreat. Another and more distant rendezvous was, however, appointed; the treasured Bible was not restored to its old place of concealment, but carried off by Totosy, the young preacher, to be reburied in a new place of refuge.

"Do you follow them?" asked Soa of Ravonino, when the others had all gone and they were about to part.

"No. My companions will come here expecting to find me if they escape. I must remain, whatever befalls. If the soldiers come, I will see them before they arrive, and give them the slip. If they give chase they will find it troublesome to catch me!"

When Soa returned to the city he went straight to the apartments of the prime minister, whom he found impatiently awaiting him.

" You have been long," said the latter.

" The distance is great," replied the nephew.

" Well ?" exclaimed the uncle, inquiringly.

" You ordered me to act as a Christian," returned the young man, with a slight smile, " and you know it takes time to do that."

" True—true. And you have brought me the list?"

" No, uncle."

" What mean you, boy ?"

" I mean that I have obeyed your first command; I have been to the Christian meeting *as a Christian*."

A puzzled, inquiring look overspread the premier's countenance.

" Well, what then ?"

" Well, then, of course I acted the part of a Christian to the best of my power. I told them why I had been sent, warned them of the evil intended them, and advised them to escape for their lives; but, as no immediate danger was to be feared, I joined them in their worship."

" And you have brought no list ?"

" None."

Rainiharo's visage, while his nephew spoke, was a sight to behold; for the conflicting emotions aroused produced a complexity of expression that is quite indescribable.

" Young man !" he said, sternly, " you have disobeyed my orders. Why have you done this? Your head must fall, for you show that you are a Christian."

With great simplicity and gentleness Soa said: "Yes, my uncle, I *am* a Christian; and if you please you may put me to death, for I *do* pray to Jesus."

Utterly confounded by this straightforward and fearless reply, Rainiharo stood for some moments gazing in silent wonder at the youth who thus calmly stood prepared to abide the consequences of his confession. At first it almost seemed as if, in his anger, he would with his own hand, then and there, inflict the punishment he threatened; but once again, as in the case of Ranavalona, love proved more powerful than anger.

"No, no, boy," he said, turning away with a wave of his hand, as if to dismiss the subject finally, "you shall not die. It is a delusion. You deceive yourself. Go. Leave me!"

Soa obeyed, and went straight to the apartment of Prince Rakota to relate to that fast friend and comrade his recent adventures, and consult with him about the dark cloud that threatened to burst in persecution over the unhappy land.

CHAPTER XVI

IN PRISON—EFFECTS OF A FIRST SIGHT OF TORTURE.

A NEW day had begun, cattle were lowing on the distant plain, and birds were chirping their matutinal songs in bush and tree when Mark Breezy, John Hockins, and James Ginger—*alias* Ebony—awoke from their uneasy rest on the prison floor and sat up with their backs against the wall.   Their chains rattled sharply as they did so.

" Well now," said Hockins, gasping forth his morning yawn in spite of circumstances, " I 've many a time read and heard it of other folk, but I never did think I should live to hear my own chains rattle."

" Right you are, 'Ockins ; ob course I 's got de same sentiments zactly," said the negro, lifting up his strong arm and ruefully surveying the heavy iron links of native manufacture that descended from his wrist.

Mark only sighed.   It was the first time he had ever been restrained, even by bolt or bar, much less by manacles, and the effect on his young mind was at first overwhelming.

Bright though the sun was outside, very little of its light found a passage through the chinks of their all but windowless prison-house, so that they could scarcely see the size or character of the place. But this mattered little. They were too much crushed by their misfortune to care. For some time they sat without speaking, each feeling quite incapable of uttering a word of cheer to his fellows.

The silence was suddenly but softly broken by the sound of song. It seemed to come from a very dark corner of the prison in which nothing could be seen. To the startled prisoners it sounded like heavenly music—and indeed such it was, for in that corner sat two Christian captives who were spending the first minutes of the new day in singing praise to God.

The three comrades listened with rapt attention, for although the words were unintelligible, with the exception of the name of Jesus, the air was quite familiar, being one of those in which English-speaking Christians are wont to sing praise all the world over.

When the hymn ceased one of the voices was raised in a reverent and continuous tone, which was obviously the voice of prayer.

Just as the petition was concluded the sun found a loop-hole in the prison, and poured a flood of light into it which partly illumined the dark corner, and revealed two men seated on the ground with their backs against the wall. They were fine-looking men, nearly naked, and joined together by means of a ponderous piece of iron above two feet long, with a heavy ring at either end which encircled their necks. The rings were so thick that their ends must have been forced together with sledge-hammer and anvil after being put round the men's necks, and then over-lapped and riveted. Thus it became impossible to free them from their fetters except by the slow and laborious process of cutting them through with a file. Several old and healed-up sores on the necks and collar-bones of both men indicated that they and their harsh couplings had been acquainted for a long time, and one or two inflamed spots told all too clearly that they had not yet become quite re-conciled.[1]

"Now isn't that awful," said John Hockins in a low voice with a sort of choke in it, "to think that these poor fellows—wi' that horrible thing that can't be much under thirty pounds weight on their necks, an' that must ha' bin there for months if not for years—are singin' an' prayin' to the Almighty, an' here am I, John Hockins, with little or nothin' to complain of as yet, haven't given so much as a thought to —— "

[1] The fetters here described may be seen in the Museum of the London Missionary Society in Blomfield Street, London, along with an interesting collection of Malagasy relics.

The choke got the better of our sailor at this point, and he became suddenly silent.

"Das so!" burst in Ebony, with extreme energy. "I's wid you dere! I tell you what it is, 'Ockins, dem brown niggers is true Kistians, an' we white folks is nuffin but hipperkrits."

"I hope we're not quite so bad as *that*, Ebony," said Mark, with a sad smile. "Nevertheless, Hockins is right—we are far behind these poor fellows in submission and gratitude to our Maker."

While he spoke the heavy door of the prison opened, and a jailor entered with two large basins of boiled rice. The largest he put on the ground before our three travellers, the other in front of the coupled men, and then retired without a word.

".Well, thank God for this, anyhow," said Mark, taking up one of the three spoons which lay on the rice and going to work with a will.

"Just so," responded the seaman. "I'm thankful too, and quite ready for grub."

"Curious ting, 'Ockins," remarked Ebony, "dat your happytite an' mine seems to be allers in de same state—sharp!"

The seaman's appetite was indeed so sharp that he did not vouchsafe a reply. The prisoners in the dark corner seemed much in the same condition, but their anxiety to begin did not prevent their shutting their eyes for a few seconds and obviously asking a blessing on their meal. Hockins observed the act, and there passed over his soul another wave of self-condemnation, which was indicated by a deprecatory shake of his rugged head.

Observing it, Ebony paused a moment and said—

" You 's an awrful sinner, 'Ockins ! "

" True, Ebony."

" Das jist what I is too. Quite as bad as you. P'r'aps wuss !"

" I shouldn't wonder if you are," rejoined the seaman, recovering his spirits somewhat under the stimulating influence of rice. The recovery was not, however, sufficient to induce further conversation at the time, for they continued after that to eat in silence.

They had scarcely finished when the jailor returned to remove the dish, which he did without word or ceremony, and so quickly that Ebony had to make a sudden scoop at the last mouthful ; he secured it, filled his mouth with it, and then flung the spoon at the retiring jailor.

" That was not wise," said Mark, smiling in spite of himself at the tremendous pout of indignation on the negro's face ; " the man has us in his power, and may make us very uncomfortable if we insult him."

" Das true, massa," said Ebony, in sudden peni-tence, " but if dere 's one thing I can't stand, it 's

havin' my wittles took away afore I'm done wid
'em."

"You'll have to larn to stand it, boy," said
Hockins, "else you'll have your life took away,
which 'll be wuss."

The probability of this latter event occurring
was so great that it checked the rise of spirits which
the rice had caused to set in.

"What d'ee think they'll do to us, sir?" asked the
sailor, in a tone which showed that he looked up to
the young doctor for counsel in difficulty. The
feeling that, in virtue of his education and training,
he ought to be in some sort an example and guide
to his comrades in misfortune, did much to make
Mark shake off his despondency and pluck up
heart.

"God knows, Hockins, what they will do," he
said. "If they were a more civilised people we
might expect to be let off easily for so slight an
offence as rescuing a supposed criminal, but you
remember that Ravonino once said, when telling us
stories round the camp-fire, that interference with
what they call the course of justice is considered a
very serious offence. Besides, the Queen being in
a very bad mood just now, and we being Christians,
it is likely we shall be peculiarly offensive to her. I
fear that banishment is the least we may count on."

"It's a hard case to be punished for bein'

Christians, when we hardly deserve the name. I can't help wonderin'," said the seaman, "that Lovey should have bolted as he did an' left us in the lurch. He might at least have taken his risk along with us. Anyhow, he could have spoke up for us, knowin' both lingos. Of course it was nat'ral that poor Mamba should look after number one, seein' that he was in no way beholden to us; but Lovey was our guide, an' pledged to stand by us."

"I can't help thinking," said Mark, "that you do injustice to Laihova. He is not the man to forsake a comrade in distress."

"That was my own opinion," returned the sailor, "till I seed him go slap through yon port-hole like a harlequin."

"P'r'aps he tink he kin do us more service w'en free dan as a prisoner," suggested Ebony.

"There's somethin' in that," returned Hockins, lifting his hand to stroke his beard, as was his wont when thoughtful. He lifted it, however, with some difficulty, owing to the heavy chain.

They were still engaged in conversation about their prospects when the prison-door again opened, and two men were ushered in. Both wore white lambas over their other garments. One was tall and very dark. The other was comparatively slender, and not so tall as his companion. For a moment the strangers stood contemplating the prisoners, and Mark's attention was riveted on the smaller man, for he felt that his somewhat light-coloured and pleasant features were not unfamiliar to him, though he could not call to mind where or when he had seen him. Suddenly it flashed across him that this was the very man to whose assistance he had gone, and whose wounds he had bound up, soon after his arrival in the island.

With a smile of recognition, Mark rose and extended his hand as far as his chain permitted. The young native stepped forward, grasped the hand, and pressed it warmly. Then he looked round at his tall companion, and spoke to him in his own tongue, whereupon the tall man advanced a step, and said in remarkably bad English—

"You save me frind life one taime ago. Ver' good —him now *you* save."

"Thank him for that promise," said Mark, greatly relieved to find at least one friend among the natives in his hour of need.

"But," continued the Interpreter, "you muss not nottice me frind nowhar. Unerstand?"

"Oh yes, I think I do," returned Mark, with an intelligent look. "I suppose he does not wish people to think that he is helping or favouring us?"

"That's him! you's got it!" replied the Interpreter, quite pleased apparently with his success in the use of English.

"My!" murmured Ebony to Hockins in an undertone, "if I couldn't spoke better English dan dat
I'd swaller my tongue!"

"Well—good-boy," said the Interpreter, holding
out his hand, which Mark grasped and shook
smilingly, as he replied, "Thank you, I'm glad you
think I'm a good boy."

"No, no—not that!" exclaimed the Interpreter,
"good *day*, not good *boy*; good-night, good morning!
We goes out, me an' me frind. Him's name Ravèlo."

Again Ravèlo shook hands with Mark, despite
the rattling chain, nodded pleasantly to him, after
the English fashion, and took his departure with
his tall friend.

"Well now, I do think," remarked Hockins, when
the door had closed behind them, "that Rav——
Ravè-what's-his-name might have took notice of me
too as an old friend that helped to do him service."

"Hm! he seemed to forgit *me* altogidder," remarked the negro, pathetically. "Dere's nuffin
so bad as ingratitood—'cept lockjaw: das a little
wuss."

"What d'ee mean by lockjaw bein' wuss?"
demanded Hockins.

"W'y, don't you see? Ingratitood don't *feel*
'thankee,' w'ereas lockjaw not on'y don't feel but
don't even *say* 'thankee.'"

A sudden tumult outside the prison here interrupted them. Evidently a crowd approached. In a few minutes it halted before the door, which was flung open, and four prisoners were thrust in, followed by several strong guards and the execrations of the crowd. The door was smartly slammed in the faces of the yelling people, and the guards proceeded to chain the prisoners.

They were all young men, and Mark Breezy and his friends had no doubt, from their gentle expression and upright bearing, that they were not criminals but condemned Christians.

Three of them were quickly chained to the wall, but the third was thrown on his back, and a complex chain was put on his neck and limbs, in such a way that, when drawn tight, it forced his body into a position that must have caused him severe pain. No word or cry escaped him, however, only an irrepressible groan when he was thrust into a corner and left in that state of torture.

The horror of Mark and his comrades on seeing this done in cold blood cannot be described. To hear or read of torture is bad enough, but to see it actually applied is immeasurably worse—to note the glance of terror and to hear the slight sound of the wrenched joints and stretched sinews, followed by the deep groan and the upward glare of agony!

With a bursting cry of rage, Hockins, forgetting his situation, sprang towards the torturers, was

checked by his fetters, and fell with a heavy clang
and clatter on the floor. Even the cruel guards
started aside in momentary alarm, and then with a
contemptuous laugh passed out.

Hockins had barely recovered his footing, and
managed to restrain his feelings a little, when the
door was again opened and the Interpreter re-entered
with the jailor.

"I come—break chains," said the former.

He pointed to the chains which bound our
travellers. They were quickly removed by two
under-jailors and their chief.

"Now—com vis me."

To the surprise of the Interpreter, Mark Breezy
crossed his arms over his breast, and firmly said—
"No!" Swiftly understanding his motive, our seaman and Ebony followed suit with an equally
emphatic "No!"

The Interpreter looked at them in puzzled surprise.

"See," said Mark, pointing to the tortured man in
the corner, "we refuse to move a step till that poor
fellow's chains are eased off."

For a moment the Interpreter's look of surprise
increased; then an indescribable smile lit up his
swarthy features as he turned to the jailor and
spoke a few words. The man went immediately to
the .curled-up wretch in the corner and relaxed his

chains so that he was enabled to give vent to a great sigh of relief. Hockins and Ebony uttered sighs of sympathy almost as loud, and Mark, turning to the Interpreter, said, with some emotion, "Thank you! God bless you! Now we will follow."

CHAPTER XVII.

MAMBA IS SUCCOURED BY ONE OF THE "ANCIENT SOOT," AND
FULFILS HIS MYSTERIOUS MISSION.

WHEN Laihova and Mamba took the reckless
"headers" which we have described in a former
chapter, they tumbled into a courtyard which was
used as a sort of workshop. Fortunately for them
the owner of the house was not a man of orderly
habits. He was rather addicted to let rubbish lie
till stern necessity forced him to clear it away.
Hence he left heaps of dust, shavings, and other
things to accumulate in heaps. One such heap
happened to lie directly under the window through
which the adventurous men plunged, so that, to
their immense satisfaction, and even surprise, they
came down soft and arose unhurt.

Instantly they slipped into an outhouse, and
there held hurried converse in low tones.

"What will you do now ?" asked Laihova.

"I will remain where I am till night-fall, for I
dare not show myself all bruised like this. When

it is dark I will slip out and continue my journey to the coast."

"To Tamatave?" asked Laihova, naming the chief seaport on the eastern side of Madagascar.

"Yes, to Tamatave."

"Do you go there to trade?"

"No. I go on important business."

It was evident that, whatever his business might be, Mamba, for reasons best known to himself, resolved to keep his own counsel. Seeing this, his friend said—"Well, I go to the eastward also, for Ravoninohitriniony awaits me there; but I fear that our English friends will be thrown into prison."

"Do you think so?" asked Mamba, anxiously. "If you think I can be helpful I will give up my important business and remain with you."

"You cannot help us much, I think. Perhaps your presence may be a danger instead of a help. Besides, I have friends here who have power. And have we not God to direct us in all things? No, brother, as your business is important, go."

Mamba was evidently much relieved by this reply, and his friend saw clearly that he had intended to make a great personal sacrifice when he offered to remain.

"But now I must myself go forth without delay," continued Laihova. "I am not well known here, and, once clear of this house, can walk openly and without much risk out of the city. Whatever befalls the Englishmen, Ravoninohitriniony and I will help and pray for them."

Another minute and he was gone. Passing the gates without arousing suspicion, he was soon walking rapidly towards the forest in which his friend Ravonino lay concealed.

Meanwhile, Mamba hid himself behind some bags of grain in the outhouse until night-fall, when he sallied boldly forth and made his way to the house of a friend, who, although not a Christian, was too fond of him to refuse him shelter.

This friend was a man of rank and ancient family. The soot hung in long strings from his roof-tree. He was one of "the ancient soot!"

The houses in the city are usually without ceiling —open to the ridge-pole, though there is sometimes an upper chamber occupying part of the space, which is reached by a ladder. There are no chimneys, therefore, and smoke from the wood and grass fires settles upon the rafters in great quantities inside. As it is never cleared away, the soot of course accumulates in course of time and hangs down in long pendants. So far from considering this objectionable, the Malagasy have come to regard it with pride; for, as each man owns his own house, the great accumulations of soot have come to be regarded as evidence of the family having occupied the dwelling from ancient times. Hence the "old families" are sometimes complimented by the sovereign, in proclamations, by being styled "the ancient soot!"

The particular Ancient Soot who accorded hospitality that night to Mamba was much surprised, but very glad, to see him. "Have you arrived?" he asked, with a good deal of ceremonial gesticulation.

"I have arrived," answered Mamba.

"Safely and well, I hope."

"Safely and well," replied Mamba—ceremonially of course, for in reality he had barely arrived with life, and certainly not with a sound skin.

"Come in, then," said the Ancient Soot. "And how are you? I hope it is well with you. Behold, spread a mat for him, there, one of you. And is it well with you?"

"Well indeed," said Mamba once again, falsely but ceremonially.

"May you live to grow old!" resumed Soot. "And you have arrived safely? Come in. Where are you going?"

"I'm going yonder—westward," replied Mamba, with charming conventional vagueness, as he sat down on the mat.

"But it appears to me," said Ancient Soot, passing from the region of compliment into that of fact, and looking somewhat closely at his friend, " it seems to me that you have been hurt."

Mamba now explained the exact state of the case, said that he required a good long rest, after that a hearty meal, then a lamba and a little money, for he had been despoiled of everything he had possessed by the furious crowd that so nearly killed him.

His kind host was quite ready to assist him in every way. In a few minutes he was sound asleep in a little chamber on the rafters, where he could rest without much risk of disturbance or discovery.

All next day he remained in hiding. When it began to grow dusk his host walked with him through the streets and through the gates, thus rendering his passage less likely to be observed—for this particular Ancient Soot was well known in the town.

" I will turn now. What go you to the coast for ? " asked his friend, when about to part.

" You would laugh at me if I told you," said Mamba.

" Then tell me not," returned his friend, with much delicacy of feeling, " for I would be sorry to laugh at my friend."

Thus they parted. Ancient Soot returned to the home of his forefathers, and Mamba walked smartly along the road that leads to the seaport of Tamatave.

He spent that night in the residence of a friend; the next in the hut of a government wood-cutter.

Felling timber, as might be supposed, was, and still is, an important branch of industry in Madagascar. Forests of varied extent abound in different parts of the country, and an immense belt of forest of two or three days' journey in width covers the interior of the island.   These forests yield abundance of timber of different colour and texture, and of various degrees of hardness and durability.

The wood-cutter, an old man, was busy splitting a large tree into planks by means of wedges when our traveller came up.   This wasteful method of obtaining planks is still practised by some natives of the South Sea Islands.   Formerly the Malagasy never thought of obtaining more than two planks out of a single tree, however large the tree might be.   They merely split the tree down the middle, and then chopped away the outside of each half until it was reduced to the thickness required.   The advent of the English missionaries, however, in the early part of this century, introduced light in regard to the things of time as well as those of eternity—among other things, the pit-saw, which has taught the natives to "gather up the fragments so that nothing be lost." Thick planks are still however sometimes procured in the old fashion.

The wood-cutter belonged to "The Seven Hundred"

which constituted the government corps. The members of this corps felled timber for the use of the sovereign. They also dragged it to the capital, for oxen were never employed as beasts of burden or trained to the yoke. The whole population around the capital was liable to be employed on this timber-hauling work—and indeed on any government work —without remuneration and for any length of time!

After the usual exhaustive questions and replies as to health, etc., the old man conducted his visitor to his hut and set food before him. He was a solitary old fellow, but imbued with that virtue of hospitality which is inculcated so much among the people.

Having replied to the wood-cutter's first inquiry that he was "going yonder," Mamba now saw fit to explain that "yonder" meant Tamatave.

"I want to see the great Missionary Ellis before he leaves the country."

The wood-cutter shook his head. "You are too late, I fear. He passed down to the coast some weeks ago. The Queen has ordered him to depart. She is mad against all the praying people."

"Are *you* one of the praying people?" asked Mamba, with direct simplicity.

"Yes, and I know that *you* are," answered the wood-cutter with a smile.

"How know you that?"

"Did I not see your lips move and your eyes look up when you approached me on arriving?"

"True, I prayed to Jesus," said Mamba, "that I might be made use of to help you, or you to help me."

"Then your prayer is doubly answered," returned the old man, "for we can each help the other. I can give you food and lodging. You can carry a message to Tamatave for me."

"That is well. I shall be glad to help you. What is your message?"

"It is a message to the missionary, Ellis, if you find him still there; but even if he is gone you will find a praying one who can help me. Long have I prayed to the Lord that he would send one of his people here to take my message. Some came who looked like praying people, but I was afraid to ask them, and perhaps they were afraid to speak; for, as you know, the Queen's spies are abroad everywhere now, and if they find one whom they suspect of praying to Jesus they seize him and drag him away to the ordeal of "tangena"—perhaps to torture and death. But now you have come, and my prayer is answered. ' He is faithful who has promised.' Look here."

The old man went to a corner of the hut, and returned with two soiled pieces of paper in his hand.

Sitting down, he spread them carefully on his knees. Mamba recognised them at once as being two leaves out of a Malagasy Bible. Soiled, worn,

and slightly torn they were, from long and frequent
use, but still readable.   On one of them was the
twenty-third Psalm, which the old wood-cutter began
to read with slow and intense interest.

"Is it not grand," he said, looking up at his young
guest with a flush of joy in his care-worn old face,
"to think that after this weary wood-cutting is over
we shall dwell in the house of the Lord for ever?
No more toiling and hauling and splitting; above
all, no more sin—nothing but praise and work for
Him.   And how hard I could work for Him!"

"Strange!" said Mamba, while the old man gazed
at the two soiled leaves as if lost in meditation,
"strange that you should show this to me.   I have
come—but tell me," he said, breaking off abruptly,
"what do you wish me to do?"

"This," said the old man, pointing to the leaves,
as though he had not heard the question, "is all
that I possess of the Word of God.   Ah! well do I
remember the time—many years past now—when I
had the whole Bible.   It was such a happy time
then—when good King Radama reigned, and the
missionaries had schools and churches and meetings
—when we prayed and sang to our heart's content,
and the Bible was printed, by the wonderful machines
brought by the white men, in our own language,
and we learned to read it.   I was young then, and
strong; but I don't think my heart was so warm as

it is now! Learning to read was hard—hard; but the Lord made me able, and when I got a Bible all to myself I thought there was nothing more to wish for. But the good Radama died, and Ranavalona sits upon his throne. You know she has burned many Bibles. Mine was found and burned, but she did not suspect me. I suppose I am too poor and worthless for her to care about! Perhaps we did not think enough of the happy times when we had them! A brother gave me these two leaves. They are all that I have left now."

Again the old man paused, and the younger forbore to interrupt his thoughts. Presently he looked up, and continued, "When the missionary Ellis was on his way to the coast I met him and asked for a Bible. He had not a spare one to give me. He was very sorry, but said if I could find any one going to Tamatave who would carry a Bible back to me, he would send one. Now you have come. Will you see the great missionary, or, if he is away, find one of the other men of God, and fetch me a Bible?"

There was a trembling earnestness in the old wood-cutter's voice which showed how eager he was about the answer. Mamba readily promised, and then, after singing and praying together, these like-minded men retired to rest.

Next morning Mamba pursued his way eastward with rapid step, for he was anxious—yet with a glad heart, for he was hopeful. Many things of interest were presented to his gaze, but though he observed them well he did not suffer them to turn him aside for a moment from his purpose—which was to reach Tamatave in the shortest possible time, so as to meet and converse with the missionary before he should quit the island.

Mamba was of an inquiring disposition. In ordinary circumstances he would have paused frequently to rest and meditate and pray. He would have turned aside to examine anything peculiar in his track, or even to watch the operations of a spider, or the gambols of a butterfly; but now he had "business" on hand, and set his face like a flint to transact it.

The distance from the capital to Tamatave was nearly two hundred miles. There were dangers in the way. As we have said, the Queen's spies were everywhere. Mamba's wounds and bruises were still sufficiently obvious to attract attention and rouse curiosity, if not suspicion.

At one part of the journey he came upon some criminals in long chains which extended from their necks to their ankles. They were doing work on the roads under a guard. He would fain have conversed with these men, but, fearing to be questioned, turned aside into the shelter of a plantation and passed stealthily by.

At another place he came to a ferry where, when he was about to enter the boat, two men stepped in before him whom he knew to be government officers and suspected to be spies. To have drawn suddenly back without apparent reason would have proclaimed a guilty conscience. To go forward was to lay himself open to question and suspicion, for he had prepared no tissue of falsehoods for the occasion. There was no time for thought, only for prayer. He committed his soul to God as he entered the boat, and then began to converse with the boatman in as easy and natural a tone of voice as he could assume. Having to face the boatman for this purpose enabled him to turn his back upon the government officers. Scarce knowing what he said in the perturbation of his spirit, his first question was rather absurd—

"Did you ever upset in crossing here?" he asked.

"Of course not!" replied the boatman, with a look of offended dignity.

"Ha! then," continued Mamba, who quickly recovered his equanimity, "then you don't know what it is to feel the teeth of a crocodile?"

"No, I don't, and hope I never shall. Did you?"

"Oh yes," returned Mamba, "I have felt them."

This was true; for it happened that when he was a little boy, his mother had taken him down to the side of a river where she had some washing to do, and while she was not looking the urchin waded in, and a crocodile made a snap at him. Fortunately it failed to catch him, but its sharp teeth grazed his thigh, and left a mark which he never afterwards lost.

"Where did that happen?" asked the boatman, when the other had briefly stated the fact—for the passage was too short to permit of a story being told.

"In the Betsilio country."

"That's a long way off."

"Yes, a long way. I left my old mother there. I'm going to Tamatave to buy her a present. Now, my friend," said Mamba, in a bantering tone, as the boat ran into the opposite bank, "take care never to upset your boat, because crocodile teeth are wonderfully sharp!"

Mamba had the satisfaction of hearing the two officers chuckle at his little joke, and the boatman growl indignantly, as he leaped ashore and sedately strode away with a sigh of relief and thankfulness for having made what he deemed a narrow escape.

The road to Tamatave was by no means lonely, for, being the highway from the seaport to the capital, there was constant traffic both of travellers and of merchandise. There were also great droves of cattle making their way to the coast—for a large part of the wealth of the chiefs and nobles of the land consists of cattle, which are exported to the islands of Bourbon and Mauritius, and disposed of to the shipping that come there for supplies.

At last Mamba reached Tamatave, footsore, worn, and weary, and went straight to the house of a friend—a native of wealth and importance in the town, and one whom he knew to be a Christian. From him he learned, to his great joy, that Mr. Ellis had not yet left the place, and that he hoped to be permitted still to remain there for some time.

It was dark when Mamba arrived, and rather late; but he was too anxious to transact his " business " to wait till morning. Having ascertained where the missionary lived, he went there direct, and was ushered into his sitting-room.

" You wish to converse with me," said Mr. Ellis, in a kind voice, and in the native tongue, as he placed a chair for his visitor—who, however, preferred to stand.

" Yes, I come from very far away—from the Betsilio country. My mother dwells there, and she is a praying one—a follower of Jesus. She loves the Word of God. I heard that you had brought the Bible to us from your own land—printed in our language, and so I have come to ask you for a Bible."

" Have you come all that long journey to procure the Word of God ? " asked the missionary, much interested.

" Yes—that is my business," replied Mamba.

Although Mr. Ellis liked the look of his visitor, and was strongly disposed to believe him, he had too much knowledge of the native character to place immediate confidence in him. Besides, the man being a stranger to him, and possibly one of the government spies, he feared to comply at once with his request, lest he should hasten his own banishment from the island. He replied, therefore, with caution.

"I cannot give you what you want to-night," he said, " but you may call on me again to-morrow, and I will speak with you."

This answer did not at all satisfy the eager heart of the poor fellow who had travelled so far and risked so much. His countenance showed the state of his feelings so strongly that the sympathetic missionary laid his hand kindly on his shoulder, bade him cheer up, and asked for his name as well as the name of some one in Tamatave who knew him.

" Now then, Mamba," he said, as they were about to part, " don't be cast down. Come here to see me to-morrow. Come early."

Comforted a little—more by the missionary's look and tone than by his words,—Mamba took his departure.

Meanwhile Mr. Ellis made inquiries, visited the friend to whom he had been referred, and found that not only was Mamba a good and true man, but that many of his family " feared the Lord greatly."

When, therefore, his anxious visitor returned very early the following morning, he was ready for him.

" I am assured that you are a Christian, Mamba," he said, " as well as many of your kindred."

" Yes, I love the Lord, and so do many of my kinsmen.   But my family is large and scattered."

" Have any of them got the Scriptures ? "

" They have seen and heard them," returned Mamba, " but all that we possess are a few pages of the words of David.   These belong to the whole family.   We send them from one to another, and each, after keeping them for a time, passes them on, until they have been read by all.   They are in my hands just now."

" Have you them with you?" asked the missionary.

Mamba did not reply at once.   He seemed unwilling to answer, but at last confessed that he had.

" Will you not show them to me ?   Surely you can trust me, brother ! "

Mamba at length made up his mind.   Thrusting his hand deep into his bosom, he drew a parcel from the folds of his lamba.   This he slowly and carefully opened.   One piece of cloth after another being unrolled, there appeared at length a few leaves of the Book of Psalms, which he cautiously handed to Mr. Ellis.

Though it was evident that the greatest care had been taken of that much-prized portion of Scripture, the soiled appearance of the leaves, worn edges, and other marks of frequent use—like the two leaves owned by the wood-cutter—showed how much they had been read.

Even Mamba's anxiety was allayed by the tender way in which the missionary handled his treasure, and the interest in it that he displayed.

"Now, my friend," said Mr. Ellis, still holding the tattered leaves, which Mamba seemed anxious to get back, "if you will give me these few words of David, I will give you *all* his words; and I will give you, besides, the words of Jesus, and of John, and Paul and Peter. See—here they are."

Saying which, he handed to his visitor a copy of the New Testament and Psalms, in Malagasy, bound together.

But Mamba did not leap at this gift as might have been expected. Either it seemed to him to be too good news to be true, or he was of a sceptical turn of mind. At all events he was not satisfied until he had sat down with the missionary and assured himself that every verse in his ragged treasure was contained in the presented volume, and a great deal more besides. Then he let the old treasure go, and joyfully accepted the new, which, he said, he was going to carry back to his mother who greatly longed for it.

Before retiring with it, however, he mentioned his friend the wood-cutter, whom Mr. Ellis remembered well, and gladly gave another Testament to be taken back to him. Then, uttering expressions of fervent gratitude, Mamba left the house.

In the course of that day the missionary inquired after his visitor, wishing to have further converse with him, but the Christians of Tamatave told him that Mamba had started off, almost immediately after quitting him, on his long return journey to Betsilio-land—doubtless "rejoicing as one that findeth great spoil."

Dust was not allowed to accumulate on the Bibles of Madagascar in those days!

CHAPTER XVIII.

UNEXPECTED DELIVERANCE AND SEVERAL SURPRISES.

At the time when Mamba started away on his expedition to Tamatave, Ravonino, as we have said, lay concealed in the forest, anxiously awaiting news from the town. At last the news came—the two white men and the negro had got involved in a row, and were in prison!

So said Laihova on entering the cave and seating himself, weary, worn, and dispirited, on a ledge of rock beside his friend, to whom he related all that had befallen.

"Give not way to despondency," said Ravonino, though he could not smooth the lines of anxiety from his own brow. "Does not the Lord reign? Let the earth rejoice! No evil can befall unless permitted, and then it will surely work for good. Let us now consider what is to be done. But first, we will pray."

In the gloom of the cavern the two men went down on their knees, and, in very brief but earnest sentences, made known their wants to their Creator.

"It is useless to remain here idle," said the guide, as they resumed their seat on the ledge.

"It is useless to go into the town," returned Laihova. "I am known now as one of those who aided Mamba to escape."

"But I am not known—at least not in my present guise," said Ravonino. "Have you seen Rafaravavy?"

"No; I tell you we had not been long in the town when this mischance befell."

"Did not Mamba tell you why he has undertaken so long a journey?"

"He did not, but I can guess," answered Laihova, with a slight smile. "The night before we left our friends in the cave in Betsilio-land I heard his mother urging him to accompany us to the capital and fetch her, if possible, a copy of the Word of God. She was joined in her persuasions by my sister Ramatoa, and you know he loves Ramatoa. I have no doubt that the two overcame his objections."

"Do you know why he objected?" asked Ravonino.

"He *said* that he was afraid to quit his mother and the others at a time when she might sorely need his protection, but other motives may have influenced him."

"If he *said* it he *meant* it," returned the guide, with some decision, "for Mamba is open and true of heart. No doubt he had other motives, but these were secondary. God grant him success and safe deliverance from the hands of his enemies !"

" Amen !" responded Laihova.

For some time the two friends sat there in silence, meditating as to what they should do in the circumstances, for each felt that action of some sort was absolutely necessary.

" My friend," said the guide at last, " it seems to me that the Lord requires me at this time to go with my life in my hand, and give it to Him if need be. I have led these Englishmen into danger. I must do my best to succour them. Rafaravavy also is in great danger of losing her life—for the Queen's fondness for her may not last through the opposition to her will which she is sure to meet with. At all risks I will enter the town and try to meet with Rafaravavy. But you, my friend, have no need to run so great a risk. The Englishmen have no claim upon you. My sister Ra-Ruth, as well as the other banished ones, need your arm to defend them, all the more that Mamba has left for a time. I counsel you to return to the Betsilio country and leave me. There is no fear. I am in the hands of God."

For a few moments Laihova was silent. Then he spoke, slowly. " No. I will not leave you. Are not our friends also in the hands of God ? For them, too, there is no fear. At present they are far from danger and in safe hiding, for even the outlaws—the robbers who infest the forests—understand something of their case; they have sympathy and will not molest them. Besides all that, Ravoninohitriniony, is there not the Blood-covenant between you and me? No, I will *not* leave you! Where you go I will go, and if you die I will not live!"

Seeing that his friend's mind was made up, the guide made no further effort to influence him, and both men prepared themselves to go to the city.

We return now to our friends Mark Breezy, John Hockins, and James Ginger, whom we left in the act of quitting their prison after being the means of obtaining some extension of mercy to an unfortunate sufferer whom they left behind them there.

The Interpreter led them up several steep streets, and finally brought them to a courtyard in which were several small houses. Into one of these he ushered them, having previously pointed out to them that the building occupied a prominent position not far from the great palace of the Queen.

"So—if you out goes—git losted—know how to finds you'self agin!"

"Das so,—" said Ebony. "You's a clibber man."

"Now you stop," continued the Interpreter, paying no attention to the remark, "for git some—some—vik—vik—vikles—eh?"

"Vikles!" repeated Mark, with a puzzled air.

"Yis—yis—vikles," repeated the Interpreter,

nodding his head, smiling, opening his mouth very wide, and pointing to it.

"P'r'aps he means victuals," suggested Hockins.

"Yis—yis—jus' so—vittles," cried the Interpreter, eagerly, "wait for vittles. Now—good-boy—by— by!" he added, with a broad grin at his blunder, as he left the room and shut the door.

The three friends stood in the middle of the room for a few seconds in silence, looked at each other, and smiled dubiously.

"Let's see if we really *are* free to go and come as we choose," said Mark, suddenly stepping to the door and trying it. Sure enough it was open. They passed out and went a short distance along the street, in which only a few natives were moving about. These, strange to say, instead of gazing at them in idle curiosity, seemed to regard them with some show of respect.

"Hold on, sir," said Hockins, coming to an abrupt halt, "you know that feller told us to wait for victuals, and I am uncommon disposed for them victuals; for, to say truth, the trifle of rice they gave us this mornin' was barely enough to satisfy an average rat. Better come back an' do as we're bid. Obedience, you know, is the first law of natur'."

"Das w'at I says too. Wait for de wittles."

"Agreed," said Mark, turning on his heel.

On reaching the house they found that two

slaves had already begun preparations for the hoped-for feast. In a few minutes they had spread on the mat floor several dishes containing rice, mingled with bits of chicken and other meats, the smell of which was exceedingly appetising. There was plain beef also, and fowls, and cooked vegetables, and fruits of various kinds, some of which were familiar to them, but others were quite new.

Slaves being present, our three travellers did not give full and free expression to their feelings; but it was evident from the way that Hockins smacked his lips and Ebony rolled his tongue about, not to mention his eyes, and Mark pursed his mouth, that they were smitten with pleased anticipation, while the eyes of all three indicated considerable surprise!

There were no knives or forks—only horn spoons for the rice; but as each man carried a large clasp-knife in his pocket, the loss was not felt.

In any other circumstances the singularity and unexpected nature of this good treatment would have stirred up the fun of Ebony and the latent humour of Hockins, but they could not shake off the depression caused by the memory of what they had seen in the prison—the heavy iron collars and the cruel binding chains. They tried to put the best face possible on it, but after a few faint sallies relapsed into silence. This, however, did not prevent their eating a sufficiently hearty meal.

R

"There's no sayin' when we may git the chance of another," was Hockins's apologetic remark as he helped himself to another fowl.

"It is very mysterious that we should receive such treatment," said Mark. "I can only account for it by supposing that our friend Ravèlo is an officer of some power. If so, it was doubly fortunate that we had the opportunity of doing him a good turn."

"Now, you leave dem two drumsticks for me, 'Ockins," said Ebony, wiping his mouth with the back of his hand. "You'll do yourself a injury if you heat de whole ob 'im."

"Well, I must confess to bein' surprised summat," said the seaman, referring to Mark's observation, not to Ebony's.

They were destined to receive some additional surprises before that day was over. The meal which they had been discussing was barely finished when their friend the Interpreter again entered and bade them follow him.

"Queen Ranavalona wish sees you," he said.

"What! all on us?" exclaimed Hockins, with elevated eyebrows.

"Yis—all."

"Oh! nonsense," he cried, turning to Mark. "It must be you, doctor, she wants to see. What can she want with a or'nary seaman like me?"

"Or a *extraor*'nary nigger like me?" said Ebony, with a look of extreme contempt.

"You kin stop in house if you choose," remarked the Interpreter, with a quiet grin, "but you heads be splitted if you do."

"Then I think I'll go," said Hockins, quietly.

"Me too," remarked the negro.

Accordingly they all went—with a slight qualm, however, for they felt slightly doubtful whether, under existing circumstances, they might not after all be going to execution.

The royal palaces, to which they were led, occupy a very conspicuous and commanding position on the summit of the hill, and stand at an elevation of more than 500 feet above the surrounding plains. They are conspicuously larger than any of the other houses in the city, are grouped together in a large courtyard, and number about a dozen houses—large and small. The chief palace, named Manjàka-Miàdana, is about 100 feet long by 80 broad, and 120 high to the apex of its lofty roof. A wide verandah, in three stories, runs all round it. All is painted white except the balustrade. The building next in size to this is the Silver House. On the eastern side of the courtyard are the palace gardens, and around it stand a number of houses which are the residences of the chief officers of the army, the Secretaries of State, and other members of the Government.

On reaching the palace gate two young officers approached to receive the visitors. They were dressed in splendid European regimentals, much bedecked with gold-lace, tight-fitting trousers, Wellington boots, sash, sword, and cocked hat, all complete! One of these, to their surprise, spoke English remarkably well.

"I learned it from the missionaries when I was leetle boy," he explained to Mark, as he conducted the visitors through the archway and across the spacious courtyard into the palace. In the second story of the verandah the Queen was seen seated beneath that emblem of royalty the scarlet umbrella, with her Court around her. Before entering the court the visitors had removed their hats. They were now directed to make a profound reverence as they passed, and proceeded along the side of the building to the further end.

A line of native troops was drawn up across the court, but these wore no uniform, only the lamba wound round their waists, and white cross-belts on their naked bodies. They were armed with the old flint-lock muskets and bayonets of the period.

Their conductor, who was an Under-Secretary of State, led them by a dark narrow stair to the balcony where the Queen sat, and in a few moments they found themselves in the presence of the cruel Ranavalona, of whom they had heard so much.

She did not look cruel at that time, however. She was dressed in a rich satin gown, over which she wore the royal scarlet lamba, and jewels of various kinds ornamented her person. She was seated in a chair raised two or three steps above the floor, with her ladies on one side and her gentlemen on the other. The former, among whom were some really good-looking brunettes, had all adopted the English fashion of dress, with parts of native costume retained. Some wore head-dresses of gorgeous colouring, composed of ribbons, flowers, and feathers in great profusion, but as no head-dress, however strongly marked by barbaric splendour, can excel the amazing feminine crests in present use among the civilised, we refrain from attempting description ! Most of the men also wore European costume, or portions thereof, some being clad in suits of black broadcloth.

The amount of ceremony displayed on all hands at Court seemed to have infected our three adventurers, for, when led before the Queen, they approached with several profound bows, to which Hockins added the additional grace of a pull at his forelock. In this he was imitated by Ebony.

For some moments Ranavalona eyed her visitors—perhaps we should say her captives—sternly enough, but there was also a slight touch of softness in her expression, from which Mark drew much comfort.

The courtiers gazed at them with evident interest, but in profound silence, for as yet the Queen had given no indication as to whether the new-comers were to be treated as friends or spies, and the recent banishment of the missionaries, and harsh treatment of Europeans by the Queen, left their minds in some doubt on the point.

Turning to the Secretary who had introduced the party, Ranavalona spoke to him a few words. When she had finished, the Secretary turned to Mark, whom he at once recognised as the chief and spokesman of the trio.

" Queen Ranavalona bid me ask where you comes from," he said.

To which Mark replied that they came from England, that they were all English subjects, though one was an African by descent.

" I have heard," continued the Queen, through her interpreter, " that you have been shipwrecked, that one of your number is a Maker of Medicine, and that you helped one of my people—even saved his life—soon after your arrival in my country. Is that so ? "

Mark explained that they had not been shipwrecked, but had been left on shore, and obliged to fly from the natives of the coast ; that he was indeed a maker of medicine, though his training had not been quite completed when he left England, and that he had rendered a trifling service to an unfortunate man who had slipped in climbing a cliff, but he could hardly be said to have saved the man's life.

While he was speaking, Mark observed that his friend Ravèlo stood close to the Queen's chair, in front of a group of officers, from which circumstance he concluded that he must be a man of some note, and that it was he who had procured the deliverance of himself and his friends from prison.

"Tell the young Maker of Medicine," said the Queen, in a loud voice, so that all the Court might hear, "that Europeans have behaved very ill here of late, so ill that they had to be banished from my country ; for I, Ranavalona, permit no one, whether his face be black, brown, or white, to meddle with my government. They fancied, I suppose, that because I am a woman I am weak and ignorant, and unable to rule ! They have now found their mistake, and Christians shall not again be permitted to dwell in my country. But I am Ranavalona, and I will do what I please. If I choose to make an exception I will do it. If any one thinks to oppose my will he shall die. The man whose life was saved by this young Maker of Medicine is my son Rakota—my beloved son. Is it not so ? "

The Queen looked round as she spoke, and the man whom we have hitherto styled Ravèlo bent his head and replied, " It is so," whereupon there were murmurs of surprise and approval among the courtiers.

" Now," continued the Queen, " as I am grateful, and as I want a physician at Court just now, I appoint this young Maker of Medicine to that post, and I appoint his black companion to be his servant. Do you all hear that ? "

All the courtiers made murmurs of assent.

" Tell them all that, Secretary," said the Queen.

Mark Breezy and his friends had considerable difficulty in concealing their astonishment when " all that " was explained to them, but they had the presence of mind to acknowledge the information with a profound obeisance. At the same time Mark explained, with much modesty, that he was not entitled to aspire to or to accept so high and honourable a position, as he had not yet obtained the standing which entitled him to practise in his own country.

" Tell him," said the Queen, sternly, " that I, Ranavalona, have nothing to do with the customs of England, and have no regard for them. If he does not accept what I offer, instant banishment— perhaps worse—will be his portion ! "

" Oh ! massa, accep' him *at once !* " murmured Ebony in an undertone, and in much anxiety.

Mark took his advice, and agreed to become

Physician to the Court of the Queen of Madagascar, without stipulating either as to salary or privileges!

"I am also told," said the Queen, with a smile of condescension to her physician, "that your English companion is full of music, and performs on a wonderful little instrument. I have a good band, which was trained by your countrymen, but they have no such little instrument. Let the Man of the Sea perform."

On this being translated Mark looked at the Man of the Sea, and could with difficulty restrain a burst of laughter at the expression of his countenance.

"What!" exclaimed Hockins, "me play my whistle afore this here Court? Unpossible!"

"You'll have to try," said Mark, "unless you wish for instant banishment—or something worse!"

"Oh! 'Ockins, blaze away *at once!*" murmured Ebony, with renewed anxiety, for the "something worse" was to him suggestive of imprisonment, torture, and death!

Thus pressed, the seaman put his hand into the inner pocket of his jacket and drew forth his cherished flageolet. In a few minutes the Queen and all her courtiers were enthralled by the music. It was not only the novelty and bird-like sweetness of the instrument itself that charmed, but also the fine taste and wonderful touch of the sailor. The warbling

notes seemed to trill, rise and fall, and float about on
the atmosphere, as it were, like fairy music, filling
the air with melody and the soul with delight.

"Good! let the Man of the Sea be also cared for.
Give them quarters in the palace, and see that they
all attend upon us in the garden to-morrow."

So saying, the Queen arose, swept into the palace,
and left her courtiers to follow.

Immediately Prince Rakota came forward and
shook hands with Mark.

"So then, your Highness," said the latter, "we are
indebted to you for all this kindness."

"It is only one small ting," returned the Prince
in broken English. "Am I not due to you my
life? Come, I go show you your house."

On the way, and after entering the house which
was appropriated to their use, Mark learned from
the Prince that their approach to the capital had
been discovered and announced by spies long before
their arrival; that it was they who had discovered
and revealed to the Queen Hockins's wonderful
powers with the "little tube." Also that it was
well known who had guided them through the
country, and that Ravoninohitriniony was being
diligently sought for in his hiding-places.

This last piece of information filled the three
friends with deep concern and anxiety.

"He has been so *very* kind to us," said Mark,

"and I know is one of the most generously disposed and law-respecting subjects of her Majesty."

"That not help for him if he tumbles into the hands of my mother," said the Prince, sadly. "He is a Christian. He has run to the forest, and has made others to fly."

"But you have much power with the Queen," pleaded Mark, "could you not induce her to pardon him?"

"Yes—if he will give up Christianity—if not do that—no!"

"That he will never do," said Mark, firmly. "I know him well. He will rather die than deny Christ."

"He is likely to die then," returned Rakota, "for my mother is fixed to root up the religion of Jesus from the land."

"But surely *you* don't agree with her," broke in Hockins at this point.

"No, I not agree," said the Prince. "But I can not command the Queen. Some time it very hard to move her even a leetle. My only power with her is love."

"Das de greatest power in de wurld!" chimed in Ebony.

"It is," returned the Prince, "and you be very sure I use the power much as I can for save your friend."

CHAPTER XIX.

THE garden party is by no means a novelty of the present day. In the early part of this century — if not much earlier—Malagasy sovereigns seem to have been wont to treat their Court and friends to this species of entertainment.

The order which the Queen had given that her European visitors should attend upon her in the garden, was neither more nor less than an invitation to a garden party, or pic-nic, to be held the following day at one of her surburban retreats named Anosy, about half-a-mile from the city. Accordingly, early in the morning—for the Malagasy are early risers—their friend the Interpreter came to conduct them to the spot, with a gift of a striped lamba for each of the white men.

"Why she not send one for *me?*" demanded Ebony, pouting—and Ebony's pout was something to take note of!

"'Cause you're black and don't need no clothing,"

said Hockins, awkwardly attempting to put the lamba on his broad shoulders.

"Humph! if she knowed what splendid lobscouse an' plum duff I kin make," returned the negro, "Ranny Valōny would hab sent me a silk lamba an' made me her chief cook. Hows'ever, dere's a good time comin'. I s'pose I aint to go to the party?"

"Yis—you muss go. All of you got to go. Kill —deaded—if you don't go."

"I'm your man, den, for I don't want to be deaded yet a while; moreover, I want to see de fun," returned the negro.

Meanwhile the Interpreter showed them how to put on the lamba—with one end of it thrown over the left shoulder, like the Spaniard's cloak, —and then conducted them to the palace, where they found three palanquins—or chairs supported by two staves—awaiting them. Getting into them they set off, preceded by the Interpreter in a similar conveyance. Ebony and his bearers brought up the rear.

The Queen and her Court had already started some time. Our party soon reached the scene of festivities, at the south-east of the city. It was a charming spot, having large gardens laid out in the European style, with goodly trees overshadowing the pleasure-house of Anosy, and an extensive lake.

The house was on an island in the lake, and was reached by a narrow causeway.

At the entrance to the place two enormous letters, " R. R.," formed in grass borders that surrounded flower-beds, indicated that Radama Rex, the first king of that name, had originated those gardens. And they did him credit; for he had made great exertions to accumulate there specimens of the most useful and remarkable trees and plants in the country—especially those that were of service in *materia medica.* Some immense camphor-wood trees were among the most conspicuous, and there were several specimens of a graceful fan-palm, as well as clumps of the long-leaved ròfia. The lake was covered in part with a profusion of purple water-lilies, and was well stocked with gold-fish. In the garden and on the upper part of the grounds were luxuriant vines, besides figs, mangoes, pine-apples, and coffee-plants.

Here, to the strains of an excellent band, hundreds of people, in white and striped lambas, and various gay costumes, were walking about enjoying themselves, conversing with animation, or consuming rice, chickens, and beef, on mats beneath the mango and fig-trees. Elsewhere the more youthful and lively among them engaged in various games, such as racing, jumping, etc.

" Come," said their friend of the previous day—

the Secretary—to Mark and his comrades, breaking in on their contemplation of the animated scene, " the Queen wishes to see you."

Her Majesty, who was dressed in a long robe of muslin, embroidered with gold, sat near the door of the garden-house, surrounded by her ladies, who all wore the simple but graceful native dress.   A guard of soldiers stood near at hand.

The Queen merely wished to ask a few ceremonial questions of her visitors.   While she was engaged with Hockins and the Secretary, Mark ventured to glance at the ladies of the Court, among whom he observed one who made a deep impression on him. She wore, if possible, a simpler dress than any of her companions, and no ornaments whatever.   Her features were well formed, and her rather pensive countenance was very beautiful.   When they were retiring from the presence of the Queen, Mark could not resist the temptation to ask the Secretary who she was.

" That," said he, " is our self-willed little Christian, Rafaravavy."

" She does not look very self-willed," returned Mark.

" True, and she is not really so—only in the matter of religion.   I fear we shall lose her ere long, for she minds not the Queen, and no one who defies Ranavalona lives long.   But come, let us sit down under this mango tree and eat. You must be hungry."

He led them as he spoke to a sequestered spot near a coppice which partially guarded them from public gaze on three sides, and on the fourth side afforded them a charming view of the gardens, the gay assemblage, and the country beyond.

At first both Hockins and Ebony hesitated to sit down to breakfast with so distinguished a person as an Under-Secretary of State.

" We aint used, you see, doctor," observed the seaman in a low tone, " to feed wi' the quality."

" Das so, massa," chimed in Ebony in the same tone ; " wittles nebber taste so pleasant in de cabin as in de fo'c's'l."

" Don't object to *anything*," replied Mark, quickly, "just do as I do."

" Hall right, massa. Neck or nuffin—I'm your man !"

As for the seaman, he obeyed without reply, and in a few minutes they were busy with the Secretary over drumsticks and rice.

The free-and-easy sociability of that individual would have surprised them less if they had known that he had been specially commissioned by the Queen to look well after them, and gather all the information they might possess about the fugitive Christians who were hiding in the forests.

Fortunately our young student was quick-witted. He soon perceived the drift of the Secretary's talk, and, without appearing to evade his questions, gave him such replies as conveyed to him no information whatever of the kind he desired.   At the same time, he took occasion, when the Secretary's attention was attracted by something that was going on, to lay his finger on his lips and bestow a look of solemn warning on his comrades, the effect of which on their intelligent minds was to make the negro intensely stupid and the seaman miraculously ignorant!

Now, while our friends are thus pleasantly engaged, we will return to Rafaravavy, whom we left standing among the Queen's ladies.

Of all the ladies there that little brunette was not only the best-looking, the sweetest, the most innocent, but also, strange to say, the funniest; by which we do not mean to say that she tried to be funny—far from it, but that she had the keenest perception of the ludicrous, and as her perceptions were quick, and little jokes usually struck her, in vulgar parlance, "all of a heap," her little explosions of laughter were instantaneous and violently short-lived.   Yet her natural temperament was grave and earnest, and her habitual expression, as we have said, pensive.

Indeed it would have been strange had it been otherwise, considering the times in which she lived, the many friends whom she had seen sacrificed by the violence of her royal mistress, and the terrible uncertainty that hung over her own fate.

After a time the Queen dismissed some of her attendants to ramble about the grounds,—among them Rafaravavy, who sauntered down one of the side-walks by herself.

She had not gone far when, on reaching a turn of the road where a small thicket of shrubs concealed her from the more public part of the garden, she heard her own name pronounced.

Stopping abruptly, she listened with intense anxiety expressed on her countenance.

"Rafaravavy!" repeated the voice again, "fear not!" Next moment the bushes were turned aside, a man stepped on the path, and Ravonino stood before her! He seized her in his arms, and printed a fervent kiss upon her lips.

"Oh! Samuel," she said, using her lover's Christian name, which she naturally preferred, and speaking, of course, in her native tongue, "why did you come here? You know that it is death if you are caught."

"I would risk more than death, if that were possible, to see you, Rafaravavy. But I come to ask you to fly with me. Our dear Lord's counsel is that when we are persecuted we should flee to a place of safety."

"Impossible!" said the girl, in a tone of decision that made her lover's heart sink. "Besides, I am not persecuted. The Queen is fond of me, and bears much."

"Fond of you she may well be, my loved one, she cannot help that; but she is fonder of herself, and the moment you go beyond a certain point she will order you out to execution. Has she not done the same sort of thing before? She is capable of doing it again. She will *surely* do it again. Come, dearest! let us fly now—this moment. I have a lamba here which will conceal most of your dress. Arrangements are made with some of our friends in the Lord to aid us. Bearers are ready. I will guide you to the caverns in the forest where my sister Ra-Ruth is longing to receive you, where many of your old friends are dwelling in security, where we worship God, and pray to Jesus, and sing the sweet old hymns in peace. Come, dear one! will you not come?"

It was evident that the intense earnestness of the lover was exerting powerful influence over the affectionate maiden, for she began to waver.

"Oh! do not persuade me thus!" she said. "I know not what God would have me do. But the Queen has been *very* kind to me in spite of my religion, and sometimes I have thought that she listens to my pleading. Perhaps God may use me as the means of bringing her to Jesus. Think what that would be—not only to her own soul but to the multitudes who are now suffering in—"

At that moment footsteps were heard on the gravel walk. They were evidently approaching the spot where the lovers stood. Before Ravonino could make up his mind to drag her into the thicket by main force, Rafaravavy had disengaged herself and bounded away. At the same moment Ravonino glided into the shrubbery and disappeared.

A few seconds later and Mark Breezy stood on the spot they had quitted. He was alone.

"Strange!" he muttered to himself, "I am almost certain that she took this path, and I fancy that the man's voice sounded like that of Ravonino. Nothing more natural than that he should ferret her out. Yet it seems to have been imagination."

"It was not imagination," said a rather stern voice at Mark's elbow. He turned quickly.

"I was sure of it!" he exclaimed.

"If you were so sure of it," said the guide, with a touch of bitterness, "why did you interrupt us and scare the maiden away?"

"You do me wrong in your thoughts," replied the student, flushing. "One of the Queen's secretaries is even at this moment coming along this track in company with Hockins and Ebony. While seated at breakfast I saw Rafaravavy walk in this direction, and somehow I took it into my head that you would surely meet her here—I know not why I thought so, unless it be that in like circumstances I myself would have acted the same part—so I hastened on in advance to warn you. Hush! do you not hear their steps?"

"Forgive me," said Ravonino, extending his hand, and grasping that of his friend. Then, speaking low and hurriedly, "You are in favour at Court. Will you befriend her?"

"I will. You may depend on me!"

There was no time for more. Already it was almost too late, for the guide had barely disappeared in the thicket when his comrades and the Secretary appeared.

"Hallo! doctor," exclaimed Hockins, "was ye arter a pretty girl that you bolted so, all of a sudden?"

"Yes, I was," answered Mark promptly. "I saw one of the Queen's ladies come in this direction and ran after her! I suppose there is no harm in that, Mr. Secretary? You don't forbid men to look at your women, do you, like the Arabs?"

"Certainly not," replied the Secretary, with a slight smile and a ceremonial bow.

"Come, then, let us follow the track, we may yet meet her."

So saying, Mark led the way along the path where

Rafaravavy had vanished, not for the purpose of overtaking her, but in order to give his friend time and opportunity to get out of the thicket un-perceived.

On the evening of that same day, after the garden festivities were over, Queen Ranavalona sat in her palace with a frown on her brow, for, despite her determination and frequent commands, the Christians in the town still persisted in holding secret meet-ings for worship. Those who knew her moods saw plainly that she was fanning the smouldering fires of anger, and that it needed but a small matter to cause them to burst out into a devouring flame.

While she was in this critical frame of mind an influential courtier appeared before her. He seemed to be greatly excited.

"Madam," he said, "I request that a bright and sharp spear may be brought to me!"

Somewhat surprised at the nature of the request, the Queen asked to know the reason.

"Madam," continued the courtier, "I cannot but see with grief the dishonour that is done, not only to our idols but to the memory of your own pre-decessors, by the doctrines of these foreigners. Our ancient customs are being destroyed and the new faith is spreading on every hand. All this is but preparatory to the invasion of Madagascar by Europeans; and, as I would rather die than see my

Queen and country so disgraced, I ask for a spear to pierce my heart before the evil day arrives."

This speech had a powerful effect on the Queen. She began to regard Christianity as not merely a sacrilege, but a political offence; for were not her people learning to despise the idols of their forefathers and to cease praying to the royal ancestors by whom the kingdom had been established, and under whom the country had become great and powerful? Might they not eventually despise herself and learn to treat their living sovereign with contempt?

For some time Ranavalona remained silent, leaning her forehead on her hand. Suddenly she looked . up with a flushed countenance.

"It is true—all true," she said. "When I was carried along in procession to-day did I not hear these Christians singing one of their hated hymns? They will not cease till some of them lose their heads. Have you got with you the formal accusation that was made before my chief judge yesterday?"

"No, madam, I have not."

"Go. Fetch it and read it to me."

The courtier bowed, left the apartment, and speedily returned with a paper containing the accusations referred to. Unfolding it, he read as follows:—

"1st. The Christians are accused of despising the

idols.   2d. They are always praying.   3d. They
will not swear, but merely affirm.   4th. Their women
are chaste.   5th. They are of one mind with regard
to their religion.   6th. They observe the Sabbath
as a sacred day."

Strange to say, this catalogue of so-called accusations deeply affected the queen with grief and rage.

"I swear," she said, with flashing eyes and
clenched hands, "that I will root out this religion
of the Europeans if it should cost the life of every
Christian in the land! Go. Leave me!"

For a fortnight subsequent to this the palace and
Court appeared as if in mourning for some public
calamity. No band played; no amusements were
allowed, and a dread of impending evil seemed to
weigh upon the spirits of all classes. During this
time, also, measures were taken to effect the final
destruction, as far as possible, of all that had been
done in the country by the teaching of the missionaries and their converts.

At last the storm burst. A Kabàry, or immense
general assembly of the nation, was called by
proclamation at the capital. The people were only
too well aware of what this signified to doubt that
the Queen was thoroughly in earnest and in one of
her worst moods. With trembling hearts they
hastened to obey the summons.

CHAPTER XX.

A GREAT KABÀRY IS HELD, FOLLOWED BY DREADFUL MARTYRDOMS.

No rank or age was exempt from attendance at the great assembly. Soldiers were sent about the city and suburbs to drive the people towards the place of assembly near the palace, and the living stream continued to pour onwards until many thousand souls were gathered together at Imàhamàsina.

Here a body of troops fifteen thousand strong was posted, and in the earlier part of the day the cannon along the heights of the city thundered out a salute to inspire the people with awe and respect for the royal authority. The highest civil and military officers were there in their varied and gay trappings, but Ranavalona herself did not appear in person. Her message was conveyed to the people by one of the chief officers of state. It was interspersed here and there with the various titles of the Queen, and was to the following effect :—

"I announce to you, oh ye people! I am not a sovereign that deceives. I therefore tell to you what I purpose to do, and how I shall govern you.

Who, then, is that man who would change the customs of our ancestors and the twelve sovereigns in this country? To whom has the kingdom been left by inheritance, by Impòin, Imérina, and Radama, except to me? If any, then, would change the customs of our ancestors, I abhor that, saith Rabòdon-Andrian-Impòin-Imérina."

After a good deal more to much the same effect, the message went on to say:—

" As to baptisms, societies, places of worship distinct from schools, and the observance of the Sabbath, how many rulers are there in the land? Is it not I alone that rule? These things are not to be done; they are unlawful in my country, saith Ranavàlo-manjàka, for they are not the customs of our ancestors; and I do not change their customs, excepting as to things alone that improve my country. And then, in your worship, you say 'Believe!' 'Follow the Christian customs!' and thus you change the customs of the ancestors, for you do not invoke all that is sacred in heaven and earth, and all that is sacred in the twelve sovereigns and the idols. And is not this changing the customs of the ancestors? I detest that; and I tell you plainly that such things shall not be done in my country, saith Ranavàlo-manjàka.

" Now I decree that all Bibles and books of the new religion shall be delivered up to be destroyed, that all who are guilty shall come in classes, according to the nature of their offences, and accuse themselves of having been baptized, of being members of the church, of having taught slaves to read—all shall come to the officers and confess; but those who conceal their offence and are accused by others shall be subjected to the ordeal of the tangena, and those who resist my commands shall die, saith Ranavàlo-manjàka."

This message was no idle threat. The people were well aware of that, and the city was filled with weeping and consternation.

It was while things were in this state that Mamba arrived at Antananarivo with his precious New Testament and Psalms in the folds of his lamba. Although well aware of what had taken place, he recklessly visited his friends in the city. From them he learned more particulars, and saw, when too late, that it would be impossible for him now to pass out of the gates with the Testament on his person, as the guards had been cautioned to search every one whom they had the slightest reason to suspect.

Hearing of the sudden exaltation of his English friends, he formed the wise resolution to place his treasure in their hands.

Boldness is often successful where timidity would fail. Without hesitation, or even consultation with his friends, Mamba went straight to the palace and demanded permission to visit the Maker of Medicine. He was allowed to pass and conducted by an official to the quarters of Mark Breezy, who was seated with Hockins and Ebony at the time.

Great was their surprise at seeing their friend.

"Why, Mamba! I thought you had gone to Tamatave?" said Mark, shaking hands heartily with him.

"Yis—yis—I goed," said Mamba, and then endeavoured to tell something of his doings in English; but his knowledge of that language was so very imperfect that they could make nothing of it. They understood him, however, when he cautiously and lovingly drew the Testament from its hiding-place and gave it into Mark's hands.

"What am I to do with it, my poor friend?" said Mark. "I know that you have no chance of retaining it, after the decree that has just been passed."

"Keep 'im—keep—for *me*," said Mamba, anxiously.

"I will do so, if I can, but it may not be possible," answered Mark.

"Yis, keep—safe. Got 'im for me mudder."

"You're a brick," cried Ebony, enthusiastically grasping the man's hand, for he had a great love for his own mother, and experienced a gush of sympathy.

At that moment there was a loud knocking at

the door, and Mark had barely time to slip the Testament into his coat pocket when Hater-of-lies entered with his silver spear and attendants. Seizing hold of poor Mamba, without uttering a word they led him away.

Hockins instantly followed, and Ebony was about to do the same when Mark laid his hand on his shoulder and checked him.

" What would you do, Ebony ? "

" Look arter 'Ockins, massa."

" Hockins is well able to look after himself. No doubt he has gone to see where they take Mamba to. One pair of eyes is enough for that. Your company would only trouble him."

A few minutes later the seaman returned with the information that the unfortunate man had been cast into the prison from which they had been so recently released.

At this time the Christians in the island possessed numerous entire copies of the Scriptures, besides a large number of Testaments and Psalms, and books of a religious character, which, having been secreted, had escaped the destruction of previous persecutions. Some of these were now given up and destroyed. Many of the more timid among the natives came forward, as commanded, and accused themselves, thus escaping punishment; but there were others who would neither give up their Bibles nor accuse themselves. Some of these were accused by their slaves, others by their so-called friends and kindred—in some cases falsely.

Next day the Prime Minister came to the Queen and reported that one lady, named Rasalama, who had not accused herself, had been accused by some of her slaves of attending religious meetings.

" Is it possible," exclaimed the Queen, " that there is one so daring as to defy me ?   Go, let her be put to death at once ! "

The intercession of friends of the accused produced no effect on the Queen, and even the pleading of Prince Rakota failed, in this instance, to do more than delay the execution for a few days.

Meanwhile Rasalama was cast into prison and loaded with chains.

" Is it not strange," she said to her jailors, " that I should be put in chains, and some of my friends should be sent to perpetual slavery and some killed, though we have done no evil ?   We have neither excited rebellion, nor stolen the property of any, nor spoken ill of any—yet we are treated thus, and our property is confiscated.   It will be wise if the persecutors think what they do, lest they bring on themselves the wrath of God.   But I do not fear. When Hater-of-lies came to my house I rejoiced that I was counted worthy to suffer affliction for believing in Jesus."

When this speech was reported to the judges, Rasalama was ordered to be put into heavier irons and severely beaten. This cruel order was carried out; and after her tender limbs had been additionally weighted, her delicate skin was lacerated with terrible stripes. Yet her fortitude never forsook her. Nay more—through the grace bestowed on her she actually sang hymns in the midst of her torment! Sometimes, indeed, her physical strength failed for a brief space. At other times the song of triumph blended with a wail of agony, but she always recovered to renew the hymn of praise.

Her tormentors were confounded. This was something quite beyond their understanding, and their only solution of the mystery was that she must be under the influence of some powerful charm. Others there were, however, who listened to her triumphant songs, and beheld her calm steadfast countenance with widely different thoughts and feelings.

But the sufferings of this poor creature had not yet terminated. The rage of her persecutors was not yet appeased. Next day the ordinary chains she wore were exchanged for others, consisting of rings and bars fastened around her wrists, knees, ankles, and neck, and these, when drawn together, forced her whole body into a position that caused intense agony—something like that which we have described as having been seen by Mark and his comrades in the same prison-house. In this posture it was impossible to use the voice in song, but, doubtless, she was not even then prevented from making melody in her heart to the Lord, for whose name she suffered so much. All night long was this terrific trial endured, but with the dawn of day came relief, for then the chains were relaxed; and so great was the change that poor Rasalama looked forward to the fate which she knew awaited her with feelings of joy.

That fate was not long delayed. Soon they led her out of the prison, and took the road which conducted towards the southern extremity of the hill on which the city stood, where was the tremendous precipice down which many a criminal and many a Christian martyr had already in Ranavalona's evil reign been hurled out of Time into Eternity. Yet this was not the gate through which Rasalama was to pass into Paradise.[1]

As she walked along, the poor martyr began again to sing a favourite hymn. When passing the place of worship, at that time closed, she exclaimed, "There have I heard the words of the Saviour." Hundreds of people accompanied her. Some even

[1] Rasalama was in truth the first martyr of Madagascar. She was slain in the year 1837. We have only transposed the date. Her story is given, without variation worthy of mention, from authentic records.

ventured to whisper words of comfort to her as she went along, although by doing so they imperilled their own lives, and one young man, utterly regardless of consequences, walked boldly by her side, speaking to her of the Saviour, till the place of execution was reached.

To this spot Mark Breezy and his companions in exile had hastened, for the Secretary had told them that some of the Christians were about to be executed, and a fearful suspicion that their friend Mamba might be among the number impelled them to hasten to the spot with some half-defined intention of interfering in his behalf. For they had gradually, and imperceptibly to themselves, acquired a great liking for the young native, whose earnest, straightforward, yet playful spirit, together with his great kindness to his mother, had deeply impressed them during the brief time they had sojourned together in the forest.

"Will we fight for 'im, massa?" asked Ebony, with anxious looks, as they ran to the place of execution, which was not far off.

"That would be useless," answered Mark. "If we were thirty Samsons instead of three ordinary men, we could not overcome the Queen's army."

"I've half a mind to try," said Hockins, with something unusually fierce in his expression.

"Many a man has run a-muck before now. I've got to die once at any rate!"

"And what good would that do to Mamba?" asked Mark. "No, I will try another plan. I have fortunately done service to the Queen in saving the life of her son. If Mamba is to be martyred, I will throw my arms round him and ask the Queen in return to spare the life of my friend."

They had by that time mingled with the dense crowd that stood on the brow of the precipice of Ambohipotsy to witness the execution. Pushing to the front with breathless anxiety, they were just in time to see Rasalama led forward by two men armed with spears. In front of them was a shallow ditch, and a little further on the brow of the precipice, from which was seen a magnificent prospect of the surrounding country. But no prospect, however sublime, could have attracted the eyes of the three friends just then, for in front of them stood two crosses supporting the bodies of two Christians who had been crucified thereon the day before. Even these, however, lost their horrible power of fascination, when they observed the cheerful holy expression of Rasalama's countenance as she was led to the edge of the ditch which was to be her grave. The bottom of that grave was already strewn with the bloody remains and the bleaching bones of other martyrs who had preceded her.

The crowd, who had followed the procession with imprecations against the Christians, now ceased to shout.

"Will you allow me a short time to pray?" asked Rasalama of the executioners.

Her request being granted, she kneeled on the rocky ground, clasped her hands, and raised to Heaven a look of calm trustfulness, as she held communion for the last time on earth with her Redeemer.

"Where is the God she prays to that he does not save her now?" whispered some. Others held their peace, but laid these things to heart.

While the poor creature was thus engaged, the two executioners, without warning, thrust their spears deep into her body. It was the custom of these men to plunge the spears into the loins of their victims on each side of the back-bone in such a position that they did not produce immediate death, but allowed the martyrs to tumble into the ditch and writhe there in agony for some time with the spears still sticking in them. Happily, in the case of Rasalama, the thrusts were—either intentionally or accidentally —more effective than usual. After a very brief struggle, her happy soul was set free to be "for ever with the Lord."

In that ditch her poor mangled body was left to

be devoured by the wild dogs that frequent all places in Madagascar where criminals suffer.[1]

"Oh, God!" exclaimed Mark, unable to repress a groan. "Let us quit this accursed spot."

"Stay, sir, stay," whispered the sailor at his elbow, "you forget Mamba. More are comin'."

More martyrs were indeed coming, as the singing of hymns proved.

Close on the heels of Rasalama, a band of nine other Christians were carried to the place of execution, each with his feet and hands tied together and slung on a pole, the ends of which were borne by two men. Straw had been stuffed into their mouths to prevent praying or singing, but several of them, managing to get rid of the straw, burst into the triumphal songs which had attracted the attention of our seaman.

Arrived at the ditch, the victims were asked if they would give up praying to Jesus. In every case the answer was a decided "No!" They were then thrust into the ditch, forced down on their knees, and made to bend forward. While this was being done, the shuddering friends of Mamba perceived that he was not among the martyrs. One by one each unfortunate was stabbed in the loins, close

---

[1] Close to the spot where the heroic Rasalama knelt to pray and die, a large Memorial Church now stands, the spire of which forms a conspicuous object in every distant view of the city.

on either side of the back-bone, but not one was terrified into recanting, although by so doing he might have been restored at once to life and liberty. The truth of that word, " As thy days thy strength shall be," was clearly and wonderfully proved in the case of these sufferers.   After all had fallen, their heads were cut off and placed in a row on the edge of the ditch.   Five of the nine belonged to one family.

One man who had been reserved to the last, for some reason or other that was not explained, was led to the brow of the precipice, and the same question was put to him that had been put to his fellow-martyrs.   From the spot on which he stood he could look down into the awful gulf, a sheer descent of sixty feet, first to a place where a ledge projected, and then, a further descent of still greater depth to the bottom, where the ground was covered with rocks and debris from the cliffs.

Unfaltering in courage and allegiance to the Master, his " No !" was distinct and decisive.   Next moment he was hurled over.   With terrific force he struck the ledge, and it must have been a lifeless body that was finally shattered on the plain below.

As the people immediately began to disperse after this, Mark and his friends hastened away from the place with an overwhelming sense of horror upon them, but thankful as well as relieved to know that their friend Mamba was not yet among the martyrs.

CHAPTER XXI.

MAMBA, SUBJECTED TO THE ORDEAL OF THE "TANGENA," ESCAPES,
BUT AFTERWARDS ACCUSES HIMSELF AND IS CONDEMNED.

IF not yet among the martyrs, it was soon evident
that Mamba stood a good chance of being among them
before long—and that the mother of whom he was
so fond, and for the gratification of whose spiritual
longings he had risked so much, would probably
never receive the Gospel of Peace from his hands.

While in prison under accusation of being a
believer in the religion of the white man, he had
debated much with himself as to what was his duty
in the present distress. Was he bound to confess
Christ and take the consequence—which, of course,
he knew to be death? To deny Him was out of
the question. He at once dismissed that idea as
untenable. But was there no other mode of escape?
Did not the Word itself advise that when persecuted
in one city he was not only entitled but advised to
escape to another? "But how am I to escape? Oh
God, guide me!" he cried, lifting his clasped hands
as he converted the question into a prayer.

The rattling of his chains seemed to bid him dismiss all hope, but he did not lose faith. He continued to pray and meditate. And the longer he meditated the more anxiously did he long to be back in the cave beside his Reni—his humble-minded loving little mother—and beside—yes, he made no attempt to conceal it from himself—beside the beautiful queen-like sister of Laihova. The more he meditated, however, the more hopeless did his case seem to become. To lie he would not—not even to gain Ramatoa. To die he would *rather* not! To escape he could not!

At last he hit upon an idea. He would **refuse to answer**. He would take refuge in absolute silence !

As might have been expected, this course of policy did not avail him much. When it was found that he would not say whether he was a Christian or not, it was resolved that the matter should be settled by an appeal to the ordeal of the Tangena.

This used to be a common and much-practised ordeal in Madagascar in days but recently past. It consisted in the administration of poison. Other ordeals existed in the island—such as passing a red-hot iron over the tongue, or plunging the naked arm into a large pot of boiling water and picking out a pebble thrown therein for the purpose of trial. Alas for both innocent and guilty subjected to either trial! But the ordeal most universally in favour was that of the Tangena.

The Tangena is in fact a poisonous nut about the size of a chestnut, which derives its name from the tree that bears it. If taken in small doses it acts as an emetic ; if in large doses it kills. Many pages would be required to give a full and particular account of all the Malagasy superstitions connected with the ordeal. Let it suffice to say, roughly, that previous to the poison being administered the accused person is obliged to swallow whole, or rather bolt, three pieces of the skin of a fowl, about the size of a dollar. Then the decoction of Tangena in rice-water is administered. If given strong it kills, and the unfortunate is held to have been guilty. If not too strong, and the sufferer be able to bear it, vomiting is the result, and the three pieces of skin are eagerly looked for. The finding of the pieces proves the accused to be innocent. The not finding of them proves him guilty, and at once, if he be a free man, he is killed, if a slave he is sold, and got rid of in some distant market. There was a very complex system of combined profit and superstition surrounding the whole affair which it is difficult as well as useless thoroughly to understand, but which it is easy to see afforded clever scoundrels the means of persecuting, defrauding, or killing any whom they chanced to dislike, or who stood in their way. Of

course it was very easy to make the potion strong
enough to kill, or to dilute it with rice-water until
it became almost harmless.

Now, when Mark Breezy heard that Mamba was
condemned to swallow the Tangena he went straight
to his friend Rakota.

"Prince Rakota," he said, earnestly, "if your
expressions of gratitude to me are sincere you will
save the life of this man."

"I will try," returned the Prince, "but the Queen
is very angry just now!"

When the Prince pleaded for the man's life Ranavalona asked of what he was accused.

"Of praying to the Christians' God."

"Does he admit the charge?" demanded the
Queen sternly.

"No—I believe not."

"Then, let the Tangena decide. It always speaks
the truth. Our ancestors thought so, and I will
not change the customs of our ancestors!" said this
outrageously conservative queen.

Rakota, however, was a determined man and not
easily foiled. Going privately to those who had the
management of the matter, he made use of those
mysterious arguments with which princes manage
to attain their ends, and afterwards told Mark the
result, which was, according to Hockins, that
"Mamba's grog was to be well watered!" As Mark

could do nothing more for his friend he went with his companions to see the result.

There was another man, accused of stealing, who was to be tested at the same time. He was a strong sturdy pugnacious-looking man.

A good deal of ceremonial of course preceded the ordeal. Among other things the poison had to be tested on two fowls. It killed them both and was deemed too strong. Being diluted it was tried on two other fowls, and killed neither. It was therefore considered rather weak. At last, having been reduced to the exact strength which killed one fowl and only sickened the other, the potion was administered to the reputed thief, after a long prayer or invocation. For two hours there was no result, but at the end of that time the pains began, and increased with much violence, yet the man maintained his innocence. His agonies were soon extreme. Amidst his torture he solicited medicine, but this was refused. His bowels, he said, were writhing as if in knots. His groans were awful. His eyes seemed ready to start from their sockets. His countenance assumed a ghastly hue, and his entire frame was convulsed with torture. Then he vomited violently, and, fortunately for him, the three pieces of skin which he had swallowed made their appearance. He was at once pronounced innocent and set free.

Poor Mamba had to witness all this before his

own turn came.   Once more he was questioned, but continued dumb.   Then he was made to swallow his three pieces of skin and to drink the Tangena.

The state of mind of his friends as they watched him after what they had just seen may be conceived but cannot be described.   In Mamba's case the poison acted differently.   Being well diluted, its effects, although severe, were not to be compared with those experienced by the first sufferer.   Still they were bad enough, and vomiting commenced much sooner.   To the great satisfaction of his friends the three pieces of skin were ejected, and Mamba, being pronounced innocent, had his fetters removed and was set free.

But when Mark hastened to congratulate him, what was his surprise to see the poor fellow clasp his hands and raise them to Heaven, while an expression of pain—very different from that resulting from physical suffering—convulsed his features.

" Oh ! no, no !" he exclaimed, in a tone of agony, "I am not innocent.   I am guilty ! guilty ! *very* wicked !   I have denied Thee, dear Lord, by my *looks,* though not with my lips !   Forgive me, O God !"   Then, turning quickly to the officers of justice, "Here—put on the chains again.   I *am* a praying man !   I love the Lord Jesus.   He will save *you* as well as me if you will come to Him !"

As this was spoken in the native language our

Englishmen did not understand it, but they had little difficulty in guessing the drift of it when they saw the officers replace the chains and lead Mamba back to prison, where the last words the jailor heard as he left him were, "Mother, mother! Ramatoa! I shall never more see your dear faces in this life—never more!"

But in this Mamba was mistaken, as the sequel will show.

Meanwhile Mark hurried back to the palace and told Rakota what had occurred. The Prince was not surprised. He had mingled much with the Christians, and knew well the spirit by which they were animated. He went at once to the Queen, who was enraged at first by his persistent pleading, vowed that Mamba should die, and gave orders to that effect. But on reconsidering the matter she commuted the sentence into life-long slavery in long chains.

There is usually but brief delay between a sentence and its execution in Madagascar. The very next day heavy chains were riveted on Mamba. These, at one end, were attached to an iron collar round his neck, at the other end to iron rings round his ankles. What sailors would call *the slack* of these heavy fetters was gathered up in one of the wearer's hands, and thus carried while he moved about at work.

The poor fellow was first set to work on a piece of road-mending just outside the city gate, with several others—martyrs and criminals—in similar condemnation. And here Mark and his companions met him unexpectedly before they were aware that the fearful punishment had begun.

At the time poor Mamba was toiling with pick and shovel. His heart was almost broken. Death he could have faced without flinching, but to be a life-long slave in galling chains, with the possibility even of seeing his mother and Ramatoa, without being permitted to go near or speak to them, was almost more than he could bear. A deep groan burst from his overcharged breast as he cried, "Oh Lord Jesus, enable me to bear it!"

It was just then that Ebony observed him and uttered a falsetto cry of astonishment.

The Secretary, who was conducting Mark and Hockins on a visit to one of the suburban places of resort, stopped and looked round.

"Dars Mamba, massa!" cried Ebony.

Mark ran to him at once, but was stopped by the guard. A few words from the Secretary, however, sufficed, and Mark was allowed to speak to the slave, which he did through the Secretary.

Despair was in Mamba's every tone and look, for the crushing calamity was too recent and too tremendous to be borne with equanimity at first. Yet through it all there ran, as it were, a tiny silver thread of hope.

"For is it not true," he said, "that 'with God all things are possible'?"

"My friend," said Mark in reply, and with a burst of enthusiasm, "I will save you *somehow!* Keep a good heart."

Mamba smiled faintly, yet gratefully, as he shook his head, gathered up the superfluous links of his chain, and resumed his toil.

"How will you save him?" asked the Secretary, with a peculiar half-amused look, as they walked away.

"I know not," answered Mark. "But we have a proverb, 'Where there's a will there's a way,' and I have a determined will to save my poor friend from this slavery. I will not cease to try—as we say in England, 'I will leave no stone unturned,'—till I have accomplished this thing. Moreover I will not cease to pray for this end. Mamba's trust in God puts me to shame. Up to this time I have only recognised by name that Saviour whom this man worships. God helping me, I will henceforth follow the Lord!"

To the surprise of the young man the Secretary turned suddenly on him and grasped his hand, and said in a low voice, as he looked cautiously round—

"It gives me joy to hear you speak so. I too am

a follower of Jesus.   I tell you this because I know, now, that you will not betray me.   There are many of us in the palace besides Prince Rakota, but we dare not speak out, for the Queen is very angry, as you know.   Hush!   Tell it not even to your companions.   Little birds have ears.   If the Queen suspects any of us, in her present state of mind, she will either ruin or kill us."

"I have heard something of this," said Mark, "from the friend who guided us to the capital——"

"I know," interrupted the Secretary, with an intelligent nod.   "It was Ravoninohitriniony.   He is well known to us.   He loves Rafaravavy, and is now in the neighbourhood of the capital, hoping to induce her to fly with him to the forests.   You are surprised, but you would not be so if you knew the number of spies that Ranavalona has out everywhere."

"Has my friend Ravonino (we call him so for brevity) been seen in—in—I mean *near* the city lately?" asked Mark, anxiously.

"Not *in* the city, certainly," returned the Secretary.   "Bold and daring though he is, he would scarcely venture that; but he has been seen and heard of more than once lately."

Mark felt relieved.   It was evident the Secretary neither knew of nor suspected the fact that Ravonino had actually attended the garden party and met Rafa-

ravavy almost under the Queen's eyes! Remembering, however, that the Prime Minister had sent
Soa to pretend to be a Christian, in order that he
might discover the secrets of the Christians, and
not having yet had much experience of the Secretary's character, he resolved to be very cautious in
his reference to Ravonino,—indeed to any one with
whom he had to do. Acting on this resolve he
changed the subject by asking questions about the
extensive rice-grounds around the capital.

The Secretary was of a communicative disposition,
and evidently fond of airing his English. He willingly followed in conversation wherever the young
doctor chose to lead, and gave him and his friends
a great deal of interesting information as to the
manners and customs of the Malagasy people—their
habits, beliefs, and laws.

Among the latter he spoke of a curious fact in
regard to criminals which gave Mark a sudden
inspiration! Hockins afterwards styled it a
"wrinkle." Ebony called it a "dodge." But,
whatever might be said on that head, it had the
effect of very materially altering the conditions of
some of the personages of this tale, as the following
chapters will show.

CHAPTER XXII.

THE COURT PHYSICIAN PRESCRIBES FOR THE QUEEN—A BLOW-UP, AND MYSTERIOUS PREPARATIONS FOR TREMENDOUS SURPRISES.

ABOUT this time the anger of Queen Ranavalona against the Christians was so great that she made herself quite ill, and more than once had to send for her Court Physician, Mark Breezy, to prescribe for her.

Our youthful medico understood her complaint, which was a simple one. He prescribed much exercise, change of air, and amusement, so as to distract her mind from the cares of State and the evil passions to which she was giving way. He hoped thus to serve the Christians indirectly, for he saw clearly that the mere mention of their existence made her ill. Some slight administrations of physic, also, coupled with judicious alterations of diet, put her Majesty in a state of such excellent health and spirits that she began to entertain quite a warm regard for her Court Physician, and congratulated herself not a little on the good fortune which had sent him to the capital.

Thus Mark was enabled to disperse, for a time,

U

the dark cloud which had been lowering over the land—not, however, in time to prevent many Christians from being slain, and some even of the officers and ladies of the palace from being degraded, their honours taken from them, and themselves and children sold as slaves.

Among the ladies, Rafaravavy had a narrow escape. For a time her life seemed to hang by a hair, for she was rebellious as well as fearless, and *would* sing her favourite hymns in spite of orders to the contrary! Love prevailed, however, as in the case of Prince Rakota, and she was tolerated as a sort of spoilt child.

Being a favourite, Mark of course became a man of power in the capital. This fact would have raised him a host of enemies had it not been for the kindness of his disposition and the urbanity of his manners. When a strapping powerful young fellow treats every one with respectful deference, keeps in the background, and neither by word nor look asserts himself, but, on the contrary, seems to entertain kindly thoughts about every one, it argues such an absence of selfishness that most people are irresistibly attracted to him. Thus, unwittingly, he escaped jealousy and enmity in a palace where both were rife, and, holding in his hands as he did the power to alleviate many of the " ills that flesh is heir to," he secured a good deal of warm friendship.

Being also an ingenious youth, he devised many little plans for amusing Ranavalona and preventing her mind from dwelling on dangerous memories. Among other things, he induced her to go in for a series of garden parties, and encouraged the people to practise their national games at these gatherings in a systematic way.

What all this was ultimately to lead to he did not know—indeed at first he had no particular end in view save the great one of preventing the Queen from ordering any more of the horrible scenes of bloodshed which he and his friends had so recently witnessed. But as time ran on his ideas became more definite and concentrated. It occurred to him that Ravonino would inevitably venture to attend the garden parties in the hope of again meeting Rafaravavy, and now that the Secretary had avowed himself on the side of the Christians, he felt that through him he might influence her to agree to her lover's proposal.

Then his plan to effect the rescue of Mamba was gradually matured.

"Ebony," he exclaimed, suddenly, one afternoon when sitting at his table preparing some villainous compound for the Queen, " go down to the laboratory, boy, and fetch me some gunpowder, sulphur, salt-petre, and charcoal."

Mark's laboratory, by the way, contained not

only the medicines which chanced to be in the capital at that time, but also a vast collection of miscellaneous articles and substances which, in the opinion of palace officials, could be classed, however remotely, with "doctor's stuffs."

"Them stuffs," remarked Hockins, who sat luxuriously in an arm-chair smoking a short pipe —for he had unfortunately obtained tobacco since arriving at the capital!—"Them stuffs are apt to cause surprisin' effects w'en properly mixed."

"Just so. That is my reason for sending for them. I shall create some surprising effects if my old cunning in pyrotechny has not forsaken me. When I was a school-boy, you must know, I was fond of dabbling in fireworks, and it strikes me that I could compound some things that would charm the Queen and astonish the natives."

"Massa," asked Ebony, powerful surprise expressed in his sable visage, while Mark spooned large quantities of the ingredients referred to into an earthenware dish, "is dem powders to be took inside arter bein' well shooken, or rubbed outside?"

"Whichever way you please, Ebony. Would you like to try?"

"No thankee, massa."

"Now, then, look here," said Mark, making some pencil notes on a sheet of paper, after arranging several plates in a row. You and Hockins set to work and mix these in the exact proportions set down on this paper. I'd do it myself, but I'm due at the palace, and you know the Queen does not like to be kept waiting. Stick to the paper, exactly, and here you have an egg-cup, a table-spoon, and a tea-spoon to measure with. Put your pipe out, I advise you, Hockins, before beginning. If Rainiharo should call, tell him he will find me with the Queen. I don't like that Prime Minister. He's a prime rascal, I think, and eggs the Queen on when she would probably let things drop. He's always brooding and pondering, too, as if hatching mischief."

"If that's a sign of hatching mischief," said Hockins, with a short laugh, "the same thing may be said of yourself, doctor, for you've done little but brood and ponder for more nor a week past."

"True, I have been plotting; but many a man plots much without much resulting."

Hurrying away, Mark found the Secretary waiting for him to act as interpreter, for the Queen understood little or no English.

After the preliminary ceremonial salutations, the young doctor asked if her Majesty would honour the gardens with her presence the following day, hold a grand reception, and make arrangements to remain in Anosy till after dark.

Yes, the Queen was quite ready to do so, but

why did her Court Physician make such a proposal ?
Had he some new surprise in store for her ?

" I have," answered Mark. " In my country we
make very grand displays with fire. But I have
various little surprises and plots in store, which
cannot be properly wrought out unless Ranavalona
will consent to go to the gardens privately—that is
to say, without public announcement, for that has
much to do with the success of my scheme."

" It shall be done, though it is against my custom," said the Queen, with a good-natured nod, for
she had begun to regard her young physician as an
eccentric creature who needed and deserved en-
couragement in his amusing and harmless fancies.

Immediately after the audience, Mark and his
sympathetic interpreter, the Secretary, obtained an
interview with Rafaravavy. The doctor began
abruptly.

" I am well acquainted with your lover, dear
young lady." At this she pouted a little, blushed
terribly, and drew her pretty figure to its full height
—which was not great ! " And," continued Mark,
" I have been very deeply indebted to him."

Rafaravavy relaxed a little, and fixed her fine
dark eyes on the youth searchingly, but said nothing.

" Now I know," Mark went on, pretending not
to observe the maiden's varying moods, " that my
friend loves you so profoundly—so deeply—that he

will risk his life to see you, and if he is caught, you are well aware that in the present state of the Queen's mind the result would be his death—almost certainly, and perhaps you would die along with him. Therefore, if you get an opportunity soon you should agree to fly with him."

During the first part of this speech the young girl's face glowed with evident pleasure, but the last part was unfortunate. It did not suit the temper of one who was brave as she was beautiful.

"I know not, sir," she said, with flashing eyes, while the little figure drew up again, "what English girls may think or do, but Malagasy women are not afraid to die with those whom they love. Your advice may be kindly meant, but I doubt if it is wise. Besides, I am a servant of my Queen, and owe allegiance to her."

"Your Queen, mademoiselle, is a servant of the devil," said Mark, whose indignation was severely stirred. "And, Rafaravavy, do you not profess to be a servant of the Christians' God—the Almighty? Does not the Book state that it is impossible to serve *two* masters?"

"Come, come!" cried the Secretary, in a sharp tone, after translating this faithfully, "it is time to go. Follow me!"

Mark's surprise at this abrupt termination of the interview was great, but as Rafaravavy retired hastily, he had no resource but to follow his friend.

"Why so sharp?" he asked, as they passed along the corridor.

"Because you have said enough," returned the Secretary, with a quiet smile. "You may understand your own women, no doubt, but not the Malagasy girls as well as I do. When a man has said *enough* to a woman he should stop and let it simmer. All the rest that he would say she will say to herself—and say it much better, too! But tell me, when do you think Ravoninohitriniony will meet Rafaravavy?"

"I don't know. All I know is that a true lover is sure to manage a meeting soon—and somehow."

He was glad to be able to make this indefinite reply; for although he trusted the Secretary, and would have revealed his own affairs fully to him, he felt that he had no right to reveal the affairs of his friend to any one.

Before they reached the palace-yard a loud report was heard. The palace shook as with an earthquake. Loud cries of soldiery were heard without, and Mark's heart sank with an undefinable dread.

To account for this report we must go back a little. When Hockins and Ebony were left, as we have seen, to mix their "powders," the former, being a reckless man, forgot to put his pipe out, and Ebony being a careless man (as regarded himself), did not observe the omission. The consequence was that the seaman kept on puffing and emitting sage reflections to his admiring friend while they mixed their compounds in concert.

" Hand me the powder, Ebony."

" Das good—ha! ha! das awrful good," cried the negro, referring to the latest sage reflection—as he pushed across the powder canister, which was a large one.

At that inauspicious moment a spark fell from the pipe! Next moment the door was burst open, the window blown out, Hockins was laid flat on his back, while Ebony went head-over-heels upon the floor!

Slowly and with a dazed look the seaman raised himself on one elbow and looked round.

" An—anything of ye left, boy?" he asked, quietly.

" I—I's not kite sure, 'Ockins," replied the negro, slowly passing his hand down one of his legs without rising from the floor. " 'Ow does it feel wid *you?*"

" All right, I think," replied the seaman, rising and presenting a remarkable exhibition of singed beard and frizzled locks, " no bones broke, anyhow."

At that instant Mark rushed into the smoke-filled

room in consternation, followed by the Secretary and a number of soldiers who formed the guard of the palace, and great was their surprise, as well as their satisfaction, to find that the two men had received no damage worth mentioning.

"Well, I *am* thankful," exclaimed Mark, beginning to pick up the debris of plates and furniture.

"So am I," remarked the sailor, "thankful to think that I've got it over at last—so easy too!"

"Why, what do you mean?"

"I means, doctor, that I've gone the whole round o' human possibilities now—leastwise I think so—and am alive to tell it! I've bin shot, an' stabbed, an' drownded—all but—an' now I've bin blow'd up!"

"So's I, 'Ockins, so you needn't boast," remarked Ebony, as he tenderly felt the place where his wool ought to have been, but where only a few irregularly-shaped patches of scrub remained.

We need scarcely say that Mark Breezy did not allow this little *contretemps* to interfere with his plans.

"You'll have to work all night, both of you—that's your punishment for disobeying orders—and without the solace of a pipe too," said Mark, when order was somewhat restored and work resumed. "The garden party, you know, is fixed for to-morrow, and it's as much as our heads are worth to disappoint the Queen of her expected amusements. Time, tide, and Ranavalona I. wait for no man! I've got to go out for an hour or so. When I return I'll show you how to make stars and crackers and red rain, etc."

"But I say, Doctor," asked Hockins, looking up from his work, "where are the cases to hold all this here stuff?"

"Time enough for that when we want 'em. I've got some fellows at work on small ones, and there's a big one that will open the Madagaskite eyes if there's virtue in saltpetre. It's made of——ah! here it comes," he added, as the door opened and two natives carried in a piece of cast-iron pipe about six feet long and four inches in diameter.

"The pistol-barrel of a giant," exclaimed the seaman.

"A young cannon!" said Ebony. "W'y, massa, you gwine to make a Roman candle ob *dat?*"

He turned for an answer, but Mark had hastily quitted the house.

Encountering the Secretary in the court-yard, he took his arm and said, "I want your help."

"Well, you shall have it. But you are so mys—mys—what is it—sterious about your leetil plans, that I fear my help is not useful."

"Oh! yes, it is. I want you to get me a paper from—I don't know who—the proper officer, whoever he is, authorising me to take a gang of convicts—four will do—to work for me."

"Good, you shall have it," returned the Secretary, with a laugh. "I see you are going to give us big surprises to-morrow."

"You are right, I am," said Mark, as the Secretary left him to execute his mission.

Armed with an order, Mark left the palace and hurried through the steep narrow streets of the town, until he reached a piece of road that was being mended by four slaves in long chains. That morning Mark had observed that his friend the crocodile was one of the four. Passing close enough to attract the attention of the poor fellow, he whispered, without stopping, "Mamba, expect me to-morrow."

This he had said in the native tongue, having by that time acquired a few sentences, of which he made the best and most frequent use possible.

Going to the guard of these slaves, he presented his paper, and said that he should come personally for them early in the morning. Then he returned to the laboratory and assisted his comrades to load the firework cases with various kinds of "fire," stars, golden rain, etc. The young cannon especially was loaded, with a succession of surprises, to the very muzzle before midnight.

"Suppose he bust!" suggested Ebony, with a solemn visage. "De Queen ob Madigascur be blow'd into middle ob nixt week—hey?"

"I shall take precautions against that, Ebony. In

the first place, I 'll have it buried in the earth up to the muzzle, and, in the second place, I 'll not place it too near her Majesty."

When all was prepared the wearied triumvirate retired to rest, each to dream of the subjects that lay nearest his heart and imagination at the moment. Hockins dreamed of tobacco-pipes and explosions; Mark of freed slaves, thunderstruck queens, eloping lovers and terrible consequences; Ebony of incomprehensible situations, crashing thunderbolts, and unimaginable coruscations of resplendent fire!

CHAPTER XXIII.

IN WHICH MARK CARRIES OUT HIS PLANS SUCCESSFULLY, AND POWER-
FULLY ASTONISHES HIMSELF AS WELL AS EVERY ONE ELSE.

IT was a brilliant lovely morning when the guests
began to wend their way to the suburban residence
of Anosy, where Ranavalona was to hold her garden
party.

The people were very gay, somewhat excited, and
very chatty, for they were aware that the young
English doctor had prepared something new and
surprising for the Queen's special benefit.

Just before the earliest of these guests, however,
had set off to the garden, our three heroes had
passed down to that part of the road where the four
slaves were already at work with pick and shovel
and clanking chain.

It was a little after sunrise when Mark went up
to the guard to relieve him.

"Take care," said the guard, when about to leave,
"that you keep the slaves well out of the way when
the Queen passes. All the others in the neighbour-

hood have been taken off long ago.   I was beginning
to be afraid you would not come in time."

" I understand," said Mark, who knew enough of
the language (and also of the situation) to follow
the drift of his meaning.

The guard thereupon turned, shouldered his
musket, and went off, apparently well pleased at the
unexpected relief from duty.

While this little incident was occurring three of
the slaves were looking on with a slight expression
of surprise in their sad faces.   The fourth, Mamba,
was standing in a dejected attitude before Hockins
and Ebony, holding a pick in one hand and his
heavy chain in the other.

" Oh ! man, I *am* sorry to see you like this," said
Hockins, extending his brawny hand, " an' I does
wish I could set you free—but you know I'm as
helpless as a babby in this matter."

Mamba dropped the pick and grasped the strong
hand, but did not look up.   His heart was too full.
He did not understand the seaman's words, but he
understood the tone.   If he had looked up he would
have seen that the tears were hopping over Ebony's
cheeks in spite of the powerful efforts of that
sympathetic soul to control them, and that he was
unable to speak because of a lump in his throat.

" Das most awrful ! " he exclaimed at last.   " Oh,
Mamby, I'd fight for you like a wild-cat wid the

cholera if that would do you any good, but it would be ob no use."

Just then Mark came forward. "Quick, follow me," he said, leading the way to a thick clump of bushes behind a wall that bordered the road. Here, quite concealed, yet able to peep through the leafy screen, he ordered his party to sit down on a heap of stones and await orders. He then went to the top of a mound that lay immediately behind them. From this he could see the road winding along for about two or three hundred yards.

Descending to his comrades he sat down beside them.

"You look anxious, doctor," remarked the seaman.

"I *am* anxious," returned Mark, "I am on the point of making a great venture, and the results may be serious. But we are in God's hands;" then, turning to Mamba, who looked at him with much curiosity and a gleam of hope on his intelligent face, "I have hope of success and have prayed for it."

Mamba, whose knowledge of English was very slight, shook his head and looked puzzled.

"Have you forgotten, Mamba, the law of your land—that the criminal who *looks* upon the Queen is from that moment entitled to claim freedom? Ranavalona is to pass along this road in less than half-an-hour."

Of course Mark said this in remarkably bad Malagasy, but Mamba understood. A gleam of intelligence shot into his swarthy visage, and his chest began to heave with strong emotion as he glared rather than gazed at the speaker. Not less surprised were Hockins and Ebony when Mark explained, for although they had indeed heard about the law in question they had forgotten it. After recovering the first shock, Mamba turned quickly and pointed to his three comrades in suffering.

"Yes, yes—I understand," said Mark, "I shall set them free at the same time. Why not? The risk will not be increased."

"A reg'lar jail-delivery!" murmured Hockins, as he drew in a long breath.

"Hush! they come!" cried Mark, crouching so as the more effectually to conceal himself, in which act he was quickly imitated by the others.

According to promise, Ranavalona had set out from her palace that morning without her wonted display and ceremonial, with only a few of her courtiers and a handful of troops around her. She did not, however, omit the scarlet umbrella of state, and it was this brilliant object which had attracted Mark's attention.

When the procession had approached close to the place of concealment, Mark whispered "Now!" and ran to the top of the mound before referred to. The

x

four slaves followed him. The summit gained they turned, lifted up their arms and chains, *looked upon the Queen*, and gave vent to the " oo !-oo !-oo !" which stands to the Malagasy in the place of a cheer. Recognising the importance of the event, Hockins and Ebony, unable to restrain themselves, gave vent to a hearty British hurrah!

At this interruption, the bearers of the royal palanquin or chair halted, the soldiers brought their muskets to the "ready," and a dark frown over-spread the features of the Queen.

Before the storm could burst, however, Mark descended the mound, went to the side of the chair, knelt on one knee, and exclaimed—

" Forgive, madam—forgive me!"

" This, then, is *your* doing," replied the Queen, sternly, through the Secretary, who was at her side.

" It is, madam. I am guilty. If punishment must descend, I alone should bear it."

There was something so modest, yet so fearless, in the youth's tone and bearing, that the Queen's brows relaxed a little.

" But why did you dare to interfere with my laws?" demanded Ranavalona, still angrily.

" I did not venture to interfere, madam," returned Mark, humbly, " I did but use one law to neutralise another. One of these slaves is my friend. I think he would be very useful in helping me to-night with my magic fires!"

There was so much of cool presumption in thus quietly changing the subject, with such charming modesty of demeanour, too, that the Queen burst into a hearty laugh.

"Strike off his fetters," she said, and gave the signal to her bearers to move on.

"Ay," said Mark to the Secretary in an authoritative tone, "and also strike off the fetters of the other three!"

"You've got cheek for anything a'most, doctor,' said the amazed and amused seaman, as they fell into the procession and followed the Queen to the pleasure-garden.

Here extensive preparations had been made for spending the day in games and festivities that far exceeded anything of the sort ever before attempted in that land. For Mark Breezy had not only an ingenious mind to devise, but an organising spirit to make use of the services of others in carrying out his plans.

When the guests were scattered about the grounds, after a good breakfast, enjoying the delightful shade of the trees, tempting the gold-fish in the lake with crumbs of food, and loitering among the by-paths, the young doctor made himself almost ubiquitous. Acting the double part of manager of the games and amusements, and private conspirator, he set an army of palace officials in motion, whom he pledged to secrecy, and led each to suppose that he was the prime mover in some plot that was to astonish and delight the Queen, in all which he was ably assisted by the Secretary. When he had thus stirred up, as it were, an air of mystery and expectation, he led the Secretary, Hockins, and Ebony, to a retired spot, and, bidding them sit down, gave them a brief address.

" You see," he said, " the time has now come for me to explain to you more fully the plans and plots with which I have been engaged for some time past. And in doing so I would impress upon you, Mr. Secretary, that I am placing my life in your hands; but I do so without fear, believing that you are a Christian and will not betray me."

Mark paused and looked full at the Secretary, who said, " But you must remember that I can do nothing that will be disloyal to the Queen."

" If you were persecuted by the Queen and threatened with death, would you consider it allowable to fly to the forests ? "

" Yes—the Word of the Lord recommends that."

" Would you consider it right to assist a fellow-Christian to fly ? "

" Truly I would ! '

" Well then, you will assist me this night, for I

have spoken to Rafaravavy. My Malagasy words
are few, but love does not require many words!
She has agreed to fly with Ravonino——"

"Have you seen Ravonino lately?" asked Hockins.

"No—I have not seen him *lately.*"

"How, then, do you know he will be ready?"

"Because," said Mark, with a peculiar look, "I
have been smitten with his complaint, and know that
it runs the same course and exhibits the same phases
in most men. Let a young fellow see his intended
bride treated with cruelty, and you may be sure that,
no matter what difficulties may be in the way, he
will hasten at the very first opportunity to meet and
carry off the sweet little fairy in spite of——"

"Das me an' my black darlin', zactly—same zif
you bin dar an' sawd us do it!" exclaimed Ebony,
with beaming interest.

"Just so," resumed Mark. "However, I have not
left things altogether to chance. Although I did
not see Ravonino lately, I saw him not *very* long
ago, and gave him to understand that when some
unusual festivities were going on in this garden he
was to be ready at the old spot for whatever might
happen! Now, here is my little plan. You know
I've been drilling fifty picked natives for some
time in that big shed at the back of the cliff on the
north side o' the city. I picked them for intelligence
as well as strength and activity. Well, I have

taught them a wild war-dance. It cost me no little trouble and many sleepless nights to invent it, but I've managed it, and hope to show the Queen and Court what can be done by a little organisation. These fifty are first of all to glide quietly among the trees, each man to a particular spot and hang on the branches fifty earthen saucers full of grease, with wicks in them. At a given signal they are to light these instantaneously and retire. At another signal they are to rush upon the open space in front of the garden-house, and there engage in a sham fight. While thus engaged, men who have been taught will set fire to the mildest of our fireworks. When these are about to go out I will myself light the big Roman candle——"

"De young cannon, massa?"

"Yes, the young cannon, and that will keep things going for a considerable time. Now, it is when the fight of the fifty begins and engrosses the attention of every one that I will myself take Rafaravavy out from among the ladies and lead her to the rendezvous. You will all stand by—to lend a hand if need be—at the south-east corner of the garden-house, that I may know exactly where to find you. My hope and expectation is that by keeping things going as long as possible our friends Ravonino and Rafaravavy will get a good start. After the flight of the latter is found out, nothing more can be done for them."

" Do they go all alone ? " asked Hockins.

" No, Laihova goes with them ; and Mamba, who knows the secret meeting-places of the Christians, will, I have no doubt, soon find out which way they have gone. Anyhow they will all certainly make for the cave in Betsilio land where so many of their friends are. May God speed them ! Meanwhile we must keep the Queen amused with races, wrestling, and such-like ; and when she begins to get wearied with mere eating and talking, I want you, Hockins, to go in for a wrestling-match with Ebony by way of varying the entertainment, and showing them what Englishmen and niggers can do."

" Wery good," said the seaman, with a sedate smile, " if that's to be the fun, you better make your will, Ebony, for I'll break your back."

" All right," retorted Ebony, with a grin, " an' I tink you'll be wise to make your last dyin' speech afore we begin, for I'll bust you ! "

The various plans which we have here sketched were carried out with such brilliant success that the Queen did not weary at all, and darkness began to descend on the scene before the day seemed to have half run its course. At this point Mark hastened to the south-east corner of the garden-house, where he found the other conspirators faithfully at their post.'

" Have you the flageolet with you ? " he asked, hastily.

"In course I has. Never goes nowheres without it," said the seaman, drawing the little instrument from his breast-pocket.

"Go then, make your bow to the Queen, and give her a tune. You know she's quite in love with your pipe—or yourself—and has been asking me about it already. She's in the verandah just now, and they are lighting the torches there."

With the silent obedience of a man-of-war's man, Hockins went off, and, without prelude, began. Dead silence was the instant result, for the small bird-like pipe seemed to charm the very soul of every one who heard it. We know not whether it was accident or a spice of humour in the seaman, but the tune he played was "Jock o' Hazeldean!" And as Mark hurried off to see that his fifty men were in readiness, he gave vent to a slight laugh as he thought of the lines :—

> "She's ower the border and awa
> Wi' Jock o' Hazeldean!"

To the surprise of the audience, no sooner had the last notes of the air died away than the performer thrust the pipe into his pocket, threw off his coat, and in a loud voice challenged the best man in Madagascar to wrestle with him. As the challenge was given in English of course no native responded. Even if it had been given in choice Malagasy we question whether any brown man there would have ventured a hug with the huge sailor. But no sooner had the challenge passed his lips than Ebony sprang forward, flung off not only his coat but his vest and shirt, and embraced his white opponent in a grip of iron.

At that opportune moment the signal was given to the fifty men, who applied their lights, and, as if by magic, the entire scene was illuminated by a blaze of intense light that almost rivalled that of the sun itself!

A tremendous "oo-oo-oo" of applause burst from the astonished company, who, having had their attention fixed on the wrestlers, did not observe how the sudden illumination had been effected.

Truly the proceedings of Hockins and Ebony would have surprised even more finished wrestlers than those of Madagascar, for the two men had entered into a sly compact not only to exert their strength to the uttermost, but to give way, each at certain points or moments, when by so doing the appearance of what they styled a "back-breaker" and a "buster" might be achieved in an effective manner. It was a marvellous exhibition. Ebony glared and gasped! Hockins growled and frowned! Nothing short of a tussle between Achilles and Hercules could have equalled it. The Court, from the Queen downwards, was awe-stricken, eye-strained, open-mouthed, and breathless, but Mark felt that it was time to cut it short. Giving a pre-concerted signal, he caused both men to fall down side by side as if exhausted but not conquered. Then he gave another signal. A moment after, fire-wheels and Roman candles began to play, and the fifty warriors rushed upon the scene, brandishing muskets and yelling like fiends.

Hastening, according to orders, to the south-east corner of the garden-house, Hockins and Ebony found the Director-General awaiting them.

"I cannot delay to fire the big candle," he said quickly.

"De young cannon!" panted Ebony.

"Yes, yes. You must fire it for me in about ten minutes or so, when the warriors seem to be getting knocked up. Follow me, Hockins, and keep close."

Another minute and Rafaravavy, who was stand-ing near the Queen's chair, felt a touch on her arm. She looked round with a start, for, like every one else, she had been fascinated and quite engrossed by the scene before her.

A glance and motion of the hand from Mark sufficed. She glided gently backwards and reached the other side of the house unobserved. Here Mark grasped her hand and Hockins followed. They walked at first, but began to run on gaining the shrubbery, which was rendered doubly dark by contrast with the glare behind them.

In a couple of minutes they reached the thicket where the previous meeting had taken place. The overarching foliage deepened the darkness so that it was impossible to distinguish features. A form was dimly seen, but it was only by the sound of the voice that they knew it to be Ravonino.

Few words were uttered. Every instant was precious.

"Farewell, dear friend," said Ravonino, grasping Mark's hand, "God grant that we may meet again in better times! Laihova waits for me beyond the garden——"

He stopped abruptly, seized Rafaravavy's hand and glided with her noiselessly into the thicket, for at that moment another figure was seen to approach them. From his unusual size they knew him to be one of Ranavalona's chief executioners. He was a cool-headed and suspicious man, a sort of natural detective, who always had his wits about him. Having observed several people gliding through the shrubbery he had quitted the sports and followed. To have been recognised by this official would have been fatal—at least to those plotters who did not take to flight. Hockins, who was prompt to conceive and act when danger pressed, at once stepped forward and gave the man of blood a right-hander on the top of the nose which instantly Romanised that feature and laid its owner on his back insensible.

At the same moment—as if the blow had been the touching of a secret spring—the whole garden was lighted up with a magnificent red glare, and they knew that Ebony had done his part and lighted the giant candle. The red glare lasted long enough to reveal the fact that Ravonino and Rafaravavy were gone, and that the man at their feet was indeed the executioner whom they had guessed him to be. Leaving him there they ran quickly back to the scene of festivities, hoping that their absence had not been observed. Before they had gone half-a-dozen steps there was an explosion like that of a big gun, a bomb went high into the air, and burst in a magnificent constellation of brilliant stars, mingled with fiery rain. The " oo-oo-oo's," became vociferous at this, and were, if possible, still more enthusiastic when the red fire changed to a beautifiul blue.

" Splendid !" exclaimed Mark, much satisfied with the result of his recent labours, "and it will keep going on for a considerable time yet."

As he spoke there was a crash like the loudest thunder, and a momentary glare as of the brightest noon-light, which was followed by intense darkness, while the garden was shaken as if by an earthquake. Loud cries and shrieks were accompanied by the falling of a shower of dust and small stones. Evidently there had been a catastrophe, and the quaking conspirators hastened to the spot, half expecting to find the Queen and Court of Madagascar blown to atoms.

"The whole consarn's busted up!" exclaimed Hockins, on coming in sight of the garden-house.

The seaman's explanation was the true one. Owing to some inexplicable mistake in the loading of the monster Roman candle, fire had communicated somehow with the lowest charge, which was a good strong one, intended to propel a glorious mass of ingenious contrivances into the air and end the matter with an effective bang. As it turned out, the bang was ten times more effective, for it not only blew out the entire charge but burst the cast-iron case, and upturned tons of earth in which Mark had taken the precaution to bury the thing up to its neck.

At first the Queen, like her people, had got a severe fright; but seeing that no one seemed to be hurt she controlled her feelings, under the impression, no doubt, that the explosion was part of the programme.

"Have you got your whistle, Hockins?" asked Mark, quickly, as he ran forward.

"Ay, sir—always here, ready for action!"

"Come, then, play up when I give the word—something quieting. Hold on! Let's do it sedately."

By this time they had got within the circle of torchlight. Reducing their run to a smart walk the two friends advanced, as Mark had suggested, sedately, in front of the Queen, while the Secretary rejoined the circle of courtiers unperceived.

As they advanced they encountered Ebony with an unused Roman candle in each hand, and an expression of horror on his black face.

"Oh! massa——" he began.

"Hush! never mind! Follow me!" said Mark, in a peremptory whisper.

Another moment and the sweet tones of the flageolet silenced the noise of the excited throng, as Hockins stood before the Queen and played one of the sweetest of Scottish songs.

Mark placed Ebony behind his comrade, made him hold up the Roman candles, quietly lighted them both, and retired. Thus Hockins, much to his own surprise, found himself, in the midst of spouting fire, producing the melodious notes of "Afton Water!"

When the little candles exploded, our Director-General advanced to the royal chair and expressed a hope that the performances had given satisfaction.

This the Secretary—ever ready in time of need—translated, and returned the answer that the Queen was charmed, after which the proceedings terminated, and Ranavalona returned to her palace to dream, no doubt, of fireworks and music instead of martyr-doms.

So engrossed was the whole Court with the exciting and singular events of the day that no one noticed the absence of Rafaravavy, and, happily, the Queen did not happen to require her attendance that night.

Even those who were in closest proximity to the fugitive's own room were so taken up with what they had seen that they either did not think of her, or supposed that fatigue had induced her to retire early.

Thus it came to pass that when her flight was discovered on the following day, Rafaravavy, carried by strong and willing bearers, and guarded by her devoted Ravonino and his faithful friend Laihova, was being swiftly borne over mountain and plain to the forest stronghold in Betsilio land.

CHAPTER XXIV.

FLIGHT AND PURSUIT OF RAVONINO AND RAFARAVAVY.

THE fury of the Queen when she heard of the flight of Rafaravavy was terrible, for this was the second of her favourite ladies-in-waiting who had become Christians and deserted her Court in fear of their lives—Ra-Ruth, the fair little sister of Ravonino, having been the first.

Fortunately Ranavalona did not think of connecting the flight of Rafaravavy with the recent entertainments, so that suspicion did not attach to Mark and his friends. Neither did the executioner with the Romanised nose suspect them, for in the profound darkness he had not been able to see who it was that knocked the senses out of him; and when afterwards he was told of the explosion that had occurred, he came to the conclusion (and told his friends) that a big stone, hurled into the air at that time, had descended on his head and felled him. Whether the "friends" believed this or not we cannot say, but certain it is that they covertly rejoiced in the accident, for naturally the man of blood was no favourite!

As might be supposed, soldiers were at once despatched all over the country in search of the fugitive; and the Queen, relapsing into one of her dark fits of cruelty, began to persecute the Christians more severely than ever. Still, Mark Breezy strove to influence her towards mercy, and in some measure restrained her.

Meanwhile Ravonino and his party pushed on in hot haste towards their place of refuge in the wild forest.

The dangers to which they were exposed and the risks they ran on this adventurous journey were too numerous to be related in detail. We can only touch on a few of them here.

Laihova, it may be mentioned in passing, failed to join them, certainly not from want of will, but because the place where he had concealed himself was discovered while he lay awaiting the signal to join his friends. Two female relations who knew of his hiding-place were caught, convicted, if we may so put it, of Christianity! and put to the torture. Although true-hearted, these poor girls were so agonised by suffering and terror that, in a moment of weakness, they disclosed the secret. But even among prison authorities there were found followers of Jesus—secretly, however, for fear of the tyrant

Queen—and one of these sent a swift messenger to Laihova to warn him. Had the youth been an ordinary man the warning would have been too late, for close on the heels of the messenger came the soldiers with his death-warrant. But Laihova was gifted with cool courage and unusual speed of foot. Trust, also, in the certainty of God's blessing, whether life or death should be his portion, filled him with that spirit of enthusiastic energy which goes so far, in all circumstances of life, to ensure success. He soon distanced his pursuers, left them out of sight behind, and, finally, found refuge with a Christian friend, who hid him over an oven in his house when he had reached the last stage of exhaustion from hard running, and could not have advanced further without rest. The soldiers came up and searched the house while he was asleep, but happily did not observe the oven ! They remained there, however, over the night, and thus rendered it impossible for Laihova to join his friends at that time.

Ravonino could not, of course, afford to delay. Knowing also that his young friend was well able to take care of himself, and that his soul's anchor was the Lord, he felt comparatively little anxiety in starting without him.

To let Rafaravavy have female companionship on the hazardous journey, her lover induced a Christian girl who had been named Sarah to accompany them.

This faithful creature was the means of saving their lives more than once by giving timely warning of approaching danger.

The first place to which the fugitives directed their steps was a village about fifty miles from the capital, where dwelt a Christian who, with his wife, offered them hospitality and protection. This man had sent a noble message to the persecuted ones in the city. It ran thus:—"Let all the Christians who are compelled to run away for their lives come to me. I will take care of them. As long as I am safe they are safe, and as long as I have food they shall share it."

Not an hour's rest was taken until the house of their friend was reached. Of course they were received with open arms. Food was placed before them, and mats were spread in a safe place on which they might rest. But neither food nor repose would the fugitives take until they had joined the Christian family in thanking God for their escape and in singing His praise.

"Sing the hymn of dear Ramanisa," said Ravonino as he seated himself at the side of Rafaravavy, after arranging her mat.

The host smiled as he turned over the leaves of a Malagasy hymn-book. "All the fugitives like that hymn," he said.

"Do you wonder?" returned his guest. "Before

the last great persecution he was one of our most faithful preachers of the Gospel, and when trouble came he always forgot himself in his eager desire to help and comfort others. Many a time has he guided and strengthened the Lord's people when they have been compelled to fly,—to travel weary and footsore by night, to wander in the dark forests, and hide in the gloomy caves. Wherever he went there was sunshine, because his heart was very full of the love of Jesus; and when he was led out to be speared, was he not faithful to the last? Perhaps we may be permitted to sing his own hymn along with him some day before the throne. No wonder that we love the words of Ramanisa. They called him Josiah when he was baptized, but he was Ramanisa when the Lord called him, and I think *that* is the name that is written in the Book of Life."

The hymn composed by this good native, which these Christians began to sing—and which is incorporated, as we have said, in the Malagasy hymnbook,—is still, and will doubtless continue to be, a great favourite with the Christians of Madagascar. The following is a translation of three of the verses.[1]

"Loud to the Lord your voices raise,
Extol His name, exalt His praise;
Publish the wonders of His hand
O'er all the earth, in every land.

---

[1] Extracted from *Madagascar, its Missions and Martyrs*, by E. Prout, for the London Missionary Society.

"Oh ! God, our God, to Thee we cry,
   Jesus, the Saviour, be Thou nigh ;
Oh ! sacred Spirit, hear our prayer,
   And save the afflicted from despair.

" Scarce can we find a place of rest,
   Save dens and caves, with hunger press'd ;
Yet Thy compassion is our bliss,
   Pilgrims amidst a wilderness."

Poor Rafaravavy had full proof of the truth embodied in these lines, both as to the affliction and
the bliss, before many days were over. The soldiers
being strong hardy men, burdened only with their
arms, and with little clothing, pushed after the three
fugitives with so much vigour that they arrived at
the place where the latter had rested on the second
day of their flight. While soldiers were thus close
to them the utmost caution and close concealment
were necessary. They remained where they were,
therefore, and every morning, before dawn, Ravonino
stole out to a neighbouring mountain with Rafaravavy and her maid. There they lay hid among the
craggy rocks until nightfall, when they returned to
their friend's house.

But soon this place of concealment became known
to the persecuting prime minister, Rainiharo, who
directed the soldiers to search the mountain before
going to the village. This they did, but did not find
the fugitives, for, as it was cold that morning, they
had agreed to run the risk of remaining in the house !

Failing to find those they sought for in the mountain, the soldiers entered the village and approached the house where they lay unperceived by human eye, and it seemed as if at last Rafaravavy's doom was sealed. Other eyes, however,— very black and sharp ones—observed the enemy, and the owners of these eyes—a flock of crows—rose in alarm at their approach.

"Oh!" exclaimed the handmaiden, Sarah, "the crows are at the rice I spread out to dry!" and out she ran to rescue it. One glimpse of the soldiers was enough. Sarah was equal to the occasion. Without even a backward glance she gave warning to those in the house, but cleverly continued her raid upon the crows, laughingly asking the men when she passed them "if they had come there to search for run-away Christians!"

"This way," whispered the host to his two guests when the warning reached him. Leading them to an inner room he made them creep under a bed and covered them with a mat. As for the chair-bearers and their burden, such adjuncts to Malagasy travel were too numerous and common in the land to attract much attention. Fortunately the soldiers were hungry, and, being eager for food, did not search the house with care, but during their stay of an hour poor Rafaravavy heard all they said respecting her and the orders that had been issued for her

arrest and death.   At the same time Ravonino
became aware that his presence in the neighbourhood was known, though his complicity in the
abduction of his companion in distress, he fancied,
had not been suspected.

That night the fugitives resumed their journey
and travelled till dawn, when they again found safe
refuge in the house of a sympathising friend.   Thus
they proceeded for several days and nights with the
utmost caution, for, wherever they went it was
found that soldiers had been sent out in pursuit.

One night they approached a village where they
knew they would be kindly received, but had
scarcely reached it when they learned that a party
of soldiers were searching the neighbourhood for
some other woman who had recently disappeared.
They were compelled, therefore, to return to the
place they had left the day before.   From this point
they changed their intended route, partly to throw
the pursuers off the scent, if possible, and partly to
seek temporary refuge at the house of an old woman
who was an aunt of Sarah.

"She's a real good Christian," said Sarah, when
advising the visit, "and she fears no one but God.
If they ever kill my old aunt she will die singing,
or praying for her murderers."

Sure enough, when they reached the hut of the
old woman, they heard her singing hymns at the

full pitch of her voice, quite regardless of the fact that she was breaking the law and that persecutors were swarming in the land.

"Shelter you!" exclaimed this old woman, when her niece had mentioned the cause of their visit, "yes, I will shelter you as long as my dear Lord gives me the power to do so."

The need for friendly aid was great, for, even while the old woman spoke, a little girl came bounding into the hut saying that a party of soldiers were approaching.

"Run! meet them, child. Then turn and run away as if you were afraid of them. Make them chase you if you can. Run!"

The girl was intelligent. She bounded away, and the old woman, with a degree of activity that was wonderful at her age, led her visitors to the back of her house and hid them in a pit. There they had to spend that night while the aunt entertained their pursuers, but next morning, after the latter had left, their old hostess led them to a plantation close at hand, where they remained concealed for several days, not daring to move, for, at various times, they saw men who were in pursuit of them pass quite near to their hiding-place.

Here it was decided that the palanquin, or chair-bearers, should proceed no further, as they only increased the danger of discovery, and that Ravonino,

Rafaravavy, and Sarah should proceed alone and on foot through the extensive forest which lay just beyond the place.

The first night all went well. The moon was clear enough to make travelling easy, and no enemies were encountered, but the next evening, a little after sunset, on gaining the crest of a hill, they met almost face to face a small band of soldiers who were travelling in the opposite direction.

To crouch behind some rocks was the work of an instant. There was no thick underwood at the spot to conceal them. As Ravonino glanced quickly round, he saw that the only hope was to turn and run. They evidently had not been perceived, but what probability was there that the two trembling girls beside him could escape by such means?

"We must fly, dear one," he said, in desperation, putting his arm round Rafaravavy's waist.

"I cannot run," she said, while a look of resignation settled on her face. "Go, *you* may escape, perhaps, if the Lord will, and bring us help. Leave us, we are ready to die."

"Leave you, Rafaravavy!" exclaimed the man, with a look almost of triumph. "No—not until my God commands. May He help us now!"

While he spoke he observed a patch of rushes growing at the side of the path. As a last resource he ran in among them, leading or rather dragging

the two girls. To their joy they found that the
rushes grew in a pool of water. It was very
shallow, but by lying down and sinking themselves
into the mud of the deepest part they managed to
cover themselves completely, except their heads,
which the rushes effectually concealed.

A few minutes later and the soldiers, reaching the
crest of the hill, halted to look round and chat. If
it had been broad day at the time the fugitives must
undoubtedly have been observed, but it was growing
dark. For a few terrible minutes the men conversed
—always on the same theme—the capture and
death of Rafaravavy! Then they resumed their
march and disappeared among the forest trees.

It was a deplorable plight in which the fugitives
now found themselves. Soaking wet, covered with
mud from their necks downwards, and without the
prospect of any shelter for the coming night save
that afforded by the open forest. Poor Sarah lost
heart entirely for a little time and burst into tears,
but Rafaravavy, putting her hand on the maid's
shoulder, said encouragingly, "'The Lord reigneth.
We will not fear what man can do unto us.' Will
you pray for us?" she added, turning to their protector.

Ravonino at once kneeled; the two girls sank down
beside him, and in few but earnest, simple words he
prayed for help in the all-prevailing name of Jesus.

The vigour of body which flowed from the prayer was no fanciful emotion or miraculous effect. The confidence resulting from faith in God, and the joy of soul and consequent flow of warm blood, were not less natural consequences of prayer than direct answers to it would have been. They rose from their knees refreshed, and walked on with renewed energy for a considerable time; but at last Rafara-vavy was fairly overcome with fatigue, and an irresistible desire to sleep. Her maid, being of a more robust physical fibre, was not so much over-come, and declared that she could still go on easily.

Ravonino at last solved the difficulty by taking his lady-love in his strong arms. She submitted with a sleepy protest, and her little head was no sooner on the man's shoulder than she was fast asleep.

And here again the power of joy to give strength became abundantly evident, for when he fairly had Rafaravavy in his arms, a glow of enthusiasm and thankfulness pervaded his entire being, so that he felt as if he had scarcely walked any distance at all that day! His endurance, however, was not destined to be further tested that night, for he had not gone far when he came unexpectedly on the hut of a wood-cutter, who received him hospitably, though, being taciturn, it was not easy to ascertain what were his views as to the religion for which so many people were then suffering.

Strange to say, during all this trying time, these fugitives found comfort not only from the Word of God, but from the *Pilgrim's Progress* of Bunyan! This work had been translated into the Malagasy language by the English missionaries, and many passages in it were found to be singularly appropriate to and comforting in the circumstances in which the persecuted people were placed. Eight copies of the great allegory had been transcribed by the native Christians themselves for their common use. These being lent from one household to another the details of the story soon spread. Naturally those who possessed strong memories learned much of it by heart, and thus it became a book which the afflicted Christians prized next to the Bible.

CHAPTER XXV.

THE FOREST REFUGE—VOALAVO IS WARLIKE, RAVONINO PEACEFUL, AND FALSE FRIENDS DANGEROUS.

WE change the scene, now, to the profoundest recesses of the tangled forest. Here, in the deep shadow cast by the overarching trees, two native girls wandered out at an early hour one morning to converse about things that interested them deeply —if the varying aspects of their expressive faces were any index to their thoughts. One was tall, dark, majestic in mien and grave of countenance. The other was comparatively fair, of small stature, and evidently of lively yet timid disposition. Need we say that they were Ramatoa, the sister of Laihova, and Ra-Ruth, the sister of Ravonino?

"I fear they will never return to us," said Ra-Ruth, laying her hand on her friend's arm.

"Say not so," replied Ramatoa, "we know not what blessings our God has in store for us. Only this we are sure of, that *all* things will work together for our good."

"But the Queen is so cruel!" objected her little

friend. "When her anger is roused she will do anything. Besides, has not the messenger told us that the soldiers have been sent in hundreds over the country to search for Christians, and spies are about everywhere. Laihova, too, has been separated from them, he says. Perhaps he has been caught.

"I like not this messenger," said the other, with a touch of sternness in her look and tone. "He seems to me like a wolf in sheep's clothing. He does not refer all things to God as 'Our Father,' and in his use of the Word he does not seem sincere. I trust that he is not one of the spies."

As she spoke her companion uttered a quick exclamation. There was a rustling in the bushes, and next moment, Laihova, springing out, clasped Ra-Ruth in his arms.

"Thank God," he said, in deep earnest tones, as he released her. "I am not too late!"

"Brother," said Ramatoa, anxiously, laying a hand on the man's arm, "are you alone?"

"Yes. Have not Ravoninohitriniony and Rafaravavy arrived?"

"No. And — and what of Mamba?" asked Ramatoa.

An expression of profound sadness crossed the features of Laihova. Dropping his eyes on the ground he stood silent. For a few moments his sister did not speak, but her breast heaved with suppressed emotion. At last she asked in a low voice—

"Has he been martyred?"

"No—he is not dead. But—he is condemned to slavery in chains for life."

Terrible though this fate was, the news of it evidently conveyed a measure of relief to Ramatoa, for it assured her that her lover was at all events not dead. Where there is life there is hope!

"I fear this will kill his mother," she said. "Poor Reni-Mamba is so full of love and gentleness, and her sorrows have been very heavy. Strange that her husband and son should share the same fate —perpetual slavery! Yet it is not perpetual. Death will set them free. Come to the cave and let us break the sad news."

As they walked through the forest Ramatoa gave her brother a rapid outline of what had occurred since the day he left.

"They will be deeply grieved," she said, "that our friends are not with you. We had all hoped that you would arrive together. A messenger who has just come did indeed tell us that you had been separated from them, but all supposed that you would easily overtake them."

"True, sister, but I overshot them. That has been the way of it," returned Laihova, regretfully.

"Still, I feel sure that they will escape," continued

the girl, "Ravoninohitriniony has such a firm trust in God, and he is so strong and brave and wise. Besides, he has the blood of the white man in his veins—he will succeed or die!"

This compliment to her brother, whether deserved or not, had the effect of raising a flush of pleasure on Ra-Ruth's little face.

"Many things have happened since you left us," resumed Ramatoa. "Razafil, the poet, has come to stay with us, and Voalavo too."

"Voalavo!" exclaimed Laihova in surprise, "is he not the chief of a tribe that does not love Jesus? And he was not a Christian when I saw him last."

"He is a Christian *now*," returned the girl, quietly, "if I may judge him by his works. He has been our main stay since you went away. Not long after you left us he came, saying that you had told him about Jesus delivering men from the power of sin, and he wanted to know about Him. You may be sure we were glad to tell him all we knew. He has never said he is a Christian, but he has stayed with us ever since, and hunted for us. He is as active as the youngest men in getting and bringing in wild fruits, and the youths are glad to have his wisdom and advice. He listens to us while we sing, and he prays in secret—I know that he does, for I have overheard him. Moreover, he has brought some of his people over to our side. He seems to be

particularly fond of Reni-Mamba, and she is fond of
him—for he is funny."

"Yes; he is *very* funny," responded Laihova, with
profound gravity.

On reaching the cavern which we have described
in a former chapter, they found that most of the
men were out, and the women were busy with those
culinary labours which tend to rejoice the hearts
of hunters when they return home.

The chief, Voalavo, was there, however, deeply
engaged in studying—yes, studying—*The Pilgrim's
Progress!* But he could not make much of it,
his education—at the hands of Ra-Ruth—having
commenced only a few weeks before. Besides
teaching the chief his letters, Ra-Ruth had read to
him large portions of the book, which had so
fascinated him that he had applied himself to his
letters with a will, and, being an able man, had begun
to make rapid progress. His desire, also, to be able
to read the Bible—when he began to understand
what it was, and to perceive the significance of some
of its soul-stirring words—stimulated his active
mind to greater exertions.

The unfortunate poet, Razafil, also fell in with the
wonderful allegory in that cave for the first time, and
it helped in no small degree to turn his mind from
brooding over the fate of his dear martyred daughter
Raniva. His mind was quicker than that of the

z

chief to perceive the grand truths which underlie the story, and he was not a little comforted. Thus these two men, so very differently constituted, sat at the feet of the fair Ra-Ruth, who being, as we have said, timid and rather distrustful of herself, was overjoyed to find that even she could help in advancing the cause of her Lord.

But it rather perplexed the little maiden when these same men, having been gifted with inquiring minds, puzzled themselves over the question why the Prince of the country in the *Pilgrim's Progress* did not kill Apollyon at once and have done with him.

" Or make him good," suggested Voalavo.

" True, that would have been better, perhaps, than killing him," assented Razafil.

Like millions of the human race before them, the two men got out of their depth here; but unlike too many thousands of the same race, they did not permit such difficulties to interfere with their unshaken confidence in the love and wisdom of that God, who certainly " doeth all things well," whatever we in our pride and partial ignorance may think of Him.

Voalavo's studies on the day we write of did not however engross him so much as to prevent his starting up in great excitement when he heard the sound of Laihova's voice. He hastened to the entrance of the cavern, and received his friend with his wonted effusive heartiness. But he was damped considerably on learning that Laihova came alone, that Mamba was enslaved, and that Ravonino and Rafaravavy were still wandering in the forest, pursued by their enemies.

"Come, my young men!" he shouted, flying into a sudden state of indignation, and clapping his hands together like a pistol-shot, "we will go and rouse our warriors. Arm, and make to the rescue! We will dethrone the Queen—this Ranavalona—usurper! Why should such a woman live on, filling the land with blood and misery!"

"My friend," said Laihova, in a soothing tone, as he laid his hand on the chief's shoulder, "the arms of Christians are not the arms of a soldier. We wrestle not against flesh and blood."

"That is idle talk," exclaimed the unpacified chief. "Did not Christian use a sword? Did not Greatheart fight Apollyon with a sword?"

"True, but these were spiritual weapons," said Laihova. "Moreover, if you did rouse your people and march to the capital, what could you do? Your whole tribe would appear but as a handful of dust in the eyes of the Hova army."

"I would that we were a handful of dust!" snorted the chief, "and we'd dash ourselves into the eyes of the Hova army and kill them while they wept!"

"But there is nothing to prevent us from going

forth to meet our friends," rejoined Laihova, "and
we can take our spears. If they stand in need of
help we may give it."

This proposition fell in entirely with the warlike
Voalavo's views, and, a band of the young hunters
and fruit-gatherers entering the cave at that moment,
he urged them to make haste with their dinner and
get ready for the war-patr.

Ever ready—as young blades usually are—for
fighting, these youths threw down their loads
quickly.

And, truly, judging from the contents of the
cavern larder that day, there was no prospect of
famine before the persecuted people. In one part
of that larder there was abundance of beef and pork,
also of game, such as guinea-fowl, pheasants, part-
ridges, peacocks, turkeys, geese, ducks, pigeons,
turtle-doves, and snipe. In another place the
vegetable and fruit-gatherers had piled up little
mounds of bread-fruit, pine-apples, cocoa-nuts, yams,
plantains, bananas, manioc-root, melons, etc., much
of which had been gathered from regions at a considerable distance from their place of abode. Thus
they had laid up store for many days, and felt somewhat elated.

But there were two hearts there which found it
impossible to rejoice, and very hard to submit to
God. Reni and Ramatoa retired to a dark recess in

the cave, and mingled their tears and prayers together.

"Oh! it would have been better if he had died!" sobbed Reni, "for then he would have been with Jesus; but now it is awful to think of the life-long slavery; and we shall never more see him on earth."

"Nay, mother, do not think thus. Whatever God does *must* be best," returned Ramatoa in a tremulous voice. "Let us try to say 'Thy will be——.'"

She broke down and finished the sentence with prayer for strength and for a submissive spirit.

Meanwhile the war-like expedition, on which Voalavo and his youths were only too ready to enter was rendered needless by the sudden appearance of Ravonino himself, with Rafaravavy and Sarah! After encountering innumerable hardships and dangers those three had at last arrived at their forest stronghold in safety.

"So then," remarked Laihova to Ra-Ruth, after the first enthusiastic reception was over, "I have only over-shot them by a few hours after all!"

"We were just going to sally forth to look for you—and fight if need be," said Voalavo.

"There was no need for that," returned Ravonino, "the Lord was our protector."

"Where is Reni-Mamba? Have you heard, mother, about your son?"

Reni and Ramatoa, who had pressed forward,
looked surprised, for their friend did not speak like
a man who had bad news to tell.

"Laihova has told me, truly," replied Reni, still
whimpering, "that my dear boy is worse than dead."

"Not so, mother," said Ravonino, taking the poor
woman's hand, "be of good cheer; Mamba is not
dead. I know not indeed where he is at this
moment, having been pressed in my own flight, but
I know that the Queen has set him free—this much
I learned from our white friend, Mark Breezy.
More I cannot tell, but is not this cause for joy and
gratitude? Come, let us return thanks to our
Father."

Most of those present were glad to give vent to
their feelings in prayer and praise, though some
there were who, having been led to join the band by
the mere force of circumstances, had little heart in
the matter. Certainly Voalavo was not among these
last, for the enthusiasm which inclined him to fight
with violence also induced him to pray with vigour.

When this appropriate act of worship was over,
food was prepared for the wearied travellers, and in
a short time the whole party was seated round the
cooking-fire, illuminated by the torches on the wall,
and listening eagerly to Ravonino as he recounted
his adventures.

"I fear much," he said in conclusion, "that another

dark season is about to fall on us. It may be like the last—or worse."

Ravonino here referred (and with bated breath) to the terrible outbreak of persecution which had occurred several years previously, when, at the lowest estimate, about two thousand men and women were severely punished, and many tortured and slain, becaused they professed or favoured the religion of Jesus.

As, one after another, various members of the party detailed the sad sufferings or deaths of relatives and friends, the feelings of all became deeply affected with grief, those of some with a considerable dash also of indignation. Among the latter of course was Voalavo.

" Why," he cried suddenly, giving his hands the accustomed pistol-shot clap that betrayed his inability to contain himself, " why do we suffer all this ? Why not assemble the tribes, go up at once to Antananarivo, take it, cut off the Queen's head, and put Prince Rakota on the throne ? "

" Ay, why not?" demanded several of the more fiery young men.

" Because the Lord tells us to overcome evil with good," answered Ravonino, quietly. Then, wishing to draw attention from the subject, he inquired for the messenger who had brought news of his own escape.

All looked round as if expecting the man to answer for himself, but no one replied.

Search was made, and then it was discovered that the messenger had hastily taken his departure from the place.

CHAPTER XXVI.

DR. BREEZY PRESCRIBES FOR THE QUEEN, AND ATTAINS TO
TEMPORARY AND " PERFIK F'LICITY."

WHILE these events were taking place in the forest, Queen Ranavalona was keeping her Court Physician and his comrades in a state of considerable uneasiness, not only with reference to the safety of their own heads, but because of her violent edicts regarding her Christian subjects.

She renewed her commands as to the necessity of every one coming forward, on pain of instant death in the event of disobedience, and accusing themselves, with the reiterated assurance that if they failed to comply and they were afterwards accused by others they should be subjected to the ordeal of the Tangena, and slain or reduced to perpetual slavery if found guilty.

The whole city was in a panic. No one felt safe. Under the influence of fear some accused themselves, expecting, no doubt, that their punishment would be lightened. Others remained quiet, hoping that they might escape detection, while many were accused by false friends as well as by enemies, and fell victims under the poison ordeal. Others, again, stood firm, and boldly proclaimed their faith in the Lord Jesus and their readiness to die if need be for His cause.

After the accusations, trials, and investigations, sentences were read which deprived four hundred officers and nobles of their honours, and levied fines on the remainder to the number of about two thousand. One would have thought that the mere necessity for such widespread punishment would have shown the Queen how deeply the new religion had taken root, and how hopeless it was to attempt its suppression, but she did not see it in that light. On the contrary, she issued a mandate requiring all books to be delivered up to her officers, and threatening death against any who should keep back or hide even a single leaf. She also commanded her subjects never again even to "think of the Christian lessons they had learned, but to blot them from their memories for ever!"

Among those who boldly held to their opinions was the Queen's own son Rakota, who, however, as we have seen, did not run quite so much risk as others, owing to his mother's affection for him. The Prime Minister's son, also, and Prince Ramonja, made no effort to conceal their opinions, though they were wise enough to refrain from exasperating the angry Queen by asserting them openly.

One morning the Prime Minister sent a message to the Court Physician, requiring his immediate attendance at the palace. Mark was seated in his own room at the time, talking with Hockins and Ebony about the gloomy state of affairs. A slight feeling of dismay fluttered the heart of each when the message came, for death-warrants were much in the air at that time.

"Oh, massa, p'r'aps dey're a-goin' to kill you!" was the negro's comforting suggestion.

"More likely they want him to cure the Queen," said Hockins.

"Couldn't you, massa," whispered Ebony, with a terribly solemn countenance, "mix a spoonful—a bery small spoonful—ob prussic acid, or creosote, or suffin ob dat sort, wid 'er physic?"

Mark laughed, and shook his head as he went out.

He found Rainiharo, with a tremendous frown on his face and deep lines of care on his brow, seated in front of our friend the Secretary, who had an open book on his knee. Three other officers of the palace sat beside them. These constituted a court of inquiry into the contents of the suspected books, and the Secretary, being the only literary character among them, was the appointed reader.

"Come here. Sit down," said Rainiharo, sternly

pointing to a seat; "we want you to explain your
books. The Queen commands us to examine them,
and, if we find anything contrary to her wishes in
them, to condemn them to the flames. But it seems
to us that there is nothing in them but rubbish
which we cannot understand."

Strange, is it not, that in barbaric as well as in
civilised lands, people are apt to regard as rubbish
that which they do not understand?

So thought the Court Physician, but he wisely
held his tongue and sat down.

"This book," said the Prime Minister, pointing
with a look of mingled contempt and exasperation to
the volume on the Secretary's knee, "is worse than
the last. The one we condemned yesterday was
what you call your Bible. We began with it because
it was the biggest book. Being practical men we
began at the beginning, intending to go straight
through and give it a fair hearing. We began at
Gen—Gen—what was it?"

"Genesis," answered the Secretary.

"Genzis—yes. Well, we found nothing to object
to in the first verse, but in the second—the very
second—we found the word 'darkness.' This was
sufficient! Queen Ranavalona does not like darkness, so we condemned it at once—unanimously—
for we could not for a moment tolerate anything
with *darkness* in it."

Mark felt an almost irresistible desire to laugh outright, but as the gratification of that desire might have cost him his head he did resist it successfully.

"Now," continued the Prime Minister, with a darker frown, "we have got to the Pil—Pil—what is it?"

"*Pilgrim's Progress*," answered the Secretary.

"Just so—the *Pilgim's Progess*. Well, we agreed that we would give the *Pil—Pilgim's Purgess* a better chance, so we opened it, as it were, anyhow, and what do we come on—the very first thing—but a man named Obstinate! Now, if there is one thing that the Queen hates more than another it is an obstinate man. She cannot abide obstinate men. In fact, she has none such about her, for the few men of that sort that have turned up now and then have invariably lost their heads. But we wanted to be fair, so we read on, and what do we find as one of the first things that Obstinate says? He says, 'Tush! away with your book!' Now, if the man himself condemns the book, is our Queen likely to spare it? But there are some things in the book which we cannot understand, so we have sent for you to explain it. Now," added Rainiharo, turning to the Secretary, "translate all that to the maker of physic and tell me what he has to answer."

It was a strange and difficult duty that our young student was thus unexpectedly and suddenly called to perform, and never before had he felt so deeply the difference between knowing a subject and expounding it. There was no escape, however, from the situation. He was not only bound by fear of his life, but by Scripture itself, "to give a reason of the hope that was in him," and he rose to the occasion with vigour, praying, mentally, for guidance, and also blessing his mother for having subjected him in childhood—much against his will!—to a pretty stiff and systematic training in the truths of Scripture as well as in the story of the *Pilgrim's Progress.*

But no exposition that he could give sufficed to affect the foregone conclusion that both the Bible and the Pilgrim, containing as they did matter that was offensive to the Queen, were worthy of condemnation, and, therefore, doomed to the flames.

Having settled this knotty point in a statesman-like manner, Rainiharo bade Mark and the Secretary remain with him, and dismissed his three colleagues.

" You see," he said, after some moments of anxious thought, " although I agree with the Queen in her desire to stamp out the Christian religion, I have no desire that my son and my nephew should be stamped out along with it ; therefore I wish to have your assistance, doctor, in turning the mind of Ranavalona away from persecution to some extent, for in her present mood she is dangerous alike to friend and foe.   Indeed I would not give much for your own life if she becomes more violent.   How is this to be done, think you ? "

The question was indeed a puzzler, for it amounted to this—" How are we to manage a furious, blood-thirsty woman with the reins loose on her neck and the bit fast in her teeth ? "

" I know not," said Mark at last, " but I will think the matter over and talk with you again."

" If I may be allowed to speak," said the Secretary.

" You are allowed," returned the Premier.

" Then I would advise that the Queen should arrange a grand journey—a procession—all over the country, with thousands of her soldiers.   This will let her have plenty of fresh air and exercise, change of scene, and excitement, and will give her something to do till her blood cools.   At the same time it will show the people her great power and perhaps induce them to be cautious how they resist her will."

" The idea is good," said Mark, with animation, " so good that I would advise its being carried out immediately—even before another week passes."

Rainiharo shook his head.   " Impossible.   There is to be a great bull-fight this week, and you know Ranavalona will allow nothing to interfere with that.   Besides, it takes time to get up such an expedition as you suggest.   However, I like the notion well. Go. I will think over it and see you again."

The bull-fighting to which the Premier referred was a favourite amusement with this blood-thirsty woman, and the spectacle usually took place in the royal court-yard. Rainiharo was right when he said the Queen would not forego it, but she was so pleased with the plan of a royal progress through the country that she gave orders to make ready for it at once on an extensive scale.

"You will of course accompany me," she said to Mark, when he was summoned to a subsequent audience, "I may be ill, or my bearers may fall and I may be injured."

"Certainly," he replied, "nothing would afford the Court Physician greater pleasure than to attend upon her Majesty on such an expedition. But I would ask a favour," continued Mark. "May my black servant accompany me? He is very useful in assisting me with my medicines, and——"

"Yes, yes," interrupted the Queen, "let him go with you by all means. He shall have bearers if you choose. And take yon other man also—with his music. I love his little pipe!"

In some excitement Mark went off to tell his comrades the news—which Hockins received with a grunt of satisfaction, and the negro with a burst of joy. Indeed the anxieties and worries they had recently experienced in the city, coupled with the tyranny and bloodshed which they witnessed, had so depressed the three friends that the mere idea of getting once again into the fresh free open plains and forests afforded them pleasure somewhat akin to that of the schoolboy when he obtains an unexpected holiday.

Great was the excitement all over the country when the Queen's intention was made known. The idea was not indeed a novelty. Malagasy sovereigns had been in the habit of making such progresses from time to time in former years. The wise King Radama I. frequently went on hunting expeditions with more or less of display. But knowing as they did, only too well, the cruel character of Ranavalona I., the people feared that the desire to terrify and suppress had more to do with the event than pleasure or health.

At last, everything being complete, the Queen left the capital, and directed her course to the south-westward. Her enormous retinue consisted of the members of the Government, the principal military and civil officers and their wives, six thousand soldiers, and a host of slaves, bearers, and other attendants; the whole numbering about 40,000 souls.

Great preparations had been made for the journey in the way of providing large stores of rice, herds of cattle, and other provisions, but those who knew the difficulties of the proposed route, and the thinly populated character of the country, looked with considerable apprehension on the prospects of the journey. Some there were, no doubt, who regarded these prospects with a lively hope that the Queen might never more return to her capital!

Of course such a multitude travelled very slowly, as may well be believed when it is said that they had about 1500 palanquins in the host, for there was not a wheeled vehicle in Madagascar at that time. The soldiers were formed in five divisions; one carrying the tents, one the cooking apparatus and spears, and one the guns and sleeping-mats. The other two had always to be in readiness for any service required about the Queen. The camp was divided into four parts; the Queen being in the middle, in a blue tent, surrounded, wherever she halted for the night, by high palisades, and near to this was pitched a tent containing the idols of the royal family. The tent of the Prime Minister, with the Malagasy flag, was pitched to the north of that of the Queen. East, west, and south, were occupied by other high officers of State, and among the latter was the tent of our friends, Mark, Hockins, and Ebony.

"Now," said the first of these, as he sat in the door of the tent one evening after supper, watching the rich glow of sunshine that flooded a wide stretch of beautiful country in front of him, "this would be perfect felicity if only we had freedom to move about at our own pleasure and hunt up the treasures in botany, entomology, etc., that are scattered around us."

"True, Massa," returned Ebony, "it would be perfik f'licity if we could forgit de poor Christ'ns in chains an' pris'ns."

"Right, Ebony, right. I am selfishly thinking only of myself at the present moment. But let us hope we may manage to do these poor Christians good before we leave the land."

"I don't think, myself, that we'll get much fun out o' this trip," remarked Hockins. "You see the Queen's too fond o' your physickin' and of my too-tootlin' to part with us even for a day at a time. If we was like Ebony, now, we might go where we liked an' no one ud care."

"Ob course not," replied the negro, promptly, "peepil's nebber anxious about whar wise men goes to; it's on'y child'in an' stoopid folk dey's got to tink about. But why not ax de Queen, massa, for leabe ob absence to go a-huntin'?"

"Because she'd be sure to refuse," said Mark. "No, I see no way out of this difficulty. We are too useful to be spared!"

But Mark was wrong. That very night he was sent for by the Prime Minister, and as he passed the Secretary's tent he called him out to act as interpreter. On reaching the tent on the north side they found Rainiharo doubled up on his mat and groaning in agony.

"What's wrong?" demanded the doctor.

"Everything!" replied the patient.

"Describe your feelings," said the doctor.

"I've—I've got a red-hot stone," groaned Rainiharo, "somewhere in my inwards! Thorny shrubs are revolving in my stomach! Young crocodiles are masticating my—oh!"

At this point his power of description failed; but that matters little, for, never having met with the disease before, we can neither describe it nor give it a name. The young doctor did not know it, but he knew exactly what to do, and did it. We cannot report what he did, but we can state the result, which was great relief in a few minutes and a perfect cure before morning! Most men are grateful under such circumstances—even the cruel Rainiharo was so.

"What can I do for you?" he asked, affectionately, next day.

A sudden inspiration seized the doctor. "Beg the Queen," he said, "to let me and my two friends wander round the host all day, and every day, for a short time, and I will return to report myself each night."

"For what purpose?" asked the Premier, in some surprise.

"To pluck plants and catch butterflies."

"Is the young doctor anxious to renew his childhood?"

"Something of the sort, no doubt.   But there is medicine in the plants, and—and—interest, if nothing else, in the butterflies."

"Medicine in the plants" was a sufficient explanation to the Premier.   What he said to the Queen we know not, but he quickly returned with the required permission, and Mark went to his couch that night in a state of what Ebony styled "perfik f'licity."

Behold our trio, then, once more alone in the great forests of Madagascar—at least almost alone, for the Secretary was with them, for the double purpose of gaining instruction and seeing that the strangers did not lose themselves.   As they were able to move about twice as fast as the host, they could wander around, here, there, and everywhere, or rest at pleasure without fear of being left behind.

CHAPTER XXVII.

IN WHICH A HAPPY CHANGE FOR THE BETTER IS DISASTROUSLY
INTERRUPTED.

ONE very sultry forenoon Mark and his party—while out botanising, entomologising, philosophising, etc., not far from but out of sight of the great procession—came to the brow of a hill and sat down to rest.

Their appearance had become somewhat curious and brigand-like by that time, for their original garments having been worn out were partially replaced by means of the scissors and needle of John Hockins—at least in the trousers department. That worthy seaman having, during his travels, torn his original trousers to shreds from the knee downwards, had procured some stout canvas in the capital and made for himself another pair. He was, like most sailors, expert at tailoring, and the result was so good that Mark and Ebony became envious. The seaman was obliging. He set to work and made a pair of nether garments for both. Mark wore his pair stuffed into the legs of a pair of Wellington boots procured from a trader. Ebony preferred to cut his off short, just below the knee, thus exposing to view those black boots supplied to negroes by Nature, which have the advantage of never wearing out. Hockins himself stuck to his navy shirt, but the others found striped cotton shirts sufficient. A native straw hat on Mark's head and a silk scarf round his waist, with a cavalry pistol in it, enhanced the brigand-like aspect of his costume.

This pistol was their only firearm, the gun having been broken beyond repair, but each carried a spear in one hand, a gauze butterfly-net in the other, and a basket, in lieu of a specimen-box, on his shoulder. Even the Secretary, entering into the spirit of the thing, carried a net and pursued the butterflies with the ardour of a boy.

"Oh! massa," exclaimed Ebony, wiping the perspiration from his forehead with a bunch of grass, "I *do* lub science!"

"Indeed, why so?" asked Mark, sitting down on a bank opposite his friend.

"Why, don't you see, massa, it's not comfortabil for a man what's got any feelin's to go troo de land huntin' an' killin' cattle an' oder brutes for *noting*. You can't eat more nor one hox—p'r'aps not dat. So w'en you've kill 'im an' eaten so much as you can, dar's no more fun, for what fun is dere in slaughterin' hoxes for *noting*? Den, if you goes

arter bees an' butterflies on'y for fun, w'y you git
shamed ob yourself. On'y a chile do dat. But
science, dat put 'im all right! Away you goes arter
de bees and butterflies an' tings like mad—ober de
hills an' far away—troo de woods, across de ribbers—
sometimes into 'em!—crashin' an' smashin' like de
bull in de china-shop, wid de proud feelin' bustin'
your buzzum dat you're advancin' de noble cause
ob science—dat's what you call 'im, 'noble'?—
yes. Well, den you come home done up, so pleasant
like, an' sot down an' fix de critters up wid pins an'
gum an' sitch-like, and arter dat you show 'em to
your larned friends an' call 'em awrful hard names
(sometimes dey seem like *bad* names!), an'—oh! I
do lub science! It's wot I once heard a captin ob a
ribber steamer in de States call a safety-balve wot
lets off a deal o' 'uman energy. He was a-sottin on
his own safety-balve at de time, so he ought to have
know'd suffin about it."

"I say, Ebony," asked Hockins, "where did you
pick up so much larnin' about science—eh?"

"I pick 'im in Texas—was 'sistant to a German
nat'ralist dar for two year. Stuck to 'im like a
limpit till he a-most busted hisself by tumblin'
into a swamp, smashin' his spectacles, an' ketchin'
fever, w'en he found hisself obleeged to go home to
recroot—he called it—though what dat was I nebber
rightly understood, unless it was drinkin' brandy

an' water; for I noticed that w'en he said he needed to recroot, he allers had a good stiff pull at de brandy bottle."

Ebony's discourse was here cut short by the sudden appearance of an enormous butterfly, which the excitable negro dashed after at a breakneck pace in the interests of science. The last glimpse they had of him, as he disappeared among the trees, was in a somewhat peculiar attitude, with his head down and his feet in the air!

"That's a sign he has missed him," remarked Hockins, beginning to fill his pipe—the tobacco, not the musical, one! "I've always observed that when Ebony becomes desperate, and knows he can't git hold of the thing he's arter, he makes a reckless plunge, with a horrible yell, goes right down by the head, and disappears like a harpooned whale."

"True, but have you not also observed," said Mark, "that like the whale he's sure to come to the surface again—sooner or later—and generally with the object of pursuit in possession?"

"I b'lieve you're right, doctor," said the seaman, emitting a prolonged puff of smoke.

"Does he always go mad like that?" asked the Secretary, who was much amused.

"Usually," replied Mark, "but he is generally madder than that. He's in comparatively low spirits to-day. Perhaps it is the heat that affects

him. Whew! how hot it is! I think I shall take
a bath the first pool we come to."

"That would only make you hotter, sir," said
Hockins. "I've often tried it. At first, no doubt,
when you gits into the water it cools you, but arter
you come out you git hotter than before. A *hot*
bath is the thing to cool you comfortably."

"But we can't get a hot bath here," returned Mark.

"You are wrong," said the Secretary, "we have
many natural hot springs in our land. There is
one not far from here."

"How far?" asked Mark with some interest.

"About two rice-cookings off."

To dispel the reader's perplexity, we may explain
at once that in Madagascar they measure distances
by the time occupied in cooking a pot of rice. As
that operation occupies about half-an-hour, the
Secretary meant that the hot spring was distant
about two half-hours—*i.e.* between three and four
miles off.

"Let's go an' git into it at once," suggested
Hockins.

"Better wait for Ebony," said Mark. Then—to
the Secretary—"Yours is a very interesting and
wonderful country!"

"It is, and I wonder not that European nations
wish to get possession of it—but that shall *never* be."

Mark replied, "I hope not," and regarded his

friend with some surprise, for he had spoken with emphasis, and evidently strong feeling. "Have you fear that any of the nations wish to have your country?"

"Yes, we have fear," returned the Secretary, with an unwontedly stern look. "They have tried it before; perhaps they will try it again. But they will fail. Has not God given us the land? Has not He moved the hearts of Engleesh men to send to us the Bible? Has not His Holy Spirit inclined our hearts to receive that Word? Yes—it has come. It is planted. It *must* grow. The European nations cannot hinder it. Ranavalona cannot stamp it out. False friends and open foes cannot crush it. The Word of God will civilise us. We will rise among the nations of the earth when the love of Jesus spreads among us—for that love cures every evil. It inclines as well as teaches us to deny self and do good. It is not possible for man to reach a higher point than that! Deny self! Do good! We are slow to learn, but it is *sure* to come at last, for is it not written that 'the knowledge of the Lord shall cover the earth as the waters cover the sea'?"

"I believe you are right," said Mark, much impressed with this outburst and the earnest enthusiasm of his friend's manner. "And," he continued, "you have a noble country to work on —full of earth's riches."

"You say noting but the truth," answered the
Secretary in a gratified tone. "Is not our island as
big—or more big—as yours—nearly the same as
France? And look around! We have thousands
of cattle, tame and wild, with which even now we
send large supplies to foreign markets, and fowls
innumerable, both wild and tame. Our soil is rich
and prolific. Are not our vegetables and fruits
innumerable and abundant? Do not immense
forests traverse our island in all directions, full of
trees that are of value to man—trees fit for building
his houses and ships and for making his beautiful
furniture, as well as those that supply cocoa-nuts,
and figs, and fruits, and gums, and dyes? And
have we not the silkworm in plenty, and cotton-
plants, and sugar-cane, and many spices, and the
great food-supply of our people — rice, besides
minerals which make nations rich, such as iron and
gold? Yes, we have everything that is desirable
and good for man. But we have a climate which
does not suit the white man. Yet *some* white men,
like yourself, manage to live here. Is not this a
voice, from God? He does not speak to us with
the tongue of man, but He speaks with a still, small
voice, as easy to understand. He has surrounded
our island with unhealthy shores. Does not that
tell the white man not to come here? Your London
Missionary Society sent us the Bible. God bless

them for that! They have done well. But they have done enough. We desire not the interference of England or France in our affairs. We do not want your divisions, your sects. We have the Word. God will do the rest. We want no white nations to *protect* us. We want to be let alone to protect and develop ourselves, with the Bible for our guide and the Holy Spirit as our teacher. You Englishmen were savages once, and the Word of God came and raised you. You only continue to be great because the Bible keeps you still in the right path. What it has done for you it will do for us. All we ask for is to be let alone!"

The Secretary had become quite excited on this theme, and there is no saying how much longer he might have gone on if Ebony had not returned, scratched, bruised, bleeding, panting and perspiring, but jubilant, with an enormous butterfly captive in his net, and the cause of science advanced.

Having secured the specimen, they set off at once to visit the hot springs, after pricking a traveller's-tree with a spear and obtaining a refreshing draught of cool clear water therefrom.

Fountains of mineral waters have been found in many parts of Madagascar, and among them several which are called Rano-mafana, or "warm waters." These vary both in temperature and medicinal properties. The spot when reached was found to

be a small cavity in the rocks which was delight-
fully shaded by the leaves of the wild fig, and by a
number of interwoven and overhanging bamboos.
The branches of the fig-trees spread directly across
the stream.

Hastening to the fountain, Hockins thrust his
hand in, but quickly pulled it out again, for the
water was only a few degrees below the boiling-point.

" Too hot to bathe in ! " he said.

" But not too hot *here*," remarked Ebony, going to
a pool a little further from the fountainhead, where
the water had cooled somewhat.   There the negro
dropped his simple garments, and was soon rolling
like a black porpoise in his warm bath.   It was
only large enough for one, but close to it was
another small pool big enough for several men.
There Mark and Hockins were soon disporting
joyously, while the Secretary looked on and laughed.
Evidently he did not in the circumstances deem
warm water either a necessity or a luxury.

That evening, after returning to camp, Mark was
summoned to lay the result of his labours before
the Queen, who was much interested in his collection of plants, and not a little amused with his
collection of insects ; for she could understand the
use of the medicines which her Court Physician
assured her could be extracted from the former, but
could see no sense whatever in collecting winged and

creeping things, merely to be stuck on pins and looked at and saddled with incomprehensible names ! She did indeed except the gorgeous butterflies, and similar creatures, because these were pretty ; but on the whole she felt disposed to regard her physician as rather childish in that particular taste.

Very different was her opinion of John Hockins. So fond was she of the flageolet of that musical and stalwart tar that she sent for him almost every evening and made him pipe away to her until he almost fell asleep at his duty, so that at last he began to wish that flageolets had never been invented.

" It 's nothin' but blow, blow, blow, day arter day," he growled as he returned to his tent one night, and flung down the little instrument in disgust. " I wish it had bin blow 'd up the time your big Roman candle busted, doctor."

" If it had been, your influence with the Queen would have been gone, John."

" Well, I dun-know, sir. Many a queer gale I 've come through in time past, but this blow beats 'em all to sticks an' whistles."

" Nebber mind, 'Ockins," remarked Ebony, who was busy preparing supper at the time, " we 's habbin good times ob it just now. Plenty fun an' lots ob science ! Come—go at your wittles. We 've hard work besides fun before us demorrow."

Ebony was a true prophet in regard to the hard work, but not as to the fun, of the morrow; for it so happened that two events occurred which threw a dark cloud over the expedition, for some, at least, in the royal procession, and induced the Queen to return to the capital sooner than she had intended.

The first of these events was the discovery of a party of sixteen fugitives who were of suspicious character and unable to give account of themselves.

They had been discovered by the Queen's spies hidden in a rice-house. When brought before the officer who examined them, they were at first silent; when pressed, they spoke a little, but nothing of importance could be gathered from them. At last they seemed to make up their minds to acknowledge who they were, for one of them stood forth boldly and said—

"Since you ask us again and again, we will tell you. We are not robbers or murderers. We are praying people. If this makes us guilty in the kingdom of the Queen, then, whatsoever she does, we must submit to suffer. We are ready to die for the name of the Lord Jesus."

"Is this, then," asked the officer, "your final answer, whether for life or death?"

"It is our final answer, whether for life or for death."

When this was reported to the Queen, all her

anger was stirred up again. She ordered the captives to be chained and sent off at once to Antananarivo. Two of the band managed to escape that
night, but the other fourteen were safely lodged in
prison.

The countenance of Ranavalona was now changed.
She took no pleasure in Mark's collections, and sent
no more for the musical seaman. To make matters
worse, there came in, on the following day, a report that some of her soldiers had captured a large
band of fugitives in a distant part of the country,
and were then marching them in chains to the
capital. As this band was at the time approaching,
the Queen gave orders to halt on an eminence that
overlooked the path along which they had to travel,
that she might see them.

It was about noon when they drew near—worn,
weary, and footsore. The Queen was so placed
among the bushes that she could see the captives
without being herself seen. Her chief officers stood
near her. Mark and his companions had taken up
a position much nearer to the forest path.

First came a band of weary little ones, driven
onwards like a flock of sheep, and apparently too
much terrified by what they had undergone to make
much noise, although most of them were weeping.
Next came a group of women. These, like the
children, were not bound, but the men, who walked

in rear, were chained together—two and two. Soldiers guarded them on every side.

"It is profoundly sad!" said Mark, in a deep sorrowful tone. "God help them!"

"Massa," whispered Ebony, "look dar! Sure I knows some ob——"

He stopped and opened wide his eyes, for at that moment he recognised Rafaravavy and Ramatoa among the women. With something like a groan, Hockins turned a glance on his comrades and pointed to the men. They required no second glance to enlighten them, for there they plainly saw Ravonino heavily ironed by the neck to Laihova, and Razafil, the poet, chained to the chief, Voalavo. Many others whom they did not know were also there. These all trudged along with bowed heads and eyes on the ground, like men who, having gone through terrible mental and physical agony, have either become callous or resigned to their fate.

As the Queen had given orders to her people to keep quiet and out of sight, the poor captives knew nothing of the host that gazed at them. Mark and his friends were so horrified that all power to move or speak failed them for a time. As for Ranavalona, she sat in rigid silence, like a bronze statue, with compressed lips and frowning brows, until they had passed. Then she gave orders to encamp where they stood, and retired in silence to her tent.

CHAPTER XXVIII.

MATTERS had now reached a crisis. Although
suffering from illness—partly brought on, or aggravated, by her unrestrained passions—the Queen gave
orders next day for the host to turn homeward.
Travelling more rapidly than she had yet done, she
soon reached the capital.

There the arrival of the captives and the news of
what had occurred prepared them for the worst.
And the worst was not long of coming. The very
day following the Queen's return, a great assembly,
or Kabery, of the whole people was called. None
were exempted from the meeting. High and low,
rich and poor, sick and healthy, were driven to the
great place of assembly near the palace—literally
driven, for officers were sent as usual to break into
the houses of the people, when necessary, and force
them to attend. And there was no way of escape,
for at the time of the summons being sent out every
outlet from the city was guarded by soldiers, and

the cannon along the heights thundered a salute by way of striking terror into the hearts of the rebellious. Well did the poor people know what all this fore-shadowed. One who was an eye-witness of the scene said, "there was a general howling and wail-ing, a rushing and running through the streets, as if the town had been attacked by a hostile army." At last the great square of the city was crowded, as full as it could hold, with hundreds of thousands of people, who were overawed by the presence of a body of troops fifteen thousand strong as they awaited the anouncement of the Queen's pleasure.

Mark Breezy was there, along with his comrades, on an elevated spot near to the place where the Queen's messenger was to make the proclamation.

"We are utterly helpless here," said Mark in a low voice, as he gazed in pity on the groaning and swaying multitude. "The Queen's countenance is changed to me. I feel sure that either we have been betrayed in the matter of Rafaravavy, or we are suspected. Indeed, if it were not that she is ill, and needs my aid, she would certainly banish us all from her dominions."

"I wish I was well out of 'em," growled Hockins. "The country is well enough, no doubt, but a woman like that makes it a hell-upon-earth!"

"Has you hear, massa, whar dey hab put Ravonino an' our oder friends?" asked Ebony.

"No, I did not dare to ask. And even if we knew we could do nothing."

The youth spoke bitterly, for he had become so much attached to their former guide, and the natives with whom they had sojourned and travelled, that he would have fought for them to the death if that could have availed them. Strong and active young men are apt to become bitter when they find that superabundant energy and physical force are in some circumstances utterly useless. To be compelled to stand by inactive and see injustice done—cruelty and death dealt out, while the blood boils, the nerves quiver, and the violated feelings revolt, is a sore trial to manhood! And such was the position of our three adventurers at that time.

Presently the highest civil and military officers came forth, one of whom, in a loud sonorous voice, delivered the message of his terrible mistress.

After a number of complimentary and adulatory phrases to the Queen herself, and many ceremonial bowings towards the palace, as if she actually heard him, the messenger spoke as follows—

"I announce to you, O people, that I am not a Sovereign that deceives. I find that, in spite of my commands, many of my people revile the idols and treat divination as a trifle, and worship the Christians' God, and pray, and baptize, and sing—which things I abhor. They are unlawful. I detest them, and they are not to be done, saith Ranavàlo-Manjaka. I will not suffer it. Those who dare to disobey my commands shall die. Now, I order that all who are guilty shall come in classes according to their offences, and accuse themselves of being baptized, of being members of the Church, of having taught slaves to read, and that all books shall be given up."

As on a previous occasion, many came forward at once and accused themselves, or gave up their Bibles and Testaments; but, as before, others concealed their treasures and held their tongue, although it was evident that on this occasion the Queen uttered no vain threat, but was terribly in earnest.

The proclamation ended, the people dispersed, and Mark and his friends were returning to their quarters when they were arrested by a party of soldiers. As usual, their first impulse was to resist violently, but wisdom was given them in time, and they went quietly along. Of course Mark protested vehemently both in English and in broken Malagasy, but no attention whatever was paid to his words. They were led to a prison which they had not before seen. As they approached the door the sound of singing was heard. Another moment and they were thrust into the room whence the sounds issued, and the door was locked upon them.

At first they could only see dimly, the place was so dark; but in a few seconds, their eyes becoming accustomed to the gloom, they could see that a number of other prisoners—both men and women—were seated round the walls singing a hymn. When the hymn ceased an exclamation from a familiar voice made them turn round, and there they saw their friend Ravonino seated on the floor with his back against the wall and chained to Laihova and to the floor. Beside him were several well-remembered natives, and on the opposite side of the room, also chained, were the women of the party, among whom were Ramatoa, Ra-Ruth, Rafaravavy, her maid Sarah, and the poor mother of Mamba.

" Ravonino !" exclaimed Mark, in tones of profound sorrow, as he sat down beside his old guide, "I little thought to find you in such a strait."

" Even so, sir," returned the man in a gentle voice, " for so it seems good in His eyes ! But still less did I expect to find you in prison—for the way they thrust you in shows me that you are no mere visitor. I fear me, the cruel woman has found out how kind you were in helping me."

" But surely dar some hope for you ! Dey nebber kill you all !" said the negro, waving his hand round as if to indicate the whole party.

" No hope, no hope," returned Ravonino, sadly. " Not even for you, Ebony, because you are only a

black man. But they won't kill *you*, sir, or Hockins.
They know better than to risk the consequences of
putting a British subject to death. For the rest of
us—our doom is sealed."

"If the Lord wills it so," remarked Laihova,
quietly.

"How do you know that the Lord wills it so?"
demanded a voice fiercely, and a man who had
hitherto sat still with his face buried in his hands
looked up. It was the stout chief Voalavo, all whose
fun of disposition seemed to have been turned to
fury. "You all speak as if you were already dead
men! Are we not alive? Have we not stout hearts
and strong limbs? While life remains there is hope!"

He leaped up as he spoke and began to wrench
at his chain like a maddened tiger, until blood spurt-
ed from his wrists and the swollen veins stood out
like cords from his neck and forehead. But iron
proved tougher than flesh. He sank down, exhausted, with a deep groan—yet even in his agony
of rage the strong man murmured as he fell, "Lord
forgive me!"

While the men conversed, and Ebony sought to
soothe Voalavo, with whom he had strong sympathy
most of the poor women opposite were seated in a
state of quiet resignation. Some there were, however, who could not bring their minds to contemplate
with calmness the horrible fate that they knew too

well awaited them, while others seemed to forget themselves in their desire to comfort their companions. Among the timid ones was pretty little Ra-Ruth. Perhaps her vivid imagination enabled her to realise more powerfully the terrors of martyrdom. It may be that her delicately-strung nerves shrank more sensitively from the prospect, but in spite of her utmost efforts to be brave she trembled violently and was pale as death. Yet she did not murmur, she only laid her head on the sympathetic bosom of her queen-like friend Ramatoa, who seemed to her a miracle of strength and resignation.

In a short time the door of the prison opened, and a party of armed men entered with Silver Spear, or Hater of Lies, at their head. An involuntary shudder ran through the group of captives as the man advanced and looked round.

"Which is Razafil?" demanded Hater of Lies.

The poet rose promptly. "Here I am," he said, looking boldly at the officer. Then, glancing upwards, and in a voice of extreme tenderness, he said, "Now, my sweet Raniva, I will soon join you!"

"Ramatoa—which is she?" said the officer, as his men removed the fetters from the poet and fastened his wrists with a cord.

Ramatoa at once rose up. "I am ready," she said, calmly. "Now, Ra-Ruth, the Master calls me. Fear not what man can do unto thee."

" Oh ! no, no ! do not go yet," exclaimed Ra-Ruth in
an agony of grief, as she clung to her friend. "The
good Lord cannot mean this—oh! take *me !* take
me ! and let her stay ! "

The sentence ended in a low wail, for at the
moment two soldiers forced the girls asunder, and
Ra-Ruth sank upon the floor, while Ramatoa was
led away.

Poor Laihova had watched every movement of
Ra-Ruth. It was, no doubt, the fiercest part of the
fiery trial he had to undergo ; and when the soldier
grasped her arms to tear her from her friend he could
restrain himself no longer. He sprang up and
made a wild leap towards her, but the chain arrested
him effectually, and three bayonets were quickly
pointed at his breast. His head fell forward, and
he sank down like one who had been shot.

Meanwhile Hater of Lies selected Ra-Ruth and
twelve others from the group of prisoners, but only
the three whom we have mentioned are known to the
reader. They were led into an outer room, where
they were further pinioned. Some of them had
their feet and hands tied together, so that, by thrusting a pole between the legs and arms of each, they
could be suspended and carried by two men. Others
were allowed to walk to the place of execution.
The rage of Ranavalona, however, was so great on
finding that the Christians would not submit to her

that she had given orders to the soldiers to torture
the martyrs with their spears as they marched along
the road.   This was done to all except Ramatoa and
Ra-Ruth, as the blood-stained road bore witness.
The comfort of being together was not allowed to
the two ladies.   They were placed in different parts
of the procession.

Mats were thrust into the mouths of the suspended victims to prevent them from speaking, but
some of them managed to free their mouths and
prayed aloud, while others sang hymns or addressed
the crowd.   Thus they passed along the road that
led to the Place of Hurling Down.

This was a tremendous precipice of granite, 150
feet high.   Thither the multitude streamed—some
influenced by hatred of the Christians, some by deep
sympathy with them, but the majority, doubtless,
prompted by mere excitement and curiosity.   And
there they crowded as near as they dared venture to
the edge of the precipice and gazed into the awful gulf.

Slowly the procession moved, as if to prolong the
agony of the martyrs.   Suddenly a young man
pushed through the crowd, advanced to the side of
Ramatoa, and grasped one of her hands, exclaiming
in a loud voice, "Dearest! I will go with you and
stay by you to the end."

For a moment the calm serenity that had settled
on the girl's fine countenance was disturbed.

"Mamba!" she said, "this is not wise. You cannot save me. It is God's will that I should now glorify the dear name of Jesus by laying down my life. But you are not yet condemned, and your mother needs your help."

"Full well do I know that," returned the youth, fervently. "Were it not for my dear mother's love and claim on me, I would now have gone with you to heaven. As it is, I will stay by you, dear one, to the end."

"Thank you, dear friend," returned the girl, earnestly. "I think it will not be long till we meet where there are no more sufferings or tears."

Soon the procession reached the brow of the terrible cliff. Here the martyrs were ranged in such a way that, while they were cast over one by one, the rest could see their companions fall.

The first to perish was the poet Razafil. After the Queen's messenger had pronounced the sentence of each, the poor man was seized and thrown violently on the ground. A rope was then fastened round his waist, and he was asked if he would cease to pray in the name of Jesus.

"Cease to pray to Jesus!" he exclaimed, while the fire of enthusiasm gleamed in his eyes—"to Jesus who saved my Raniva, and who holds out His blessed hands to me—even me—to take me to Himself? *Never!*"

Razafil was instantly slung over the precipice, and held suspended there in the hope that the awful nature of his impending fate might cause his courage to fail, while the executioner knelt, knife in hand, ready to cut the rope.

"Once more, and for the last time," said the officer in command, "will you cease to pray?"

The answer was an emphatic "No!"

Next moment Razafil went shooting down headlong into the abyss. There was a projecting ledge of rock about fifty feet down the precipice. On this the body of the martyr struck, and, bounding off into space, reached the bottom with incredible violence, a shattered and mangled heap.

With trembling hearts and straining gaze the other victims watched the descent. It seemed to be more than human nature could endure to voluntarily face such a fate when a word would deliver them. So thought many of the spectators, and they were right; mere human nature could not have endured it, but these Christians were strengthened in a way that the ungodly will neither believe nor understand. One by one they were led to the edge of the cliff, suspended over the edge, and had the testing question put to them, and, one by one, the answer was a decisive "No!"

But where was the tyrant Queen while this scene of butchery was being enacted? In her chamber

in the palace—comparatively, yet not altogether,
regardless of the matter.

Her son Rakota stood beside her. Our friend
the Secretary stood at the door.

"Mother," said the Prince, quietly, "they are
being hurled down now—and little Ra-Ruth is
among them."

The Queen looked up, startled. "No, no!" she
said, hesitatingly. "Ra-Ruth must not—but—but—
I must not seem to my people to be weak—yet I
would save her."

Rakota gave a gentle nod to the Secretary, who
instantly vanished. He reached the place of execution only just in time. The rope was already round
the girl's slender waist, and the testing-question had
been put—but her timidity had flown, and was replaced by a calm, almost angelic, expression, as she
gazed up to Heaven, clasped her hands, and, with a
flush of enthusiasm, exclaimed—

"No—Jesus—no, I will *never* cease to worship
Thee!"

A murmur of mingled surprise and pity broke
from the crowd. At that moment the Secretary
came forward.

"The Queen," he said, "has sent me to ask you,
Ra-Ruth, whether you will not worship our gods
and save your life."

"No," answered the girl, firmly. "I have been

weak—a coward—but now God has sent me strength by His own Holy Spirit, and my fixed determination is to go this day with my dear brothers and sisters to Heaven."

"You are a fool! You are *mad!*" exclaimed an officer standing by, as he struck her on the head.

"Yes, she is *mad*," said the Secretary to the officer in command. "Send a messenger to tell the Queen that Ra-Ruth has lost her reason. Meanwhile, let her be taken away and guarded well till the Queen's pleasure regarding her is known."

But although this poor girl was thus snatched from death at the last moment, no mercy was extended to the others. All were thrown over the cliff and dashed to pieces at that time except Ramatoa. When the question was put to her, last of all, she, as might have been expected, was not less firm in her reply than her companions; but, instead of being thrown over, she was informed that as it was not allowable to shed the blood of one of noble birth she was to be burnt alive!

At this dreadful announcement she turned paler than before, but did not flinch. At the same moment poor Mamba lost control of himself. He sprang to her side, put an arm round her waist, and shouted—

"This shall not be! I, too, am a praying man. Ye shall not touch her!"

He glared fiercely round, and, for a moment, the

soldiers did not dare to approach him, although he was totally unarmed. But they sprang on him from behind, and he was quickly overpowered by numbers. At the command of their officer, they tore him from Ramatoa, carried him to the cliff, and hurled him over. His head struck the ledge, and his brains were dashed out there. Next moment he lay dead among the rocks at the bottom.

This awful sight Ramatoa was spared, for, at the same instant, they had dragged her away to the spot where a pile of wood had been prepared for herself. Four stakes were fixed in the midst of the pile, as three other Christian nobles were to be burnt along with her, one of whom was a lady. While Ramatoa watched the preparations for her death, her fellow-sufferers arrived—singing, as they walked, a hymn which begins with "When our hearts are troubled," and ends with "Then remember us." Ramatoa raised her voice and joined them. There was no wavering or shrinking from the fiery ordeal. When all was ready the martyrs quietly suffered themselves to be bound to the stakes ; and, strange to say, when the flames roared around them, the song of praise still went on, and the voices of praise and prayer did not cease until they had culminated in glad shouts of praise and victory before the throne of God !

We write facts just now, reader, not fiction ! Men

talk of the cruelty of devils! Assuredly there is not a devil in or out of hell who can sink to lower depths of cruelty than fallen man will sink to when left to the unrestrained influence of that hateful thing—*sin*—from which Jesus Christ came to deliver us, blessed be *His* name!

It is said that while these four martyrs were being fastened to the stakes, an immense triple-arched rainbow stretched across the heavens, one end of which appeared to rest upon them, and that rain fell in torrents. This so terrified many of the spectators, that they fled in consternation from the scene.

But the cup of iniquity was not yet filled up. While the martyrs were still in the fire, and praying "O Lord, receive our spirits, and lay not this sin to their charge," a shouting yelling band arrived, dragging after them the corpses of the men and women who had perished at the Place of Hurling Down. These were tossed upon the pile to serve as fuel to the fire. The poor unrecognisable remains of Mamba were among them; and thus, even in their death, he and Ramatoa were not divided!

At this time of terrible suffering and trial—as in the previous persecutions during the reign of this tyrant queen—hundreds of Christians willingly submitted to the loss of position, wealth, and liberty for the sake of Jesus, besides those who witnessed a good confession, and sealed their testimony with their blood. Thirty-seven native preachers, with their wives and families, were consigned to a life of slavery. More than a hundred men and women were flogged and sentenced to work in chains during their lives. Some were heavily fined, and many among the "great and noble" were stripped of honours and titles, reduced to the ranks, and forced to labour at the hardest and most menial occupation.

Among these last was Prince Ramonja, who had been the means of sheltering, secreting, and saving many Christians. Fortunately Prince Rakota retained his influence over his mother, and his power to do good—a circumstance for which our three adventurers had ultimately reason to thank God, though, for a considerable time after that, they remained in prison, in company with their friends Ravonino, Voalavo, Laihova, and others.

These last were not delivered from their chains, but lived in hourly expectation of being led out to execution. After Ra-Ruth's removal, Laihova was at first overwhelmed with despair, but when a friendly jailor informed him of her having been spared under the supposition that she was insane, hope revived a little, though he could not help seeing that the prospect ahead was still very black.

Another prisoner who was inconsolable was poor Reni-Mamba. From the time that she was told of her son's fate she seemed to sink into a state of quiet imbecility, from which no efforts of her friends could rouse her. She did not murmur or complain. She simply sat silent and callous to everything. around her. She, Rafaravavy, Sarah, and the other females, were removed to another prison, and for a long time their male friends could learn nothing as to their fate.

"It is this prolonged uncertainty that's so hard to bear," remarked Ravonino to Mark one day, lifting his hands high above his head, and letting them fall, with the clanking chains, into his lap.

"True, true," replied the youth, shortly—for confinement was beginning to tell unfavourably on himself.

"Das w'ere it is," remarked Ebony, endeavouring to brighten up a little, but with only moderate success, "it's sottin still an' doin' nuffin dat kills. What you tink, 'Ockins ? "

"Ay, ay," assented the seaman ; and as for a long time nothing more than "ay, ay" had been got out of Hockins, Ebony relapsed into silence.

Things had reached this lugubrious pass when an event occurred which materially affected the condition of the prisoners, and considerably altered the history ol Madagascar.

CHAPTER XXIX.

THREATENED DEATH AVERTED—BURIED ALIVE—END OF THE TYRANT QUEEN—REVOLT CRUSHED AND RADAMA II. CROWNED.

ONE morning, shortly after sunrise, Mark was awakened by the entrance of their jailor. By that time he had grown so accustomed to clanking chains, shooting bolts, and such-like sounds, that he looked up sleepily and without much interest, but a thrill or qualm passed through him when he observed that the jailor was followed by Hater of Lies with his silver spear.

Still more were he and his awakened comrades horrified when the names of Ravoninohitriniony and Voalavo were sternly called out. Both men promptly stood up.

"At last!" said the former, quietly, and without a trace of excitement. "Well, I am glad, for it is the Lord's will. Farewell, my friends," he added, looking back as he was led away, "we shall all meet again in great joy—farewell!"

Evidently Voalavo did not take things so quietly. His lips were firmly compressed, his face was deeply flushed, and his brows were sternly contracted, as they led him out. But for his chains the chief would certainly have given his jailors some trouble.

The whole thing passed so quickly that it seemed to those left behind like a dream when they found themselves alone. Ebony sat down, put his face on his knees, and fairly burst into tears.

" Oh ! Lord," he sobbed, " send 'em quick for me, an' let 's hab it ober ! "

It seemed as if the poor fellow's prayer was about to be answered, for again the door opened, and the Secretary entered.

" Be not afraid," he said, observing their alarm, " I come not to summon you to death, but to ask you, doctor, to come and see the Queen—she is ill."

" Oh ! massa, pison her ! *Do*, massa ! Nobody would call it murder," said the negro, with fervent entreaty.

Paying no attention to this advice, Mark followed the Secretary, and the bolts were again drawn on his friends.

He found Ranavalona suffering severely. Indeed, for some time previous to that her health had been failing, and she would gladly have had the advice of her Court Physician, but seemed to be ashamed to send for him after the way she had caused him to be treated. There is this to be said for her, that she would probably have liberated him long ago, but for the advice of her minister, Rainiharo, who was jealous of the young Englishman's growing popularity as well as a hater of his religion.

After prescribing for the Queen and affording her some relief, he gave orders that she should be kept very quiet; that no noise was to be permitted in or near the palace. Then he left her apartments with the Secretary.

As they traversed one of the corridors, the latter told Mark that the order had been given for the execution of Ravonino and Voalavo.

"Was that order given by the Queen?" demanded Mark, flushing with indignation, while a gush of anxiety almost choked him.

"No, it was given by Rainiharo, who takes advantage of his position and the Queen's illness."

Just then a step was heard at the further end of the passage, and Hater of Lies advanced towards them with his badge of office, the silver spear, in his hand.

Like a flash of light an idea entered the young Englishman's head! He had no time to think or plan—only to act. In the same moment, however, he offered up a silent prayer for help.

As the officer was about to pass, Mark snatched the spear from his hand and brought the handle of it down on its owner's crown with such good-will that the Hater of Lies was laid flat upon the floor !

Thunderstruck, the Secretary gazed at his young companion.   " You are ruined now ! " he said.

" True, and *you* must be ruined along with me! Here, take the spear and act the part of the Hater of Lies."

For a moment the Secretary hesitated—then, as if suddenly making up his mind, he said—

" Come, I am with you heart and soul ! "

" Lead to the place of execution—quick," cried Mark.

" We will take the prison in passing," said his companion, grasping the spear and hastening onward.

The prison was soon reached.   The guards were a little surprised at the change of the bearer, but no one dared to think of opposing the passage of the well-known and awful emblem of office!

" Come, Hockins, Ebony, Laihova, follow us," cried Mark, springing in.

He did not wait to explain.   The Secretary, acting his part well, stalked with grand solemnity down the streets towards the western gate of the city.   His four friends followed.   Every one made way.   Hockins and the negro, not knowing what they might be called on to do, took the first opportunity that presented, each to seize and carry off a garden-stake, as a substitute for cudgel or quarterstaff.

The guards, as before, let them pass without

question. Once outside the town they quickened their pace, and finally ran.

"We may be too late!" gasped Mark.

"It may be so—but we have not far to go." As he spoke they distinguished sounds as of men engaged in a struggle. On turning a point of rock they came in sight of a party of twelve soldiers. They were struggling fiercely with one man, whom they tried to bind. But the man seemed to possess the power of Samson.

"It's Voalavo," cried Hockins, and rushed to the rescue.

"Das so," cried the negro, following suit with blazing eyes.

Snatching the silver spear from the Secretary, Mark sprang forward like a wild cat, and, sweeping it right and left, brought down two of the men. His comrades overturned two others whose muskets they seized, while Voalavo, with the power of a giant, hurled two others from him as if they had been boys. He did not stop to speak, but, to the surprise of his rescuers, ran straight into a neighbouring coppice, and disappeared.

For one moment the remaining soldiers lowered their bayonets as if to charge, but the Secretary, grasping the Hater of Lies, said, in a commanding tone—

'What means this haste? Ye shall answer to the

Queen for what you have done! Go! Return to your quarters. You are under arrest. Carry your comrades with you!"

Cowed by this speech, for they all knew the Secretary to be a man of position and power in the palace, the soldiers humbly picked up their fallen comrades and retired. The victors immediately ran into the coppice in search of Voalavo, whom they found on his knees, digging up the earth with both hands as if for very life! Just as they came up he had uncovered the face of Ravonino, who had been buried alive, and was already as pale as if he were dead.

"Have they killed him?" gasped Laihova, as he dropped on his knees with the others, and began to dig.

"No—they do not kill when the sentence is to bury alive," said the Secretary, "but no doubt he is half-suffocated."

The grave was very shallow—not more than a foot deep, and a living man might without much difficulty have struggled out of it, but the poor man had been bound to a long pole, which was buried along with him, so that he could not move. They soon got him out, and were about to cast him loose when there arose a cry in the city which quickly increased to a mighty roar.

"They have found out our trick," said the

Secretary. "Nothing can save us now but flight. Come—take him up. This way!"

In a moment Hockins and Ebony had the ends of the pole on their shoulders, and bore their still unconscious friend after the Secretary. The noise and shouting in the town increased, and it soon became evident that they were pursued, being led, no doubt, by the soldiers who had been so roughly handled.

"This way," cried their guide, turning sharp into a by-path which led them into a small garden, "a friend—a Christian—dwells here."

The friend turned out to be an old woman who was rather deaf, but she heard enough to understand the situation.

"Here!" she said, tottering into a back-yard, in which was a quantity of straw and rubbish. "Go down there."

She pointed to a hole. It was the mouth of a rice-hole. Down went the Secretary, without a word, and turned to receive the end of the pole which Hockins passed carefully in. The rest followed. The old woman put on the cover and threw over it some of the rubbish.

Being pitch dark, the nature of the place could not be distinguished by the fugitives, but they could hear the shouting of the soldiers who searched the house for them. They could also hear the angry queries that were put to the owner of the place, and they could perceive that the old woman had miraculously become dumb as well as stone deaf!

Soon the quietness overhead led them to hope that the soldiers had left. In a short time the cover of the rice-hole was removed, and the old woman, putting her head down, informed them that all was safe, at least in the meantime.

They now unfastened Ravonino from the pole, and found, to their great joy, that he was yet alive, though considerably shaken. A little rice-soup, however, and a night's rest, put him all right again.

In that hole, carefully tended by the deaf old woman, these six were compelled to secrete themselves for a week, during which time the soldiers were scouring the country in all directions in search of them. They had to keep so close, and to be so careful, that they did not even dare to let the old woman go near the neighbours to inquire what was going on in the town, though naturally they were very anxious on that point.

At the end of that week, while the fugitives were taking a breath of fresh air in the yard, they were surprised by hearing the tramp of approaching soldiers. To dive into their hiding-place and be covered over by the old woman was the work of a few seconds. Anxiously they listened while the renewed search was going on. The sounds sometimes showed that the searchers were retiring from the yard, at other times drawing near to it. At last a step was heard on the rubbish heap above them; then a blow resounded on their covering, as if with the butt-end of a musket. This was followed by a shout, a clamour of voices, and a hasty clearing away of the rubbish.

"All is lost!" exclaimed the Secretary in his native tongue.

"Not while we have arms," growled Voalavo.

"You need not count on me to help you," said Ravonino, quietly, in the native tongue; "why should we slaughter men uselessly? If we had a chance of making a dash I would fight. But we can get out of this hole only one by one, and no doubt a hundred men await us!"

"Is we a-goin' to fight, massa?" asked the negro, hopefully.

"Of coorse we are," said Hockins.

"No, my friend, we are not," said the Secretary, "our only hope, now, is in God."

"It seems to me," rejoined Ravonino, "that God is our only hope at *all* times—whether in danger or in safety; but He makes it plain just now that our duty, as well as our wisdom, lies in quiet submission."

Ebony received this remark with a groan, and Hockins with something like a growl. Just then the covering of their hiding-place was thrown off, and several bayonet-points appeared.

"Come out, one at a time, quietly, else we will shoot you where you stand!" exclaimed a stern voice.

The Secretary translated this. At the same time Ravonino clambered out of the rice-hole, and was instantly seized and bound.

"It's all over now—may the Lord have mercy on us!" exclaimed Hockins, dropping his weapon and following his friend.

Whatever might have been the various feelings of the unfortunate party, the example thus set was accepted, for each one submitted, and when Mark looked round on the large band of armed men by whom they were surrounded, he perceived the wisdom of Ravonino's advice, and how hopeless would have been any attempt on the part of himself and his friends to break through and escape.

Silently, and without a word of explanation, the officer in command led his captives into the town. They were too much overwhelmed by their calamitous circumstances to pay much attention to anything, yet they could not help observing that greater crowds of people than usual were hurrying through the streets, and that every one wore, more or less, an air of excitement.

Our friends had expected to be cast into their old

prison, but they were led straight to the palace, where they were handed over to the officer on duty. In spite of the depression of his spirits, the Secretary could not resist his feelings of curiosity, and asked what all the stir meant, but he received no answer.

The prisoners were now conducted into a large room, where they found Prince Rakota standing, surrounded by a crowd of people—male and female. Beside the Prince was his cousin, Ramonja. Ravonino and Laihova observed—with a gush of feeling which may be understood but not described—that Rafaravavy and Ra-Ruth were among the ladies. Poor Reni-Mamba was also there, her mild face showing unmistakable traces of the suffering caused by the loss of her only son.

"Welcome, my friends," said Rakota, hastening forward to receive the prisoners. "You are now safe and free!"

"Safe? free?" repeated the Secretary, in surprise.

"Yes. Have they not told you the news?" he asked, while an expression, as of pain, passed over his face, "my mother—the Queen—is dead! But come," he added quickly, as if he wished to avoid the subject, "I wish to consult with you, for serious dangers threaten us. Come."

He left the room quickly, followed by the Secretary, while Ravonino and Laihova were drinking in the news from the respective lips that pleased them best.   The facts were soon communicated to all the party.

The Queen, they said, who had been declining in health for a considerable time past, had latterly become much worse.   No doubt her failure to stamp out Christianity must have aggravated her complaint, for the effect of her extreme severity was rather to advance than hinder the good cause.   The persecutions—the banishments—the murders—of twenty-five years, instead of checking, had spread the Gospel far and wide over the land, for, as in the first days, 'they that were scattered abroad went everywhere preaching the Word,' and the amazing constancy, and courage, and tenderness to their enemies, of the noble army of martyrs, had given a depth and power to the Christian life which might otherwise have been wanting.

At all events, whatever the cause, Ranavalona I. sank rapidly, and, on the 15th of August, 1861, after a reign of thirty-three years, the Tyrant Queen of Madagascar passed away to the tribunal of the King of Kings.

Her son, Prince Rakota, was her successor; but his succession was not to be unopposed.   He had a rival claimant to the throne in his own cousin Rambosalàma, an able, wary, and unscrupulous man, who, on perceiving that the end was approaching, had laid his plans secretly and extensively for

seizing the reins of government. Prince Rakota, however, was so much beloved that all his cousin's plans
were revealed to him by his friends, but the disposition of the prince was too humane to permit of his
adopting the usual savage means to foil his foe.

"All has been told to me," he said to the Secretary. "My cousin has gained many to his side—
especially of those who hate the Christians. He
has even hired men to kill me! I know it, because
one of the assassins came last night and warned me.
At the same time he confessed that he had intended
to commit the crime."

"But have you not taken steps to thwart your
cousin!"

"I have. For some time past every allowable
measure for our protection has been taken, but the
religion of Jesus, as you know, forbids me to resort
to poison, the chain, or the spear. My reign shall
not begin with bloodshed if I can help it. You know
that my good friend the Commander-in-Chief of the
troops, Rainiharo's son, is on our side. Finding that
my cousin went about armed, he recently issued an
order that no one should be allowed to carry arms
in the palace. As I myself bowed to this order,
and submitted to be searched, of course Rambosalàma had no excuse for refusing. Then, as a precaution, we have concealed from all except sure
friends the orders which, from day to day, have

regulated the movements of the troops. I have met daily in council those on whom I can depend, and our course of action is all arranged. Only one point remains unsettled, and it is that which I ask you to undertake—for your will is resolute."

"Whatever my Prince requires of me shall be done—if it be not against the laws of my God," said the Secretary.

Rakota looked pleased with the reply. "I want you," he said, "to stand in the passage here, till Rambosalàma appears. He is sure to pass, being now in the death-chamber, to which I return speedily. His followers will be in force in the palace-yard—I hear the multitudes assembling even now. When he passes this way it will be to give the signal of revolt. You will stop him. If he resists, use force—you are strong! You understand?"

The Secretary looked intelligent, and bowed as the Prince rose and left him. Then he hastily sought for and found his friend Ebony, with whom he had struck up a sort of happy-go-lucky friendship.

Meanwhile the multitudes, who had heard early in the morning that the Queen was dying, had crowded every street that led to the palace. Some had even pressed into the courts in their anxiety to know the truth. Laxity seemed to prevail among the guards, for many people who carried weapons

ill-concealed in their lambas, and whose looks as
well as movements were suspicious, were allowed to
enter. These were the partisans of Rambosalàma.
Indeed it is probable that even among the guards
themselves there were adherents of the Pretender.

But the faithful Commander-in-Chief was on the
alert, and had laid his plans. He stood in the
chamber of death where the mourners were weeping.
He watched with keen eye the movements of Rambosalàma, and when that Prince left the room for the
purpose of giving the signal to his followers, he
slipped quietly out and gave his counter-signal,
which was the waving of a scarf from a window.
Instantly a trumpet sounded, and more than a
thousand trusty soldiers who had been in waiting
marched into the palace courts.

Hearing the trumpet, the Pretender hastened
along the passage that led to the court. At the end
of it a door opened, and the Secretary, stepping out,
confronted him.

"Well met, Rambosalàma," he said, taking his
arm in a friendly but firm way, "I have somewhat
to say to you."

"Not now, not now!" exclaimed the other,
hastily. "I am wanted outside! Another time——"

"No time like the present," interrupted the
Secretary, tightening his grasp, "come this way."

Rambosalàma, taking alarm, tried to wrench himself free, but the Secretary was strong. At the same moment a powerful black hand grasped the nape of his neck.

"Come now, sar, you go 'long quiet an' comf'r'able an' nobody hurt you. Dis way. Das a sweet little chamber for de naughty boys."

With a force that there was no resisting Ebony pushed the prince into a small room with a very small window. The door was shut, the key turned, and the danger was past!

Immediately afterwards the Commander-in-Chief appeared on the balcony of the palace, announced the Queen's death to the multitude, and, amid demonstrations of wildest joy, alike from soldiers and people, proclaimed Rakota King of Madagascar, under the title of Radama II.

In the afternoon of the same day the King presented himself to the people, arrayed in royal robes, with a crown on his head, and surrounded by his chief nobles.

So overjoyed were the people at the blessed change from the tyranny of a cruel woman to the sway of a gentle prince, that it was some time before they could be quieted. When silence was obtained, the King, in a few and simple words, assured his subjects that his great desire was, and his aim would be, to devote himself to their welfare, and that of the country over which he had been called to reign.

CHAPTER XXX.

THE LAST.

THE vigour with which Prince Rakota put down
the attempt at usurpation was followed by characteristic deeds of leniency and kindness. Instead of
taking the usual method of savage and semi-civilised
rulers to crush rebellion, he merely banished
Rambosalàma from the capital, and confined him in
a residence of his own in the country ; but no fetters
were put on his limbs, and his wealth was not for-
feited, nor was he forbidden to communicate with
his friends.

Moreover, before the sun of that day in 1861 had
set, the new King caused it to be proclaimed far and
wide that all his subjects might depend upon
receiving equal protection ; that every man was free
to worship God according to the dictates of his own
conscience; that the prison doors should be thrown
open to those who had been condemned for conscience sake, and their fetters knocked off. He also
sent officers to announce to those who had been
banished to the pestilential districts that the day
of deliverance had come.

To many of these last, of course, the good news came too late for this life. Disease, and hard labour and cruel fetters, had done their work; but the deliverance that came to these was grander and more glorious than the mere removal of earthly chains and pains.

It was a glad day for Madagascar, and the people of the capital were wild with joy, for condemned ones who had long been given up as lost, because enslaved or imprisoned for life, were suddenly restored to family and friends, while others could entertain the hope that those who had been long banished would speedily return to them. Many a house in the city resounded that day with hymns of praise and thanksgiving that the tyrant Queen was dead, and that the gentle Prince was crowned.

But the change did not bring equal joy to all. Some there were whose smitten hearts could not recover from the crushing blows they had sustained when the news of loved ones having perished in exile had been brought to them—though even these felt an impulse of pleasure from Christian sympathy with the joy of their more fortunate friends.

Among these last was poor Reni-Mamba. She, being very meek and submissive, had tried hard to join in the prayer and praise; but her voice was choked when she attempted to speak, and it quavered sadly when she tried to sing.

"Oh! if it had only pleased God to spare thee, Mamba—thou crumb of my life!—my dear, my only son!" She broke out thus one day when the sympathetic Ra-Ruth sought to comfort her. "I was beginning to get over the loss of his father —it was so many years ago that they took him from me! and as my boy grew up, the likeness to my Andrianivo was so strong that I used to try to think it was himself; but—now—both——"

"Are with the Lord, which is far better," said Ra-Ruth, tenderly laying her hand on Reni's arm.

"You are young to give such comfort," returned Reni, with a sad smile.

"It is not I who give it, but the Lord," returned Ra-Ruth. "And you forget, mother, that I am old in experience. When I stood on the edge of the Rock of Hurling, that awful day, and saw the dear ones tossed over one by one, I think that many years passed over my head!"

"True—true—" returned the other, "I am a selfish old woman—forgetting others when I think so much of myself. Come—let us go to the meeting. You know that the congregation assembles to-day for the first time after many, many, years—*so* many!"

"Yes, mother, I know it. Indeed I came here partly to ask you to go with me. And they say that Totosy, the great preacher, is to speak to us."

Many others besides these two wended their way to the meeting-house that day. Among them was a group in which the reader is perhaps interested. It consisted of Mark Breezy, John Hockins, Ebony Ginger, Samuel Ravoninohitriniony, Laihova, and Voalavo.

" Well now, this is the queerest go-to-meetin' that I 've had to do with since I was a babby," remarked Hockins, as he looked from side to side upon the varied crowd of men and women, black, brown, and yellow, rich and poor, noble and slave, who were joyfully and noisily thronging to the house of God!

" Das true,—an' look dar ! " said Ebony, pointing to a young woman who was standing as if thunder-struck before a worn-out, feeble, white-haired man in tattered garments, with a heavy iron collar on his neck.

Recovering from her surprise, the young woman uttered the word " Father " with a wild shriek, and rushed into the old man's arms.

"Easy to see that he is a banished one returned unexpectedly," observed Mark, as the young woman, after the first wild embrace, seized the old man's arm and hurried him towards the meeting-house, while tears of joy streamed from her eyes.

And this was not the only case they witnessed, for constantly, during the days that followed the accession of Radama II., exiles were hastening home, —men and women in rags, worn and wasted with want and suffering—reappearing in the city to the astonishment and joy of friends who had supposed them long since dead. Yes, the long-desired jubilee had come at last, and not only was there great rejoicing over those lost and found ones, but also over many who, through the power of sympathy, were brought at that time to the Saviour and repentance.

Referring to that period, one of those returned exiles writes thus :—" On Thursday, 29th August 1861, we that were in concealment appeared. ' Then all the people were astonished when they saw us, that we were alive and not yet buried or eaten by the dogs. And there were a great many people desiring to see us, for they considered us as dead, and this is what astonished them. On the 9th of September, those that were in fetters came to Antananarivo, but they could not walk on account of the weight of the heavy fetters and their weak and feeble bodies."

It was a strange gathering, and there were many surprises in the church that day, and some strange music too, besides that of psalms and hymns and spiritual songs, for, during the service, several exiles who had just arrived, hearing what was going on, had hastened to the scene of reunion without waiting to have their fetters filed off, and entered the house in clanking chains.

The preacher's duty was one of unusual difficulty, for, besides these peculiar interruptions and the exclamations of surprised friends, the sympathy of his own heart nearly choked his utterance more than once. But Totosy was equal to the occasion. His heart was on fire, his lips were eloquent, and the occasion was one of a thousand, never to be forgotten. Despite difficulties, he held his audience spell-bound while he discoursed of the "wonderful words of God" and the shower of blessing which had begun to fall.

Suddenly, during a momentary pause in the discourse, the clanking of a very heavy chain was heard, and a man was seen to make his way through the crowd. Like Saul, head and shoulders above his fellows, gaunt, worn, and ragged, he had been standing near the door, not listening, apparently, to the preacher, but intent on scanning the faces of the congregation. Discovering at length what he looked for, he forced his way to the side of Reni-Mamba, sank at her feet, and with a profound sigh —almost a groan—laid his head upon her lap!

Mamba, grown to a giant, seemed to have come back to her. But it was not her son. It was Andrianivo, her long-lost husband! For one moment poor Reni seemed terrified and bewildered, then she suddenly grasped the man's prematurely grey head in both hands and covered the face with passionate kisses, uttering every now and then a shriek by way of relieving her feelings.

Great though the preacher's power was in over-coming the difficulties of his position, Reni-Mamba's meek spirit, when thus roused, was too much for him. He was obliged to stop. At the same moment the gaunt giant arose, gathered up Reni in his great arms as if she had been a mere baby, and, without a word, stalked out of the meeting to the music of his clanking chains. A Malagasy cheer burst from the sympathetic people.

"Praise the Lord! Let us sing!" shouted the wise Totosy, and in a few seconds the congregation was letting off its surplus steam in tremendous and jubilant song, to the ineffable joy of Ebony, who must have burst out in some other way had not this safety-valve been provided.

But there were more surprises in store for that singular meeting. After the sermon the preacher announced that two marriages were about to be solemnised by him in the simplest manner possible. "My friends," he said, "one of the bridegrooms is only half a Malagasy, the other half of him is English. He objects to ceremony, and his friend, the other man to be married, objects to everything that *he* objects to, and agrees to everything that *he* agrees to, which is a very satisfactory state of mind in a friend ; so they are to be married together."

Immediately after this speech Ravonino led forward Rafaravavy, and Laihova advanced with
Ra-Ruth, and these two couples were then and there
united in matrimony.   Radama II. himself, and
Prince Ramonja, who had been recalled and rein-
stated with the Secretary, and Soa, and other
courtiers, graced the wedding with their presence.

From this time, Radama II.—or Rakota, as we
still prefer to call him—began systematically to
undo the mischief which his wicked mother had
done.   He began to build a college ; he re-opened
the schools throughout the country which had been
closed in the previous reign, and acted on principles
of civil and religious liberty and universal free
trade, while the London Missionary Society—which
had sent out the first Protestant Missionaries in
1818-20—were invited to resume their beneficent
labours in the island—an invitation which, of
course, they gladly accepted, and at once despatched
the veteran Mr. Ellis, and other missionaries, to the
re-opened field.[1]

But all this, and much more historical matter of
great interest, we must leave untouched, in order
that we may wind up the record of our heroes'

[1] Those who wish for fuller information will find it in such works
as *Madagascar and its People*, by James Sibree, Junr. ; *Madagascar,
its Missions and its Martyrs ; The History of Madagascar*, etc., by
Rev. William Ellis ; *Madagascar of To-day* (a threepenny volume),
by G. A. Shaw, F.Z.S., etc.

fortunes, or misfortunes; as the reader pleases to consider them.

The events which we have described occurred in such rapid succession that our trio—Mark, Hockins, and Ebony—had scarce found breathing-time to consider what they should do, now that they were free to do as they pleased.

"Go home, ob course," said Ebony, when the question was mooted. "Aint my black darlin' awaitin' ob me dar?"

"I incline to the same course," said Mark, for my——well, I won't say who, is awaiting me there also."

"Unless she's falled in lub wid some one else, tinkin' you was dead, massa, you know," suggested Ebony.

"Ditto, says I," answered Hockins, when appealed to, "for, to the best o' my belief, my old ooman is awaitin' for me, too, over there—he pointed to England with the stem of his pipe—to say nothin' o' three thumpin' boys an' a gal—also an old gran'-mother an' a maiden aunt, etceterer—all a-waitin' with great patience, I have no manner o' doubt."

"But how's we to git dar? Das de question; as Hamblit said to his moder's ghost."

The question was answered sooner than they expected, for while they were yet speaking, a summons came from the King commanding the immediate attendance of the Court Physician. The object was to offer Mark his appointment permanently, but Mark respectfully, yet firmly, declined the honour.

"I feared that," said the King, "for I doubt not that you has friends in your native home which draws you. Well, you wishes to go. I say Go with my good-will. There is Breetish ship loading at Tamatave now. If you and you's friends mus' go, there be your chance, and I will send you to Tamatave in palanquins. We all very sorry you go, for you was useful to us, and you was be kind—to my mother!"

Of course Mark gladly availed himself of the opportunity, thankfully accepted the king's offer, and went off to inform his comrades and make preparation.

It was a sad occasion when they met in the house of their old guide Ravonino, to spend the last evening with him and Rafaravavy, and Laihova, and Ra-Ruth, Reni-Mamba and her husband, Voalavo, Soa, Totosy, the Secretary, and other friends, but it was also a time of pleasant communing about days that seemed so long past, although so recent. They also communed of days to come, and especially of that great day of re-union in the Better Land. And intensely earnest was the final prayer of the native pastor Totosy, as he commended his friends to the loving care of God.

Next day they set sail for the seaport town of Tamatave.

And here we might appropriately terminate our narrative, for the bright days that had begun to dawn on Madagascar have never since been darkened by persecution—though they have not been altogether cloudless or free from the curse of war; for, with its enormous capacities and important position, the island has long been a morsel coveted by some of what men style the " Great Powers."

But we may not close our tale without at least touching on one dark spot, the contemplation of which cannot fail to grieve the heart of every sincere Christian. Rakota, the gentle, humane, courageous Prince, who had always favoured, and suffered hardship for, the cause of Christ, who had shielded and saved many of the Christians at the risk of his own life, and seemed to be—indeed was— a very pillar in the infant church, Rakota fell into gross sin and ultimately perished by the assassin's hand.

We have no right to judge him. Only this we know, that "the blood of Jesus Christ cleanseth from *all* sin;" and if his life and death throw light upon any passage of Scripture, they seem to bring out in strong relief the words, " Let him that thinketh he standeth take heed lest he fall."

*   *   *   *   *

It was a bright breezy morning when our three heroes stood on the deck of a homeward-bound vessel and gazed wistfully over the taffrail at the fast-receding shore. When the island sank like a little cloud into the horizon and disappeared, Mark and Ebony turned their eager eyes in the direction of old England, as if they half expected that celebrated isle of the west to appear! Possibly the one was thinking of a fair one with golden hair and blue eyes and a rosebud mouth. It is not improbable that the other was engaged in mental contemplation of a dark one with "a flat nose, and a coal-scuttle mout', an' *such* eyes!" As for Hockins, he stood with his sea-legs wide apart, his hands in his breeches pockets, and his eyes frowning severely at the deck. Evidently his thoughts, whether of past, present, or future, were too deep for utterance, for, like his comrades, he maintained unbroken silence.

Leaving them thus in pensive meditation, we regretfully bid them—and our readers—farewell!

THE END.

PRINTED BY T. AND A. CONSTABLE, PRINTERS TO HER MAJESTY,
AT THE EDINBURGH UNIVERSITY PRESS.

LIST OF WORKS

Mr. R. M. BALLANTYNE.

"In his tales of the sea, of the forest and the flames, and in all that he writes, there is a fidelity to nature and a knowledge of many paths of life which are not surpassed by any author in his special field of literature."—*Morning Post.*

With Illustrations. Ex. Crown 8vo. 5s.

THE WALRUS HUNTERS.
A TALE OF ESQUIMAUX LAND.

With Illustrations. Crown 8vo. 3s. 6d. each.

THE HOT SWAMP.
A ROMANCE OF OLD ALBION.

"Full of action and adventure."—*Scotsman.*

THE BUFFALO RUNNERS.
A TALE OF THE RED RIVER PLAINS.

"Mr. Ballantyne tells an admirable story of 'the struggle for life' valiantly and victoriously fought by the early colonists of the Red River region in North-Western America."—*Daily Telegraph.*

CHARLIE TO THE RESCUE.
A TALE OF THE SEA AND THE ROCKIES.

"In 'Charlie to the Rescue' Mr. Ballantyne supplies his con-stituency—which is now a large and well-satisfied one—with a sufficiency of battles, sieges, and escapes; the troubles of ranchmen, whose lives are threatened both by white and black scoundrels, are admirably reproduced. It is a capital story."—*Spectator.*

BLOWN TO BITS;
Or, THE LONELY MAN OF RAKATA. A TALE OF THE MALAY ARCHIPELAGO.

"A capital story, written in the author's old style, and full of life and action from beginning to end."—*Standard.*

BLUE LIGHTS;
Or, HOT WORK IN THE SOUDAN. A TALE OF SOLDIER LIFE IN SEVERAL OF ITS PHASES.

"The soldier's career is graphically depicted, and the story is in every way a good one."—*Literary Churchman.*

With Illustrations. Crown 8vo. 3s. 6d. each.

THE FUGITIVES;
Or, THE TYRANT QUEEN OF MADAGASCAR.

"There is plenty of adventure in the shape of imprisonment and combats with men and animals, and a negro and a sailor between them supply a comic element of the best quality. Everything considered, this is one of the best stories even Mr. Ballantyne has published."—*Academy.*

RED ROONEY;
Or, THE LAST OF THE CREW.

THE ROVER OF THE ANDES.
A TALE OF ADVENTURE IN SOUTH AMERICA.

"An admirable boys' story."—*Scotsman.*

THE YOUNG TRAWLER.
A STORY OF LIFE AND DEATH AND RESCUE IN THE NORTH SEA.

"Few men have laboured so steadfastly in their generation to provide sound, wholesome fare for 'our boys' as Mr. Ballantyne, and 'The Young Trawler' is worthy of his reputation."—*Academy.*

DUSTY DIAMONDS, CUT AND POLISHED.
A TALE OF CITY-ARAB LIFE.

THE BATTERY AND THE BOILER;
Or, THE ELECTRICAL ADVENTURES OF A TELEGRAPH CABLE-LAYER.

"The interest never flags."—*Academy.*

THE GIANT OF THE NORTH;
Or, POKINGS ROUND THE POLE.

"Of variety of perilous adventure, and peril ingeniously surmounted, there is no lack."—*Daily News.*

THE LONELY ISLAND;
Or, THE REFUGE OF THE MUTINEERS.

"Mr. Ballantyne weaves the romantic episode of the mutiny of the 'Bounty' into a most effective narrative."—*Graphic.*

With Illustrations. Crown 8vo. 3s. 6d. each.

POST HASTE.
A TALE OF HER MAJESTY'S MAILS.

"The book should find a place in every boy's library; it is full of interest."—*Leeds Mercury.*

IN THE TRACK OF THE TROOPS.
A TALE OF MODERN WAR.

"Mr. Ballantyne has blended with the incidents of war on the Danube a story of personal adventure spiritedly told."—*Daily News.*

THE SETTLER AND THE SAVAGE.
A TALE OF PEACE AND WAR IN SOUTH AFRICA.

"A capital story of South African life. Mr. Ballantyne, through the medium of a thoroughly manly and healthy tale of sport and war, frolic and danger, full of stirring yet not exaggerated scenes, presents a sketch of a very important period of the early history of our colony at the Cape of Good Hope."—*Times.*

UNDER THE WAVES;
Or, DIVING IN DEEP WATERS.

"Mr. Ballantyne enlarges the already gigantic debt due to him by the young by his 'Under the Waves,' a story meant to illustrate the practice and peril of diving in deep water, which it does in not only an interesting, but often in an amusing manner."—*Times.*

RIVERS OF ICE.
A TALE ILLUSTRATIVE OF ALPINE ADVENTURE AND GLACIER ACTION.

"A tale brimful of interest and stirring adventure."—*Glasgow Herald.*

THE PIRATE CITY.
AN ALGERINE TALE.

"The story is told with Mr. Ballantyne's usual felicity, and, as it is plentifully sprinkled with horrors, no doubt it will be greatly enjoyed by some boys."—*Athenæum.*

BLACK IVORY.
A TALE OF ADVENTURE AMONG THE SLAVERS OF EAST AFRICA.

"A captivating story. We heartily recommend it."—*Record.*
"Boys will find the book about as delightful a story of adventure as any of them could possibly desire."—*Scotsman.*

With Illustrations. Crown 8vo. 3s. 6d. each.

THE NORSEMEN IN THE WEST;
Or, AMERICA BEFORE COLUMBUS.

"This thoroughly delightful book is an adaptation of the Saga of Iceland, and also of Mr. Laing's 'Heimskingla; or, Chronicles of the Kings of Norway,' supplemented by Mr. Ballantyne's own experience and adventures in the wilderness of America. These ingredients are put together with the skill and spirit of an accomplished story-teller; and the result is a book that cannot possibly be laid down till the very last word of the last line has been read."
—Athenæum.

THE IRON HORSE;
Or, LIFE ON THE LINE. A RAILWAY TALE.

"A captivating book for boys."—*Guardian.*

ERLING THE BOLD.
A TALE OF NORSE SEA-KINGS.

"A capital tale of the Norse Sea-Kings."—*Times.*

FIGHTING THE FLAMES.
A TALE OF THE FIRE-BRIGADE.

"Many a schoolboy will find keen enjoyment in the perusal of 'Fighting the Flames,' and assure his little sisters with suitable emphasis that Mr. Ballantyne is 'a stunning good story-teller.'"— *Athenæum.*

DEEP DOWN.
A TALE OF THE CORNISH MINES.

"By reading Mr. Ballantyne's admirable story a very large amount of knowledge concerning Cornish mines may be acquired; whilst, from the fact of the information being given in the form of a connected narrative, it is not likely very soon to be forgotten. . . . A book well worthy of being extensively read."—*Mining Journal.*

THE FLOATING LIGHT OF THE GOODWIN SANDS.

"The tale will be especially interesting to adventure-loving boys."—*Record.*

SHIFTING WINDS.
A TOUGH YARN.

"A hearty, vigorous, bracing story, fresh with the pure breezes and sparkling with the bright waters of the everlasting seas."— *Athenæum.*

With Illustrations. Crown 8vo. 3s. 6d. each.

THE LIGHTHOUSE.
Or, THE STORY OF A GREAT FIGHT BETWEEN MAN AND THE SEA.

"Thoroughly at home in subjects of adventure, the author has made this, like all his stories for boys, smart in style, thrilling in interest, and abounding in incidents of every kind."—*Quiver.*

THE LIFEBOAT.
A TALE OF OUR COAST HEROES.

THE GOLDEN DREAM.
A TALE OF THE DIGGINGS.

THE RED ERIC;
Or, THE WHALER'S LAST CRUISE.

GASCOYNE, THE SANDALWOOD TRADER.
A TALE OF THE PACIFIC.

"Full of cleverly and impressively drawn pictures of life and character in the Pacific."—*Caledonian Mercury.*

FREAKS ON THE FELLS,
AND
WHY I DID NOT BECOME A SAILOR.

THE WILD MAN OF THE WEST.

THE BIG OTTER.
A TALE OF THE GREAT NOR'-WEST.

With Illustrations. Crown 8vo. 2s.

THE KITTEN PILGRIMS;
Or, GREAT BATTLES AND GRAND VICTORIES.

"We have copied the title-page of this amusing and instructive quarto for little folks. Nothing further is necessary. Mr. Ballantyne stands at the head of all our children's story-tellers *facile princeps.*"—*Churchman.*

With Illustrations. Crown 8vo. 2s. 6d.

BATTLES WITH THE SEA;
Or, HEROES OF THE LIFEBOAT AND THE ROCKET.

With Illustrations.   Crown 8vo.   2s. 6d. each.

HUNTED AND HARRIED.
A TALE OF THE SCOTTISH COVENANTERS.

A COXSWAIN'S BRIDE;
Or, THE RISING TIDE : And other Tales.

THE GARRET AND THE GARDEN;
Or, LOW LIFE HIGH UP :
And JEFF BENSON ; or, THE YOUNG COASTGUARDSMAN.

THE CREW OF THE WATER WAGTAIL.
A STORY OF NEWFOUNDLAND.

THE MIDDY AND THE MOORS.
AN ALGERINE TALE.

THE PRAIRIE CHIEF.

LIFE IN THE RED BRIGADE.
A FIERY TALE.   AND FORT DESOLATION ; or, SOLITUDE IN THE WILDERNESS.

THE ISLAND QUEEN;
Or, DETHRONED BY FIRE AND WATER.   A TALE OF THE SOUTHERN HEMISPHERE.

TWICE BOUGHT.
A TALE OF THE OREGON GOLD FIELDS.

THE MADMAN AND THE PIRATE.

PHILOSOPHER JACK.
A TALE OF THE SOUTHERN SEAS.

THE RED MAN'S REVENGE.

MY DOGGIE AND I.

SIX MONTHS AT THE CAPE.
LETTERS TO PERIWINKLE FROM SOUTH AFRICA.   A RECORD OF PERSONAL EXPERIENCE AND ADVENTURE.

Crown 8vo.   Price 3s. 6d. each.

TALES OF ADVENTURE BY FLOOD, FIELD, AND MOUNTAIN.

TALES OF ADVENTURE;
Or, WILD WORK IN STRANGE PLACES.

TALES OF ADVENTURE ON THE COAST.

MR. R. M. BALLANTYNE'S

Miscellany of Entertaining and Instructive Tales.

With Illustrations.   1s. each.

Also in a Handsome Cloth Case, Price 20s.

The "Athenæum" says :—"There is no more practical way of communicating elementary information than that which has been adopted in this series.   When we see contained in 124 small pages (as in 'Fast in the Ice') such information as a man of fair education should possess about icebergs, northern lights, Esquimaux, musk-oxen, bears, walruses, etc., together with all the ordinary incidents of an Arctic voyage woven into a clear connected narrative, we must admit that a good work has been done, and that the author deserves the gratitude of those for whom the books are especially designed, and also of young people of all classes."

I.

FIGHTING THE WHALES ; or, Doings and Dangers on a Fishing Cruise.

II.

AWAY IN THE WILDERNESS; or, Life among the Red Indians and Fur Traders of North America.

III.

FAST IN THE ICE ; or, Adventures in the Polar Regions.

IV.

CHASING THE SUN ; or, Rambles in Norway.

V.

SUNK AT SEA ; or, The Adventures of Wandering Will in the Pacific.

VI.

LOST IN THE FOREST; or, Wandering Will's Adventures in South America.

VII.

OVER THE ROCKY MOUNTAINS; or, Wandering Will in the Land of the Redskin.

VIII.

SAVED BY THE LIFEBOAT; or, A Tale of Wreck and Rescue on the Coast.

IX.

THE CANNIBAL ISLANDS; or, Captain Cook's Adventures in the South Seas.

X.

HUNTING THE LIONS; or, The Land of the Negro.

XI.

DIGGING FOR GOLD; or, Adventures in California.

XII.

UP IN THE CLOUDS; or, Balloon Voyages.

XIII.

THE BATTLE AND THE BREEZE; or, The Fights and Fancies of a British Tar.

XIV.

THE PIONEERS: A Tale of the Western Wilderness.

XV.

THE STORY OF THE ROCK.

XVI.

WRECKED, BUT NOT RUINED.

XVII.

THE THOROGOOD FAMILY.

XVIII.

THE LIVELY POLL.   A Tale of the North Sea.

LONDON: JAMES NISBET & Co., 21 BERNERS STREET, W.

www.ingramcontent.com/pod-product-compliance
Lightning Source LLC
Chambersburg PA
CBHW031825270326
41932CB00008B/551